TigerFish

Hoàng Chi Trương

ISBN-13: 978-0999162705
ISBN-10: 0999162705

Book Cover Designed by Marsa Morse
Author Photograph on Back Cover by Johnathan Woodson

Report errors found in TigerFish to chismith@chibeingchi.com

PRAISE FOR TIGERFISH

"*TigerFish* is a story of love, fear, and sacrifice in the name of family. Hoàng Chi takes you to her upbringing as the daughter of a Vietnamese Army Colonel and into the day to day activities of a young lady during war time. Her descriptions of the streets and landscape are so detailed that you see yourself in the story and the middle of the action. When the Vietnam war hits close to home, you can feel the danger and heartbreak Hoàng Chi and her family faced, including the difficult choice to leave their beloved country behind and move to the United States as refugees.

Life as a refugee was tough but Hoàng Chi's fighting spirit never gave up, and she now graces us with her story in this fascinating book."

Tatiana Froes, LLM. *Reader and Blogger*

"I'm not one to read autobiographies or memoirs, but I am sincerely glad that I chose to read this one. Not only is this an amazingly well written 'coming of age' story, but it also provides, with excellent descriptive style, the challenges faced transitioning from the more strict, disciplined and tradition-based Vietnamese culture, to the free-flowing, opportunistic and ego-driven American culture. All during the tender, vulnerable, teenage years that are hard enough without these additional challenges.

My praise to the author, both for surviving this turbulent and challenging time in her life, and for having the courage to tell it with passion, confidence, and respect."

Michael Chrobak. *Author*

"Many parts of the world are suffering a refugee crisis as we speak and it is easy to forget that waves of forced emigration have been happening for years and even centuries, most predominantly in times of war. Trương reminds of us of the struggles faced by Southern Vietnamese families who were forced to flee death or imprisonment after the fall of Saigon, as the Vietnam war came to a close in 1975. Her memoir, *TigerFish*, is a fascinating tale of what it was like for Trương and her large family, to adjust from their privileged life in their home country, to refugee status in America, starting all over again. The story of the family's assimilation, told through the innocent eyes of the young 'Chi', is an endearing one. No doubt it will resonate with many who have faced similar circumstances, out of their control, and survived to share their experiences."

Brydie Wright. *Author*

"I found *TigerFish* to be fascinating! I loved how Trương was able to share her story in a way that was both moving and relatable, bringing together some of the horrors of war and the refugee experience, with humor and wonder in her coming-of-age story. Though originally written for her children, I believe Trương's story is especially poignant at this time. Too often, it's easy to label those of another skin color, country, or religion as "other." Yet in sharing her story, Trương gives us a powerful reminder that beyond the labels, refugees and immigrants are human beings, just like us. Through this inspiring account of her experience as a refugee and building a new life in America, Trương thoughtfully reminds us that we (all of humanity) have so much in common, if we will only have the courage and compassion to reach out and connect."

Becky McCleery, *a reader*

"*TigerFish* is a wonderfully engaging, brave, and deeply personal story of a young girl's childhood in wartime Vietnam, the refugee experience, culture clash, and the power of true love. Hoàng Chi Trương wants her story to benefit not only her children and larger family, but also the growing number of refugees in the world today. She hopes her experience can help humanize the dislocated, those compelled by war or want to leave their homelands with no promise of return. It is a very timely tale. Trương shows that a key in meeting the challenges facing refugees, and the challenges of negotiating cultural difference more broadly, is simple mutual respect, seeing humanity in otherness. Or, as she advises her daughter, treating people with compassion and love. Indeed, Trương's extraordinary life and story are a testament to the power of compassion and love. What the world needs now."

Tad Ballew, Ph.D. *Cultural Anthropologist, Translator*

"*TigerFish* is a detailed and heartfelt love letter to her children. Not only does this book feature her life, but it captures the sights, smells, fears and cries of innocence robbed. Trương shares historical and cultural details to the reader, to the point that we can travel back in time with her. *TigerFish* gives shocking, yet poignant details of how each family member survived the horrors of war. She was able to illustrate sympathy, empathy, fear, and love – not just for her family, but for everyone she met along the way.

TigerFish invited me to question my beliefs about war, history, religion, culture clashes and loyalty while the author wove sacrifice, respect, commitment, unconditional love, and honesty throughout this book. Trương leaves no stone unturned as she pours out her heart and soul to connect her words to the reader.

Everyone can benefit from reading this book. You cannot remain unchanged as you partake in her journey. *TigerFish* shares the past and reveals the present. It allows us to use tragedies as springboards to the future. The book makes it possible to discover our own '*TigerFish*,' and it has encouraged me to feel pain, move on, never forget and to continue to love."

Phyllis Banks, *a reader*

"Trương has written a wonderful story, emotional at times, and I shed tears as she shared her family's experiences leaving their beloved homeland to escape the war and make America their new home. It wasn't easy, and Trương and her family are remarkable in how they stayed together, persisted through many trials and eventually thrived!

The author's descriptive phrases discussing the bakery and the pastry her father bought made my mouth water and piqued my sense of smell. I could almost see the "soft wrinkles from a lifelong kindness" used to describe a relative. I hope there is a sequel to *TigerFish*.

TigerFish made me think and see the Vietnam war from a different perspective. I thank Trương for sharing with us this treasure she's written for her daughter."

Denise Gildon, *a reader*

ACKNOWLEDGEMENTS

TigerFish is my first book, and I have many people to thank. The first person on my list, to whom I owe my utmost gratitude for being the biggest cheerleader, would categorically be my thoughtful and loving husband, Chris.

I left my government job nine months ago to fully dedicate myself to this book. From day one, I sat down writing, editing, setting up my website, niching down to my ideal readers, and building an author's social media platform and following. The subsequent months included more editing, finding and working with editors, book cover designers, beta and advanced readers, a formatter, and proofreaders – all new processes to me – while minimizing our household of two empty nesters, my husband and I, a dog, and two cats.

Without fail, I sat at my desk from morning to evening, making my best effort to not work at night or on weekends when my husband was home, but sometimes I was not successful. Chris not only fully supported me leaving my job to pursue my life's goal and passion, but he also cheered me on when I ran into obstacles, reminding me not to get burnt out, cooking dinners for me while I worked. He's been championing for me since we met in high school. A significant portion of my journey includes Chris, and this book will elaborate on that point.

I started writing this book for my daughter, and then also for my son who was born three years later. They are the pride and joy of my life as any mother feels passionately about theirs. This book is for them, for their family history, as one day their offspring and grandchildren will want to know their heritage. Here's to you both, Natasha and Jeremy, with my deepest and most profound expression of love.

I want to express my deepest gratitude and profound love to my parents. My father who continuously fought in Vietnam and America to provide us a better future and opportunities. My mother, whose life was always selflessly devoted to her children and husband. I learned discipline from my father and compassion from my mother. I persevered in writing this book to document my history because I've watched and learned how they strived all their lives to give us a better life. Here is a Vietnamese proverb which I will cite to express my debt of gratitude to my parents:

Công cha như núi Thái Sơn
Nghĩa mẹ như nước trong nguồn chảy ra
Một lòng thờ mẹ, kính cha
Cho tròn chữ hiếu mới là đạo con

Father's labor is as extraordinary as Thái Sơn Mountain
Mother's love is as sacred as water flowing from the source
With undying devotion, I pledge my loyalty and respect to my parents
To uphold my family honor while fulfilling my duty in our family name

(Thái Sơn Mountain or Taishan Mountain, Taishan, Tai'an, China)

Authors don't create works in a vacuum. I've been an avid reader all my life but have taken books for granted, not knowing the enormous amount of work that goes into writing, editing, proofing, printing, publishing, and marketing. Every night, I read a paperback at bedtime, and savor the delicious words authors labored to put down just for my enjoyment, without thinking twice about their effort.

I'd like to thank a few of my writing's biggest supporters, besides those who I've already acknowledged. To start, my earliest "family focus group": Mimi, Steve, and Julie, when I first embarked on this journey. To my friend Tatiana Froes, whose moral support and reading of my manuscript have helped me through many hurdles during my writing process; to a fellow author Michael Chrobak for selflessly and tirelessly proofing my manuscript; to our true blue friend, Tad Ballew, who sprinted to the finishing line and helped with the final proofing; and to my loyal and faithful early adopters who believed in my mission and writing about the refugee experience and Minimalism. This story no longer belongs to me, it belongs to our nation, to lend a voice and a face to the refugee and immigrant crisis we are currently experiencing in our highly divisive country via the immigration bans.

My utmost appreciation goes to my brother Thảo and his wife Liên for promptly reading my manuscript and providing feedback, fact-checking, and new insights into our family history which I missed, or had no knowledge as I was a younger sibling.

To all my brothers and sisters, especially the older ones, Kim Chi, Thọ, Thông, thank you for your sacrifices when we first came to America, for postponing your college education and working to support our family so that I could continue with my schooling. I also thank all of my siblings for your understanding in writing this memoir. I retold my life story as accurately as I can remember. These events were significant to me but may not have registered in your memory, and vice versa. In the spirit of storytelling, some conversations were created to provide context for the events and were not verbatim.

Last but not least, I owe my debt of gratitude to David Brown, Bạch Tuyết Lê, David's wife, and Liên Lê. They generously and selflessly vouched for my family at the United States Embassy in 1975. They brought us to America for a chance at a new life full of promises and opportunities–and saved our lives. Mere words cannot sufficiently express how grateful I am to all three of them; each played a unique role, took risks, and responsibility for our family's escape from communism and a new life in America. I would like to use this book as a platform to dedicate an evergreen and enduring expression of gratitude to each of them. I could not thank you enough for what you've done for my family and me. I could only pay it forward, in your honor, and in my modest way of sharing my refugee journey and lessons learned.

I wanted to write my story, so those who lived through it won't feel like you went through it alone, although your experience may have been more painful. For those who are going through the acculturation process right now, have hope, and know that it will get easier. For those who are waiting to get accepted by a new country, please have hope that good will win over evil, and that the land of opportunity may just be in your grasp. Never give up.

PROLOGUE

I originally wrote this memoir for my children to pass down our family history. I wanted to describe how vastly different my life had been in comparison to theirs. I wanted them to know how I survived the war and successfully fled the communists at the Fall of Vietnam in 1975. My ultimate goals are to describe and portray my ensuing journey in acculturating and assimilating in America, and how I eventually met their father.

Little did I know I would continuously revise my memoir as time went by, addressing the story to my daughter when she began kindergarten, through junior high, high school, college, and again as she graduated.

Now I know it can no longer wait as my daughter will soon be married. My story will be the ultimate and eternal gift to her and her brother, to their children, grandchildren, and for many generations to come.

I must tell my story. It tugs at my heart, my soul and all the fibers of my body. It's not a "want" to tell this story, but a "need" and a "must-do" life goal of mine.

In the following pages, as a letter to my daughter, I will recount and share my childhood, coming of age, and the challenges I eventually overcame with humility, loyalty, and grit. I hope that my lessons learned will inspire others to overcome their life's obstacles as refugees or immigrants.

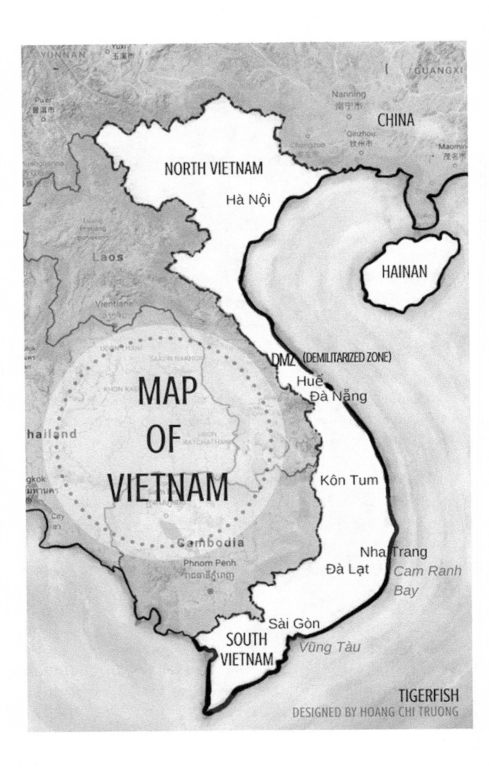

MAP
OF
VIETNAM

CHINA

NORTH VIETNAM

Hà Nội

Laos

HAINAN

DMZ (DEMILITARIZED ZONE)

Huế
Đà Nẵng

Thailand

Kôn Tum

Cambodia

Nha Trang
Đà Lạt   Cam Ranh
Bay

Sài Gòn

SOUTH
VIETNAM   Vũng Tàu

TIGERFISH
DESIGNED BY HOANG CHI TRUONG

TIGERFISH

With love and gratitude, I dedicate this book to my selfless Mother

PART ONE

CHAPTER 1

Our Woven History

Dearest daughter,

I was born in the year of the Tiger, 1962, an inauspicious birth year for a girl in Vietnam because people still believed in the Chinese astrology from their one thousand years of domination. According to this belief, women born under this sign were stubborn and strong-willed, taking control of domestic matters and not submissive to their husbands in the traditions of Confucianism.

Given the education you've had, the way we raised you, and the books that you read from my bookshelves—such as Betty Friedan's *The Feminine Mystique*—I know it will be difficult for you to fathom. I accepted being labeled the Tiger Girl at such a young age. I've been self-conscious ever since and aware of others beliefs about me. Older relatives fervently cautioned my parents to keep a watchful eye on me. They lowered their voices, furrowed their brows, and with a well-rehearsed, quiet sophistication, shook their heads in disappointment and disapproval. They found me guilty of my potential wrongdoings before I even reached puberty, when one was supposedly capable of such bad behavior. I grew used to the stigma and almost always expected this premature judgment.

Don't feel bad for me. This stigma didn't make me sad or bitter; instead, it strengthened me, the same way an old cypress anchors its roots deeply to stand up to the relentless, seaward wind. Do you see how beautifully this hardship has shaped and formed the stretching branches and foliage, like long slender fingers pointing toward the sea?

Year of the Tiger

To tell you as complete a story as possible, I'm gathering a few precious documents and photos on the dining room table that survived our exodus to America. Studying my birth certificate, yellowed and brittle to the point of crumbling between my fingers, brings me closer to my parents. It is the same piece of paper my mother and father once held in their young hands on a bone-chilling cold and rainy day in January so long ago.

I imagine they gave a few crumpled paper notes to a half-asleep official behind the counter. Perhaps he was an indifferent man with a smoldering cigarette haphazardly dangling from his thin leathery lip, reluctantly pecking on typewriter keys. He awarded them an official red stamp, proof of authenticity, squinting his cloudy veiled eyes as he typed my parents' names and professions on the preprinted form. Father: Soldier. Mother: Housewife. My mom restlessly comforted her infant whose red face contorted from endless crying. That was me, squirming in a tightly bound bundle.

My father shifted uneasily in his starched, military, olive-drab colored uniform, alternating left to right, feeling the urgency to return to his post in Kôn Tum. My mother's high mandarin collar stiffened as she leaned down to my face and softly hummed a lullaby. Sitting amongst the bus passengers on the way home, my parents discussed ways to get more help for my mom with the new child.

I met my six siblings and paternal grandmother later that day. They cooed and caressed my pink cheeks, marveling at my tiny fingers and curled toes. They called me "Bé Chi," or Little Chi. Every day I learned a bit more about each sibling. Kim Chi wore a long ponytail and lovingly watched my mother sponge bathe me for the first time. She sat securely in a wicker chair, and my mother plopped me squarely into her arms. She swayed me while singing a French lullaby, "Frère Jacques." The cream-colored ceiling fan whirred overhead in witness to our first exchange of sibling tenderness. My brothers on the other hand, only whirled about in my outer orbit, barely recognizable or registering in my stratosphere. Their syncopated and sometimes shrapnel-loud voices ricocheted sharply off of the walls and resident geckos.

Rain insistently shrouded Nha Trang, like the ubiquitous leeches in the rice paddies, cleaved tightly on farmers' ankles and calves. The days were long and cold, and my siblings were fidgety inside, which made my grandmother increasingly impatient. I kept them awake at night, crying from wet diapers and bouts of hunger. My family woke up markedly ill-tempered and perhaps didn't know why. Grandmother found comfort in criticizing my mother and siblings, but my mom continued making the cooing sound to soothe me, as she unpinned my cloth diapers and bottle-fed me. During the days, she wrapped me up tightly and paced on the veranda when I cried. Her sublimely gentle world of rain deepened the charm and grace of the drenched bougainvillea and intoxicating jasmine flowers. The scented earth quietly nodded off. Drip, drip, drip.

In my protected and sheltered days, I could only hear the peaceful orchestra of rustling leaves, poetic raindrops and the melodic rushing of the rain-swollen creek. My beginning years possessed an almost ethereal and dreamlike quality, acutely punctuated with vivid colors and sharp, pungent scents.

Nha Trang

Nha Trang sat modestly between dark blue-green jungle to the west and the blessed beauty of the Pacific Ocean to the east. A group of brightly painted fishing boats gently rocked on the tide, their painted eyes coming to life, eager and poised for their nightly seaward trek, hoping to sustain their kindred owners. On the pale salmon-colored sand, women and men rocked casually on their heels while mending nets, and barefoot children ran serpentine laps between the basket-boats and their parents. Some chased the surf and burst into a delighted sort of frightened laughter, a seemingly rehearsed pandemonium.

All roads led to the beach. All homes respectfully devoted their prized windows eastward, properly greeting the sun rising over the ocean, whose rays gave infinite hope to the life-lusting residents. Randomly-sized homes nestled amongst narrow streets, creeping lazily towards the distant mountain ranges. Generations shared these households; loneliness was a hard-pressed notion. Life spilled out onto the streets, children played in front, and adults chatted with neighbors and friends. Public displays of domestic spats erupted and extinguished as quickly as they became aflame. Privacy was a novel concept.

My parents had a modest home on Nguyễn Trung Trực street, several streets west of the beach and within walking distance to the open-air market. Our house was painted white with a red tile roof that grew mossy green from the torrential monsoons. The matching green shutters that graced the front windows were only a coincidence but looked well planned. Our parents kept us protected behind the stucco half wall, topped with decorative wrought iron spires, a sharp silhouette dramatically softened by the climbing vines of bougainvillea with their vibrant blooms.

Inequity abounded throughout the town and the country. Mustard-colored walls and wrought iron gates segregated the French villas and their parked Citroens from the noisy, communal streets. Colonists were now long gone, but traces of their existence remained. They bled and robbed their subjects, driving many to their eventual deaths. They erected grand buildings and furnished them with the finest imports from France. "Blood wealth," I heard my relatives murmur.

Bitter reminders of French brutality were etched in these buildings where the wealthy Vietnamese resided behind elaborately designed gates. They employed servants who might not see their families for months at a time. Servants were not only for the well-offs, as even middle-class families were accustomed to having at least one or two, and sometimes even children were servants. They wore ragged clothes that, like their lives, had been patched by a potpourri of colors and textures. They might never set foot in school and might someday be turned out to the streets to peddle trinkets or sell lottery tickets. They would later marry, then repeat the vicious cycle, if the war did not kill them or they were not lured into drugs and prostitution.

The quintessential street vendors, food and nonfood alike, dominated the landscape. Steamy hot peanuts, barbecued corn slathered with a chive sauce, and the silkiest soybean with warm, ginger caramel syrup were only a few of my childhood favorites. The women, straining under the weight of their baskets full of goods, walked in a rhythm that enabled them to endure the excessive burden. On so many levels, these were strong women, and I was mesmerized by them.

In those days, we lived apart from my father, because, as military personnel, he had to live full-time on the base near the dangerous battle zone. For our safety, we lived in Nha Trang and out of harm's way. Occasionally, he received home leave to see his family, and this was one of my first and most treasured memories of my father. During one visit, he took us to the French bakery to get my favorite pastry called Choux à la Crème. My oldest sister skipped and bounced around my mom and me while I was being spoon-fed the last taste of sweet, white sand dab and steamed rice. She buried her face into mine with her big brown eyes and sung, "Dad eees taking uh us to the bakerry!" then bounced and skipped around the room with unabashed excitement.

I was only three, but I remember riding on my dad's gleaming, aquamarine Vespa. I recall the sensation of the wind brushing my face and of the inertia when he took the curves. The pastries were a gastronomic pleasure indeed, but that wasn't what made us giddy. We crammed ourselves in the Vespa, giggling, and filling up our reserve tanks of "Daddiness" before he left again. The anticipation of being at the bakery with my father far exceeded the actual act of being there, or of eating the exceedingly sweet vanilla creme. Viscously and generously, it oozed over every single one of my taste buds. The happy moment with my father soon disappeared just as quickly as he appeared, like the mountain clouds west of Nha Trang and just as unpredictable. We filled up our reserves and returned to our normal life, fighting back the hot tears that welled up when he left by running to the backyard to play.

My mother and aunties raised us while my father fought far away battles in Kôn Tum. In those days, adults didn't think about causing concerns or worries for their children. They didn't conceal their thoughts or their frustrations, and continually showed their disapproval of the corrupted government, making tsk-tsk sounds, like the mischievous sand-colored geckos that lurked in the dark. The women looked concerned and whispered in a huddle, so as not to be heard by the secret police. Later in life, I learned that they worried and speculated about the direction of our country, as there were rumors of a possible coup against President Diệm and his brother in

1963, but back then, I worried because of their tone of voice, though I always quickly drifted into a slumber and felt safe that the adults would protect us no matter what happened.

Đà Lạt

"I will drop by and check on grandmother while you are gone," my auntie convinced my mother the day we left Nha Trang for Đà Lạt, the central highlands where we lived while my father attended the military academy. Just like that, we moved, without my grandmother. A small family suite in an old French hotel became our new home, La Catina, as far as I could decipher from my mother's accent. This hotel housed the military cadet families. The young wives, like my mom, gathered and folded their home-sewn cloth diapers, told their secrets, and watched their toddlers play together. Here, my mother met Auntie Xuyến, who became her lifelong friend. She, perhaps, was the only friend my mom ever had, and they became very close as their husbands climbed the ranks together.

Dark roasted coffee permeated our modest apartment every morning as my father routinely readied for school. He patiently waited for his coffee while rustling and reading the newspaper. The static of the BBC station transmitted over the Philips shortwave radio filled our kitchen with a sense of connectedness to the rest of the world. On the table, the one-serving tin coffee press primly perched on his cup, slowly dripped one drop at a time, keeping rhythm with the tick-tock of the grandfather clock. I watched and listened to my father's collective morning sounds and the occasional dialogue between my parents.

In the evenings, upon my dad's return, he methodically and gingerly slipped a shiny black record from its sleeve and placed it on the phonograph. We listened to a tête-à-tête of a Parisian man and woman. My father repeated the phrases while eyeing his book and occasionally making notes. My mother regarded him with remote deference as she quietly set the chopsticks and rice bowls on the dinner table. She promptly glared at us and raised her index finger to her tight lips to hush us so that he could rehearse his French lessons.

Đà Lạt was a picturesque highland plateau and a romantic place for lovers to rendezvous and exchange their courtship croons, and a famously popular choice for honeymooners from the cities. In my two-year-old memory, I could only recall being kept mostly inside, spending hours observing the world through the window. I stood on the squeaky vinyl chair, captivated with people and vehicles many stories below us, insignificantly small and inconsequentially moving about on the streets below like scattered ants. At times, I could see my mother emerge from the hotel then fold into the crowd to board the market-bound bus. Men clung to the sides like monkeys, bouncing rhythmically over each pothole. Baskets of fruits and vege-tables were tied to the roof, pigs noisily squealed, and ducks flapped their wings, leaving fluffs of downs in their wake. Diesel fumes thickly enveloped the air, then dissipated as the bus swayed and roared its way over the pothole-filled terrain called roads. I often worried whether I would see my mother again, much the same as I felt whenever my father had to return to work on his army base where it was unsafe for civilians.

The world was infinitely vast when I was two, especially when separated from my mother on the hotel grounds while she collected laundry from the communal clothesline. Once, as the sun was going down, I watched as my mom unpinned and gathered the last dry diapers. The next time I looked up, she was gone. No one was around, and I could only hear the crickets and their mocking strings section. The damp, cold air descended as I called out for my mother. Suddenly, the hotel's ghost story came alive with an image of a woman who hung herself on the hotel's landing. As I said, adults in those days wouldn't think twice of talking about things that would traumatize children, unlike the way most modern parents would shield their kids from scary stories. They didn't filter for children because children were invisible little human beings, in waiting to become adults. There I was, at the landing, where I could vividly imagine the display of the unhappily departed. I stood on that stairway landing and cried, my legs paralyzed, not knowing how to find my way home. It seemed a recurring theme, as a child, the fear that I wouldn't see my mother and father again.

CHAPTER 2

Ancestral Land ~ Ninh Hòa

We moved back to Nha Trang after my father graduated from the Academy. Two years had passed, and political unrest continued to mount. Protesters flooded the streets armed with banners and raised fists. Passionate and idealistic youth, their necks swollen with raised blue veins, shouted anti-government slogans. Some crackdowns sent Buddhist monks, as well as high school and college students, scattering in the streets like bees disturbed from the hive. Some ran through our neighborhood and climbed through our side fences to escape civilian and military police. I was merely four years old but felt a rumbling thunder beneath the surface of my security. For the first time, I felt unsafe and unprotected by my parents. I visualized the faces of Communists, like the elusive monsters under my bed that were capable of assuming multiple shapes and forms. I feared they would eventually consume my secure childhood and home.

My father became an officer and received a transfer to the First Division Infantry in Đà Nẵng, a locale of strategic and vital political interests. He left for his new post while my mother made arrangements to rent our home in Nha Trang. Until my father found a place for us in Đà Nẵng, our interim home was in Ninh Hòa, an hour bus ride from Nha Trang. We lived with my maternal aunt's family at their ancestral home.

My aunt Dì Năm was a sweet-natured woman who was quick to smile. She wore soft wrinkles from a lifelong kindness, so one could never tell the hardship she had endured. Her husband left her and five young children for another love interest in Sài Gòn on one of his many buying trips. He never looked back except to write that he wouldn't be sending home any more money. "City living is too costly," he relayed through a relative.

To save her honor, she didn't display her pain but forged on, raising her children on the ancestral land the best way she knew how. The villagers didn't scorn or pity her. Instead, they loved and protected her and her children for her enduring sacrifices. As a child I worried that my father might leave us as my uncle had left her. I was reprimanded for asking if he would, my mother noting that it was disrespectful and might bring this situation upon our family. It wasn't my mom's fault that she was so harsh. It was the time in which we lived when daily lives were full of superstition and folklore.

My mother's family was the third generation in Ninh Hòa, and the elders in the village knew my grandparents well. Smiling family friends and relatives dropped by continuously, carrying baskets of fruit and deliciously homemade treats for my family. I've never seen my mother happier than when she was in Ninh Hòa with her relatives and friends. She smiled and often laughed, even with the prospect of facing uncertainties in Đà Nẵng. Some days, my mother and relatives spent hours under the shade of the mango trees polishing the brass urn and candelabra for the ancestral altar. They polished the amber gold sheen to a mirror-like perfection. Other days, they shucked corn, plucked duck feathers, or gutted and scaled fish.

We barely saw our mother and aunties during our stay there. Our cousins showed us hidden groves to spy on grownups as they winnowed the rice hulls from the chaff and where to pick the best fresh fruit in the village. We sprawled out under the shady, ancient Banyan tree, spreading out our loot and gorging on sweet ripe papayas, mangos, and dragon fruit. We spent hours wading and splashing in the shallow river, scooping up handfuls of clams to steam with lemongrass for snacks later in the day.

At dusk, the frogs hopped out one by one until the front porch was dark with their bodies. My uncle gave me piggyback rides so I wouldn't have to touch the frogs with my bare feet, and we dined outdoors under the feeble light of an oil lamp, flickering to and fro. Crickets chirped, geckos clicked their tongues, and a melody of full-throated tenor frogs echoed off some distant riverbank. My auntie let me lie in her lap and rubbed my back after dinner while she talked, and there I stayed listening to their soothing voices, retelling their childhood stories.

"You don't remember because you were too young," an older relative said to my mother, "but your father had to fire his hunting rifle to scare the elephants away. Otherwise, the whole herd would come and trample the crops and rice paddies." He paused for effect and leaned toward her face, "And you know what? They can run fast. They could pick you up with their trunks and carry you away if they're mad at you!" I envisioned the elephant chasing after our grandfather and neatly tucking him underneath its tusks and trunk as it ran off with him into the thick jungle.

My grandfather retired from the Civil Service with a generous pension and acquired many hectares of land in Ninh Hòa. He put in rice paddies and built a house for his wife and children. They also had fruit orchards of citrus, mangos, papaya, and a generous vegetable garden. They raised chickens, ducks, geese, and pigs. The villagers respected my grandfather, and they often came to him for advice, bringing tea and cakes to show their gratitude and appreciation. The government granted him the rare permission of owning a rifle for hunting game, and he occasionally hired a hunts-man for deer and other wild game for food.

My maternal grandmother died at the young age of forty-one, shortly after the birth of her last son. Western medicine was not available then, and no one knew the cause of her death, although most suspected that it was due to childbirth complications. My grandmother's death necessitated the hiring of nursemaids in the village for the newborn until he could digest rice soup.

My grandfather faced more tragedy shortly after his wife's de-mise. One of his sons got shot as he emerged from the jungle by the South Republic Army on suspicion of being a communist sympa-thizer, and it was unclear what activities he'd engaged in to be killed this way. From this allegation, they demolished my grandparents' home, leaving only the concrete foundation. They seized my grand-parents' sacred, ancestral altar, made of beautiful mahogany and inlaid with mother-of-pearl, and everything else of value.

After the upheaval and deaths in the family, my grandfather sold most of his land. Without his wife and son, he no longer had the desire to farm. His health declined, and he passed away ten years later. My oldest aunt, Dì Ba, was married and lived away and had since returned home to care for my mother and the youngest uncle. My mom lost her mom when she was seven years old, then her father when she was seventeen. She frequently commented that she was very fortunate to have my aunt and her kind husband who was very loving and hardworking. They fulfilled their duties and raised my mother until she was properly married to an upstanding soldier.

My aunt Dì Ba and her husband were very protective of my beautiful, young, eligible mother. They shielded her from the Re-public soldiers and their harassment. The country folk like my mom's family had two enemies, the Republic government in the daytime, and the Việt Minh, or the communist sympathizers at night. The whole family fled on foot at night with their bedrolls, food, and water to their "safe house" or camped in their hiding places in the woods to prevent a possible kidnapping of her or worse, like possible sexual assaults, bringing dishonor to the family.

When my mother talked about education, she had a longing look and wished she could have attended school and become a teacher like her younger brother. "Education," she would say, "I want this, first and foremost for you and your sisters so that you can make a living should your husbands ever leave or die." She wanted this impossible and unattainable goal to be within our grasp — a dream she couldn't achieve due to the constraints of her circumstances, culture, and generation.

My parents in Đà Lạt, 1956.
Left to Right: Father, Bá, Thảo, Tâm, Mother holding Kim Chi

Consequently, my mother stayed home and learned embroidery, knitting, and sewing. She mastered the art of domesticity, shopping, cooking, honoring and caring for her husband's three sons, mother, and his younger siblings while he worked in faraway battle zones. My mother earned a modest living by sewing and embroidering intricate designs for ceremonial matrimonial pillows, baby pillows, clothes and handkerchiefs – all prized possessions. She also became a highly skilled knitter who took in assignments for sweaters, caps, and baby booties. While she stayed home and honed her skills, her younger brother, not faced with similar threats or challenges because he was male, finished high school and college and became a high school math teacher.

My mother was born in 1935, the year of the Dog, in Bình Thành, Ninh Hòa, a farming village in central South Vietnam. She was second to the youngest of five surviving children in her family. At eighteen, my mother was a beautiful lady who had many admirers. Young, eligible bachelors discreetly admired her, but very few had the courage to obtain courtship permissions from my uncle and aunt. My mother fondly recounted her earliest admirers, one of whom was a young officer who conceded when he discovered that his friend, my father, was about to approach her for courtship. My dad was bold and determined, which served him well in the end. My uncle and aunt gave him the blessing to court my mother, which consisted of two chaperoned visits at their home. Shortly after that, my parents wed in 1955.

In his brief courtship with my mother, my father revealed that he was a widower with three young sons, all under six years old, and inquired if my mom objected to raising them. At eighteen, my mother was full of confidence in her ability to raise the boys. She'd been looking after her nieces and nephews and consented to my father's proposal. My mother immediately gained the responsibility of three kids after my parents were married and with the bittersweet sentiment, my mom moved to Kôn Tum with her new husband.

My parents in their first home in Kôn Tum, 1959

CHAPTER 3
New Life in Đà Nẵng

As I mentioned earlier, my father became an officer and received a transfer to the First Division Infantry in Đà Nẵng. Since this development came suddenly, my parents only had a short time to find housing for the family at the new location. My father scrambled and exhausted all his connections, only to find a small two-room apartment in a large, two-story colonial French building. This building had provided military housing before the French had been soundly defeated in 1954 in the battle of Điện Biên Phủ and had high tailed back to France.

We begrudgingly said goodbye to our relatives in Ninh Hòa and headed for the unknown, faraway territory with trepidation. It was a short flight on Air Vietnam. The simple green dragon logo, emblazoned across the belly of the plane, contrasted with the beautiful flight attendants, seemingly floating in the aisles, hypnotizing everyone with their silky, bright blue áo dài uniforms.

They offered small clear glasses of fizzy Tiger orange soda, and we drank it for the very first time as children. The carbonated beverage made us burp, to our complete surprise, and we laughed heartily,

19

choking on the gaseous bubbles. My siblings sipped the drinks, again and again, trying to repeat the new sensations, each time cackling, until our mother put an end to our silliness.

The attendants smiled and winked as though they were in complicity with us and brought more trays of colorful candies, inviting us to go ahead and grab a handful. We were never offered this much candy when it wasn't the New Year's celebration, and before now we were never allowed to have soft drinks. Emboldened by this service, I asked if they had Choux à la Creme, but their eyes widened as they said they didn't. I knew then in my four-year-old mind that this was going to be the beginning of many disappointments if they didn't have my favorite treats where we were going.

We arrived in Đà Nẵng on a workday, and my father was not there to meet us. There were nine of us in our not-so-small family: my mother and her five children, two stepsons, and my female cousin, who was my mom's temporary helper. My oldest brother Thảo stayed behind in Nha Trang to finish his senior year at Võ Tánh High School. We felt lost on the tarmac, standing in the blazing hot sun. Within a few minutes, my mother scanned the area and located an army guard station where we clumsily lugged our bags, and my mom borrowed a phone to call my father. He couldn't meet us, he said and advised her to take the bus instead. The soldier overheard her conversation and waved a soldier nearby in his Jeep to take us to the station. "This is Captain Trương's family. Please bring them to the bus station."

When we arrived, the crowded bus was pulling away, and we all plopped down our bags, eyeing my mother for further directions. No one was talking. We were tired. The city was dusty, and the bus exhaust spewed indiscriminately, shrouding nearby pedestrians, peddlers, motorcyclists, and cyclists. We were all quiet when we finally boarded the bus and sat in awe, watching the unsightly new city we now called home. Stretches of concrete light poles and overhead power lines untidily crisscrossed the streets. We looked forward to seeing our father at the end of the bus ride, and found him standing in the front of the apartment buildings. We couldn't run up fast enough to say our respectful greetings, "Thưa Ba!" That was the silver lining for me. I finally got my stay-at-home father, which meant he'd be home every night instead of being at an outpost for extended periods of time.

I didn't like Đà Nẵng. None of us did. There was no ocean breeze, and you could smell the muddy brown Bạch Đằng, the river that dissected the city. The locals made fun of our southern Nha Trang accent, but I knew it wasn't us or the way we pronounced our words. Quite the contrary, I was sure they had an odd way of speaking and an even more bizarre vocabulary. Surely, they were the strange bunch. We didn't know how long we had to be in this godforsaken place, but hoped it would be temporary and that we'd return home before school started in a few months. We didn't know we would stay there for a very long time, right to the bitter end!

Catholic School Days

Since our family was not Catholic, my parents worked hard at every angle and connection to enroll Kim Chi and me at Sacred Heart. Allegedly, it was an excellent school, and therefore, we must receive our education there. To this day, I'm not sure why my parents started me in kindergarten so early, as I was only four years old. I believe I had so many troubles at Sacred Heart because I was much younger than the other students to learn the school's religious rituals.

On my first day of kindergarten, my father later told me, he stayed outside the classroom all morning to make sure I would be all right. I couldn't help staring at the nuns who wore peculiar white gowns and black leather sandals that crisscrossed their white-socked feet. Most of them looked like they'd eaten something very sour which made their faces pucker up, perhaps the unripe starfruit.

There were even rumors that they were love-spurned and joined the convent to escape the loss, and when that didn't work, they took their frustration out on snotty-nosed children like us. I worshiped the older students and believed their story. I noticed something else about the nuns, they all had the same squeaky-clean scent of Ivory soap. Not that this was bad, but I always equated that smell with being smacked on the knuckles.

Kindergarteners didn't wear white uniforms like the rest of the student body. We wore regular clothes. I remember vividly, proudly wearing the new blue jeans my father gave me the night before school. My dad thoughtfully chose these pants and bought them from the Sears Roebuck catalog that an American officer had given him. He had ordered a red peacoat for Kim Chi and a pair of the button-fly blue jeans for me. I remember them so well because almost immediately upon seeing me, the kids pointed and laughed that I was wearing boy pants. Didn't I know that only boys wore front button-fly, so they could, you know, pee the way boys do? Apparently, in those days, girls only wore pants with side zippers or buttons. I quickly convinced myself the other kids didn't know anything about American fashion, but still, I was humiliated and wished I could run home.

Before I attended school, I didn't know anything about Catholicism. Now I knew one thing for sure: the nuns crossed themselves and invoked Jesus' name incessantly, whether they were worried, displeased, or in disbelief, as this was their way to salvation, I supposed. For a non-Catholic, it looked like they had a nervous tic or an involuntary, knee-jerk reaction. Naturally, I mimicked them to blend in, but soon I was baffled to learn that this was not such a great idea.

At the end of kindergarten, I learned two things. Lesson one: Nuns were mean. Lesson two: There were two sets of rules, one for school and one at home. It was okay and acceptable to exclaim

"Jesus" and cross myself at school, but my parents didn't allow this practice at home. "We are not Catholic. We don't do that!" They didn't offer further explanations, and I didn't dare ask, but I made a mental note to observe the strict demarcation between my Catholic school and my Confucian home.

My older sister adjusted quite beautifully at school, and the nuns loved her. At Christmas time, she asked my mother to donate a tree to the school, and of course, my mom said she could, so the nuns were ecstatic. Now they could expand and arrange their manger scene with the shepherds, sheep, and baby Jesus. What an excellent addition to the classroom. Indeed, the nuns very much adored her. That week, my mother sent our driver into the forest to cut down a pine tree fit for the school display, and he carefully delivered it to Sacred Heart.

I observed and tried to learn, but couldn't see the big picture of how adults communicated and managed their relationships. I wanted to please the nuns, much the same way my sister did with the gifted tree. I fantasized that if I also gave them a tree, I'd be in their good graces. I asked my mother to give my class one, and I heard that I could. I promised the nuns that our classroom would have a tree. When the day came, I stood at the doorway and waited for the driver to deliver a freshly cut pine. Time passed, and the nuns asked me to sit down in my seat, filled with terrible disappointment when the tree didn't arrive. Apparently, my mother didn't take my request very seriously. I was mortified, horrified, and disgraced. The nuns didn't like me much before, and now they definitely hated me.

Truthfully, I didn't understand their disapproval of me. Did I cry too much when in kindergarten and first grade? Was I one of the crybabies in the classroom? From the deepest and darkest memories, I realized that at Sacred Heart, I was indeed one of those children who cried during class, instead of obediently reciting prayers with the nuns. The nuns threatened that I would be well on my way to that hot place where no angels sang if I didn't stop crying.

In first grade, I earnestly sang and prayed in class. My grades were as poor as ever, and the nuns were relentless with their wooden rulers on my knuckles for not getting any smarter. After two years at Sacred Heart, I begged my parents to take me elsewhere. I was then enrolled in the all-girl public school at the beginning of second grade, partly because of our relocation, but mostly because I wasn't doing well socially or academically. My older sister stayed happily with her nun teachers.

I tell this, not for dramatic effect, but to explain how I began testing boundaries and their consequences. One of the earliest examples scared my parents, though we were surprised by the happy outcome.

In Kindergarten, I walked home when my mother was late to pick me up. I only started walking, on autopilot, the same routes I had always walked with my mother. I didn't dawdle, and I was not scared. When I got home, to my surprise, my parents were unbelievably angry, but they immediately scooped me up and hugged me, crying. They made me promise that I would never do that again. Contrary to their belief that I was a stubborn child, I was only a curious child and didn't think it hurt anyone if I walked home.

American Soldier and Communist Defectors

To share another story to illustrate how I continued to be the black sheep of my family, my older sister often accused me of not listening to her, not following her rules. In first grade, I saw my first real-life American, as opposed to the black and white television versions in *Gunsmoke, The Big Valley, Star Trek, Hawaii Five-O,* and *Mission Impossible,* all the shows the American station had broadcast to entertain their troops.

It was a hot and stifling day. I sat on the sidewalk in front of the school waiting for our ride home, and again, our driver was late. Kim Chi and I kept searching for our car, but each time the cars were for someone else, and one by one, all the students were picked up except for us. We sat there wilting, listening to our empty stomachs growl. From afar, I spotted an American, dressed in civilian clothes, walking towards us. He approached and squatted only knees apart from us to take our picture.

He was, as I recall, a strange yet beautiful creature. Vietnamese didn't have blue eyes, and ours aren't set as deeply, causing the brows to be more prominent. His eyes sparkled with different hues of blue like glass marbles, and they possessed certain ethereal qualities. His high bridge and sharp-angled nose had yet another captivating effect. I don't remember his hair color, but his skin was a golden color, surely from the intense tropical sun, looking very much like the color of my mother's perfectly fried egg rolls. When he spoke, I was both scared and intrigued. I was scared because I had never seen an actual real-life American before, and this man had such a formidable stature. At the same time, I was intrigued by how beautiful he was.

His voice was deep, and he must have asked if he could take our pictures and proceeded to snap several. It happened quickly, and I was motionless, but my sister always knew what to do in awkward situations like these, so she deftly hung a white handkerchief over her face. Through gritted teeth, she mumbled as though he understood Vietnamese, "Don't let him take our picture! Cover your face," she stammered, "Uh, with your school bag!" I was slow to comprehend and didn't see any harm in it, just mildly embarrassed for a stranger to take our pictures in these wretched uniforms. I sat there motionless, not obeying my sister, studying the American, as beautiful as a movie star, except in person and color. It was not worth the reprimand of my mother, but how I wish I could have that priceless picture now, to see how horrified my sister was, and how completely baffled, smitten, and transfixed I was, staring into the viewfinder.

Kim Chi and I did many things together since Minh Châu was only two years old then, too young for me to hang around with daily. Our home in Đà Nẵng was very different from the one in Nha Trang. We lived in an upstairs apartment unit, one of many. The residents shared the bathrooms at one end of the building and showers at the opposite end.

We used to pair up for our morning constitution and sat in adjacent stalls. On one occasion, my sister broke the silence from sheer boredom and asked if I was daydreaming. I truthfully replied that I wondered why boogers were salty. My sister shrieked with outrage and asked how I knew they were salty unless I had tasted them myself, and no one with manners would go around picking their noses, let alone tasting it. She didn't want me to continue my filthy habit and told me just to wait until my mother heard about it.

After that, I didn't share my thoughts with her. In my mind, my older sister started to act like an adult, like the nuns, so I began to retreat from her. And yet, as siblings, we were bonded together, so I could not be angry with my dear sister for long.

My siblings made fast friends with kids in the same building. I can't remember if I had any friends there. Does friendship form that early? I can't even remember anything about my younger sister Minh Châu, who became my best playmate in later years. What I can say, unequivocally, is this was the place for which I hold the fondest memory of feeling loved and doted on by both parents. Then and only then, in that preciously small and finite window of time, I had both parents to myself. They cuddled and bounced me, and my father let me sit on his feet, craning me up and down while sitting in his chair, as though I was inside a John Deere tractor's bucket, a fun game that made me endlessly giggle and cry out, "More, more! Again, again!"

On these evenings, we listened faithfully to our BBC radio programs on the same Philips shortwave radio my father had since his academy days. Sometimes they had a reporter with a strong northern accent, and when that combined with static, we barely understood the content but got the gist of the state of the war. Every day, just like today's *NPR's Marketplace* radio program "doing the numbers" of the Dow Jones Industrial Average, this program did the numbers too, except it was of the defected Việt Cộng who denounced communism to join the South Vietnamese armed forces or become civilians. The theme song for this program was hauntingly sad, about a lost bird finding its way back home. To this day, I can still sing the lyrics.

I had a vivid imagination as a child and pictured a bedraggled Việt Cộng trudging toward the line in the sand with both arms up, looking scared. He prayed that the South Vietnamese would not fire shots at him. I was sure he was hungry, looked tired, and wore black, rubberized tire tread sandals. When I was very young, I thought they defected from war injuries and famine. Later on in life, I figured the defectors no longer believe in Uncle Hồ's idealized communism. They'd experienced otherwise for too long, and utopia would never occur as long as humans remained fallible. Then as I grew even older, I believed that it must have been a sadly staged propaganda from the South Vietnamese regime, the testimonies scripted somewhere in a dimly lit office, attempting to reach the guerrilla fighters moving in the Củ Chi tunnels between the North and the South. But I will never know the truth.

CHAPTER 4

Remote Outpost ~ Sơn Chà

We moved yet again to a remote outpost called Sơn Chà shortly after our year in Đà Nẵng. I had enjoyed the short stint with our stay-at-home father, but now that he was stationed in Huế, I struggled with his career success and not having him under the same roof. I felt the loss personally. He was now the lieutenant colonel, the captain commander of the 3rd Battalion of 48th Infantry Regiment Separate. We were driven to schools, on outings, and lived by a new set of rules with increased security and safety measures. Suddenly there was a buffer around us.

Our new house on the base had a landscaped front yard, set behind a barbed wire fence. We lived within the compound that was adjacent to the office building where soldiers saluted the flag at formation and performed their drills in the mornings. Some left in their GMC trucks and Jeeps to their mission destinations, and others disappeared into the buildings. I watched them with fascination from my front porch swing, much the same way I watched the world outside my window in Đà Lạt when I was two years old. The soldiers scurried to their tasks, only stopping momentarily to greet and salute one another. What did the soldiers say to one another? Perhaps it was something like, "Yes, the C-rations came in this morning, and we'll need to unload them," or maybe, "Don't look now, but the lieutenant colonel's kid is still spying on us at position two o'clock." I had an active imagination and it was full of self-importance because the soldiers were too busy to notice children in their proximity.

I was at an age where I loved to spy on other people, and it didn't help that we watched too many episodes of *Ironside* and *Get Smart* on American TV stations. I was in luck because across the street, the American mess hall and kitchen were within my line of sight, just perfect for my daily observations. In the Quonset hut, the warm flood of yellow lights illuminated the American soldiers in their white baker hats and aprons, baking bread and preparing meals for the troops. On those evenings, I savored the sweet scent of baked bread and rolls and learned the fragrance of American comfort food—beef stew with potatoes and carrots—that wafted over my front porch, a curiously blending juxtaposition of my mother's aromatic fried fish and jasmine rice.

Sơn Chà was a rural, backwater hamlet about half an hour away from Đà Nẵng. Its elementary school had kindergarten to fifth grade and a high school from sixth to twelfth, a typical school structure in Vietnam. The elementary school I attended had three small buildings arranged in a U-shape. It must have been new; its barren landscape dotted only by a few oleanders in the center courtyard where the flagpole stood. Off to the sides were two outhouses, one for students and one for teachers.

If you believed in luck, then you might say mine had changed when I met my second-grade teacher in this small hamlet. Teacher Hương, which incidentally means fragrance, greeted us each morning at the door and patted our heads as we passed and said her goodbyes the same way at the end of the day. She patiently waited for us to answer a question when she called on us, and many raised their hands, wanting her attention, so eager to please or impress her with their knowledge. I didn't know teachers could be this gentle and wondered why my parents waited so long to bring me here.

Surprisingly, she didn't carry a ruler. Instead she spoke kindly and smiled frequently. School had a new meaning to me, and I no longer doubted my academic ability. Math became my favorite subject, and I discovered that I wasn't such a bad student after all, as the nuns had convinced me. My teacher's tender ways made her even more beautiful than she already was. Once she knelt down at my desk and asked, "Why so sad, and why all the tears?" Though I immediately regretted that I told her too much, confessing that I saw my mother cry when my father left, and wondered why he was always leaving, if he loved us as much as we loved him. Was it something we did?

During dinner conversation, my mother inadvertently learned about my conversation with the teacher and became very upset that I had revealed our family affairs for the world to see. Slowly, from that day on, I learned about propriety and boundaries, that there were things one could say and things one could never say. From that day on, I also began slowly learning about family honor, that there were things we did and said because we pledged complete and utter loyalty to our family.

Sơn Chà Public School Days

In the late sixties, elementary school children had six school days, but we finished at noon. Starting in first grade, we graduated from writing with pencils to writing with ink pens, the kind that had metal nibs to dip in inkwells after every few words. Beyond elementary school, we were required to use fountain pens, and most of us would have the best penmanship from years of training while preparing for college. I carried tennis ball-size inkwells with a little handle like one would carry a lunch pail. Often, about once a week, the wells spilled blue ink on my white shirt, as the lids fitted poorly. My right hand was constantly ink-stained, and my right middle finger where the pen pressed against was callous and bulbous from endless hours of penmanship.

Our blue ink came from store bought pellets the size of dried peas. We diluted them with warm water in a container, then transferred the mix to the tin inkwells. Their design was such that the ink wouldn't spill when they were tipped over, but they always did, and my uniforms were telltales of such regular incidents. In second grade I had two lined notebooks, one for math and one for language arts such as spelling, writing, and grammar. The best notebook brand was the Cyclos, with an ink drawing of a man pedaling the pedicab on the covers. Its high-quality paper made writing and blotting an improved experience, as the ink glided and soaked into the thick fibers.

My parents brainwashed us at a very young age not to be wasteful, not to tear the pages when we made mistakes because these were very expensive. They told us, "It's like tearing up money and throwing it away." But sometimes I had to "tear up money" when I erased them too much, leaving an unsightly, gaping hole on the page. We used ink blotters. These were soft pressed paper squares, to absorb the ink of freshly written words to keep them from smearing. At a very young age, we were scared into submission and learned to write neatly, or the teachers would give us a sound rapping over the knuckles. We avoided pain and stayed within the confines of right and wrong. It was wrong to ask questions, even for the sake of learning, as it was perceived to be questioning authority, and that would undoubtedly lead to civil disobedience.

Our country was at war with the North Vietnamese or the Việt Cộng, also known as the VC, and our job was to learn and be patriotic. Here I was, in a patriotic classroom where I could see the Vietnamese flag, its three red stripes representing the bloodlines of our regions, North, Central, and South set against the yellow background representing our skin color. Every morning we sang the national anthem at formation then orderly, two-by-twos, we filed into our classrooms. These classes held up to fifty students each, and neatly, we tucked ourselves into long wooden desks. We kept our inkwells and pens in the troughs in the top half of the tables and our book bags on the floor.

There were three rows of desks, about five deep. The studious children sat in the front rows, while the lazy ones hid in the back where they were more likely to get away with talking and not paying attention to class. The teacher had a full-size wooden desk, on an elevated platform, where she had a good view of the students. The blackboard hung in front of the classroom with its matched length platform, so anyone who was called to write on the board could walk across it and reach the top. Every day the class leader took roll call and recorded it in the left-hand side box, such as 42/50 for forty-two children present out of fifty total. She also wrote the date and the teacher's selected proverb as part of our lessons, where she would explain its meaning and socially redeeming values.

Our uniforms were basic white shirts and blue skirts or pants. Our shirts had tags to show our names and the class identification. We followed our teacher's orders without question and were taught to revere them as much as our parents and ancestors, if not more, following the Confucian teaching. My school year in Sơn Chà culminated with a peaceful and successful end. I received awards for excellent academic achievement, whatever that might mean in second grade. We assembled in front of the whole student body and proudly received our red cellophane-wrapped awards and gifts of miscellaneous school supplies. This academic year was the turning point in my life where I knew that the maltreatment from the nuns was behind me, and given the right mentor and teacher, I could be at the top of the class, basking in the glory of hard work and rewards.

The Foiled Plot

Despite the war, up until this point, we lived a rather uneventful life. I know I have complained incessantly about not having my father around, but let me be more truthful to say he was very strict when he was home. Most of the time, he held family meetings to reiterate the rules and restrictions he wanted my mother to carry out and reinforce in his absence. He handed out award monies for our good report cards, and we lined up as if we were getting New Year's Lì Xì money in red and gold envelopes, but he also scolded us when we received bad grades or didn't follow the rules. I imagined my grandmother and mother kept a running tally of all our mischiefs and wrongdoings, so he could address them all at once when he came home. Both of my parents worked hard to teach us to be upstanding citizens and sheltered us from harm, not only from the war but also the ills that it brought. We were lucky that we didn't know losses like others experienced on a daily basis, at least not up until this point. But soon, the VC retaliated against my father for his collaboration with his US Advisor and First Marine Division on guerrilla warfare.

They went after our family to retaliate against my father's tactical assistance and guidance to the US forces, resulting in massive destruction of the VC's infrastructures. His collaboration also included methods on how to win the hearts and minds of the villagers, so that top commanders and soldiers could avoid more casualties from booby traps. My father once said that 65% of the 1st US Marine Corps injuries in vital areas of Đà Nẵng such as Dodge City were from the booby traps. For example, Colin Powell was injured by these in the Ashau Valley.

My father worked with the US commander and troops to stop their practice of indiscriminate deployment of air support or artillery, also known as "prep fires," or heavy shelling on a village before entering to kill the VC. Unfortunately, the casualties were mostly innocent women and children—because the enemy was quicker to escape into their secret tunnels. But more importantly, my father emphasized that the reason villagers set booby traps to hurt the US forces was in reaction to their prep fires practice before entering the village. But all of his US collaboration and success had a price.

A rescue mission of 26 Marines encircled by Main Force Saper of Quảng Da Special Zone of Central Vietnam, known as Dodge City, in the vicinity of Meade River. This was a Search and Destroy Operation in an area of 7 square kilometers, South of Đà Nẵng, 1968.

In those days, like clockwork, the driver, "Uncle" Thăng, would drop my mother off at the outdoor market for grocery shopping every day. One day, after my mom had left, the driver abandoned the jeep, leaving Minh Châu in the car by herself. She recalled that a man in everyday, civilian clothing came up and offered her a can of soda, which she refused and didn't think much of after he walked away.

That day, my mother returned to the car earlier than usual, and Thăng had barely made it back, only minutes before she arrived with her basket full of fish and vegetables for that day's meal. After they had arrived home, my mother prepared lunch and sat down to enjoy it with Minh Châu, but they were interrupted by a deafening explosion that came from the direction of the Jeep.

As it turned out, there was an attempt on my family's life, and the explosive planted in the vehicle would have killed my mother and sister, had her shopping trip lasted as long as it usually did. Luckily for all of us, my mother left the market a lot sooner than expected. No one knew the cause of the blast until the police came for an investigation. They asked Minh Châu many questions as she was the only person in the Jeep at the market. They wanted to know about the time frame, the man, what he looked like and what he said to her. They also found shreds of the Coke can with traces of plastic, thus concluding the cause of the explosion. The driver was immediately transferred to the frontline combat for failing his duty and abandoning the Jeep.

We learned that Thăng died some time after that in battle, and I was afraid to be alone anywhere at home, even while using the bathroom. I was afraid to run into his ghost because I thought he might blame our family for sending him away to his death. As for Minh Châu, she suffered nightmares and slept with my mother every night after that incident. Thăng's replacement, "Uncle" Lai reported to work as our new family driver, after he'd been carefully screened by the Military Police. Lai had a stellar record and would later guard and protect our family from another assassination attempt.

The End of Innocence

I remember when it first happened. It was the year before the Tết Offensive in 1968, when my then college-age and oldest brother Thảo came home for the summer. He called our driver in the middle of the night on the military phone to take my mother to the doctor. Earlier that day and evening, my mother felt her labor pains and was in frequent communication with my father to keep him apprised of the developments. He planned to escort her to the hospital, but they lost communication. Her pain intensified, and my mother needed to deliver the baby sooner than she'd expected.

Opting for a quicker route for her instant delivery, the driver took my mother to a small birthing clinic nearby. It was indeed a quick delivery, and the midwife swaddled the baby, handing him over to my mom, then discharged them the following evening. Shortly after they arrived home, my jubilant father joined my mother and proudly named the new baby boy, Thi.

Having had five children, my mom knew something was terribly wrong with Thi when he had trouble breathing. He quickly developed a fever, and spasms contorted his tiny body. My father rushed them to the hospital in Đà Nẵng where the doctor promptly diagnosed Thi with tetanus and said he wouldn't live.

In an instant, my mother's whole world was obliterated. He was her beautiful little boy. Anger and grief are such mild words to describe her pain. Our family wanted to punish the midwife for taking Thi's life when she cut his umbilical cord with tainted scissors, but that wouldn't bring him back, it was too late.

My siblings and I visited my mother at the hospital on our way to school, where we saw the nurse take Thi away. I was merely six years old. It was surreal, in slow motion, my mother floating out of her hospital bed, flapping her arms around her baby, and then slumping to the cold floor with him. I didn't want to leave my mother there in her pain, convulsing, and sobbing, but it was time for us to go to school. I could hear the deafening sound of teardrops hitting the impersonal and cold tile floor. As the driver whisked us away, I glanced over my shoulder at my broken-hearted mother on the floor.

I never quite knew how to grieve for Thi, but I'm grieving now, even as I'm writing about my little brother, who would have been almost fifty this year. I didn't understand death at such a young age. I only knew it devastated my parents and my oldest brother. Time suspended that day, slowly and languidly fluttering like a spider web in the breeze.

Thi's funeral was somber and profoundly heart-wrenching. His doll-like body wrapped in white linen. A piece of white cloth loosely placed on the top of his face. His coffin sat in the brightly lit living room on a table where red candles and sandalwood incense burned for him on the ancestral altar. An unfamiliar scent that reminded me of ground turmeric overpowered the room. My eyes burned and my vision blurred from the constant flood of my tears, and they distorted the shapes of all things before me. My parents told us that he was safe with our ancestors now and they would care for him. They prayed to Buddha and our ancestors for their blessings then placed Thi in his tiny coffin.

We started the procession of cars to the cemetery in the forest of Sơn Chà. The morning was gray, and the wind whistled among the pines as we began our walk to his gravesite. Somehow I was displaced from my parents and siblings. In the midst of confusion and grief, I got separated from my family, and when we arrived, I took off running to find my family. There were many people in front of us, all wearing white clothing and white headdress for the funeral, all heading in the same direction. I ran and called out my siblings' names, passing everyone, until I got to a place where everyone was gathering. I found my mother and hung on to her áo dài. At last, I was where I belonged, right next to my mom, her whole body quivering with grief, flanked by my oldest brother and father with their arms around her.

The pine trees towered over the funeral procession. They howled and hissed at the attendants while whipping the sand over the headstones and graves. I felt lost, confused, and cold. The violent wind creaking and whistling of the trees reminded me of the propaganda on television against opium and marijuana. "If you used these drugs," the narrator said, "you'll end up like ghosts flying through the air in cemeteries like these." I immediately visualized the TV ghosts circling and growling their grievances all around us.

Peering through the openings in the crowd before me at the gravesite, I witnessed Thi's coffin slowly lowered into the ground. My father and brother had to restrain my mother; she didn't want the earth to swallow him. Much later, my parents lit candles and incense and burned written paper prayers to heaven for my brother, and we watched the white ash ascend skyward. I was sure I saw my baby brother's spirit spiral up and away. In the presence of the sheer walls of the Marble Mountains, I felt dwarfed and insignificant to the earth that engulfed my brother.

My oldest brother Thảo was the chief source of comfort for my mother, as my father had to return to work. A month later, we came back to the cemetery for Thi's "Gate-Opening" ceremony, a ritual to release his spirit to roam and finally meet our ancestors. My mother brought a little broom to brush away sandstorm dunes that had been building up on his grave from the nearby beaches. She pulled small, flowering weeds from around the gravesite, cleaned and filled up the water cups, replaced the flowers, and lit new candles and incense. She arranged plates of clear cellophane wrapped cookies and fresh fruit at the headstone, and with three lit incense sticks, she closed her eyes and whispered prayers to Buddha and ancestors to protect and guide him as well as our family here on earth, especially her husband, who was fighting on the battlefront.

As I am telling this story, I wish I could hold my mother and hug her tightly. When we were growing up, we didn't talk about sacred things; we just soldiered on, with sadness and pain. We didn't talk about our feelings, maybe because it would break us into tiny fragments. Many years later, my mother finally spoke about Thi. In the short time that she knew him, she said he was a beautiful baby who barely cried at all. If I could talk to my mother now, I would want to know how she found the enduring and extraordinary strength to live on after such devastation. I think she slept a lot in her room, but we all took naps in the afternoons, so I didn't think it was anything out of the ordinary.

As I write, the depths of my memories begin to surface, and I understand my poor mother suffered a lot more than I ever realized as a kid. I was six, and she was thirty-three years old. She was young, raising three stepsons and her five children while her husband was at war, and then to suffer the loss of her baby boy. I can barely stand to imagine her struggles and the loneliness she must have felt. If I could go back, I would comfort her instead of being a stubborn girl, crying and squirming when she combed and braided my hair. I would tell her, "I love you, Mommy. I'm sorry that I'm such a pill. I didn't know that you had to endure so much suffering and so many losses. See, I can stand still so you can braid my hair, and I won't cry for silly reasons like fighting with my sisters and brothers. I love you so, Mommy!"

After the "Gate Opening" ceremony, we returned to Thi's gravesite at least once a month to offer flowers, incense, candles, and sometimes paper clothes, toys, and money, so my brother would not be left wanting. Another child's grave was next to my brother, and we cleaned up his grave whenever we visited Thi's. We almost always left blocks of Bánh In, the dense rice cakes with beautiful flower imprints, on their stones. The food always disappeared by the next time we came, and I believed then that my brother and his neighbor ate them together under the stars and the moon of Sơn Chà.

CHAPTER 5

Sadness and Tragedies

We carried on after Thi's death. Life resumed for my younger sister and I. Minh Châu was the baby of the family again, and she was my best playmate. We were first introduced to the "Westerns" when the Americans aired their television shows to entertain their troops. Minh Châu and I loved to pretend to be cowboys. We were so enamored and fascinated by their unusual and wild ways of riding horses, sleeping on the ground, drinking black coffee out of tin cups, cooking over the fires, and speaking their strange language.

With active imaginations, we climbed in the empty and large cupboards at floor level in the dining room, pretending to be in our stagecoach. We reenacted a highway robbery, one of us played the robber riding alongside the wagon, and one of us sat inside the cupboard stagecoach.

The highway robber game provided us hours of fun, of course, until one day, the robber kicked the door in a little too hard, just like the cowboys did on the TV shows, and the door jammed shut. One of us got trapped inside the dark, cramped space. We wiggled and shoved the door until it fell off its hinges and we felt like heroes. Normally, we would have been in serious trouble, but my mother didn't care about our antics. She buried herself in her bedroom, sleeping most of the day and came out to have dinner with us when the cook served it at our round table.

We couldn't believe our luck that we escaped the feather duster spanking this time. My mother usually didn't spare the rod; rather she used the long handle feather duster to whack us on our bottoms when we misbehaved. Between my two older brothers and me, it seemed like we got punished every other week.

Minh Châu, and I didn't have many toys and relied on our resourcefulness for play. We lost ourselves in building fortresses, playing house and school. We pretended to be our most and least favorite teachers and mimicked their idiosyncratic ways. We experimented with cooking outdoors and stole rice from the pantry for our experiments. My older brothers helped us gather bricks and made a three-sided oven, using scrap wood to build the fires and an old C-ration can for a rice pot. Not having any experience in cooking rice, we burned the rice at the bottom and had very wet and crunchy rice in the middle. We dug for red clay and molded small earthen pots, plates, and bowls, like those we saw at the market. We gathered assortments of leaves for make-believe vegetables, then neatly placed them in a stack to cut thin strips for salad, the way our mother did. In retrospect, one the benefits of having a big family was that my mom didn't always know where we were or what we were doing. We were each other's friends, and we rarely needed other kids for playmates.

As we played, my father engaged deeply in battles, sometimes sleeping in the foxhole alongside his soldiers, working hard to keep us safe, healthy and in school. He was a military commander, and as such, even when he was shot down from a helicopter and severely wounded, the army postponed several days before informing my mother, for unknown "security reasons." They told my mom only when he returned to stable condition. We were allowed to visit my father at the American army hospital, where the staff treated us to single serving cups of Foremost vanilla ice cream, something we had never had before. Its silky texture rollicked on my tongue and in my mouth. I liked how slowly it melted and coldly slid down my throat. I treasured every little crystal of the ivory colored cream and savored this new delicacy.

Strangely, I enjoyed being in the American Quonset hospital. There were two rows of cots for recuperating American soldiers, one row against each curved wall. The men were peaceful. They sat up playing cards, reading, and talking to each other. Some were sleeping, perhaps dreaming about being sent home to America. I wished I could have spoken English then. I always had an unexplainable fascination with the English language and its foreign words full of the "s" sounds. Minh Châu and I used to talk to each other in our made-up English language, full of "s" sounds because this was what it sounded like to us.

My father returned to work after his long convalescence. We were very fortunate that he survived the alleged friendly fire from an American helicopter. In this war, not everyone was as lucky as my father. A woman once came to my mother for help. Her husband died in battle. For his sacrifice, the widow received twelve months' salary from the government. She came to our house, asking my mother for a special favor. Between sobs, she asked for a few bags of concrete to build a proper grave for her late husband. The widow convinced my mother that she didn't have anyone to turn to, and she had young children at home. She promised she wouldn't return with additional requests.

I watched the grief-stricken woman, crying before my mother. I couldn't wait to find out what my mom would do, but their conversation went on for a long time, and I ran off to play with my sister. People like this woman came to my mother for help routinely because she was known for her generosity. Refugees who fled the communists from the countryside stopped by our house asking for food and shelter. These strangers came to our doorstep for the night, their children's hollowed eyes and caved-in stomachs crying for hunger relief. Their ragged clothes and dirty bare feet frightened me. I watched them eat their rice with salted cabbages and fish so fast, I feared they might choke. I worried that they might die during the night, as they slept on straw mats on our back porch.

Sơn Chà was a poor town, and most people had no land or skills to eke out a living. Some made cardboard, tarp, and corrugated tin shacks by rummaging through the town's dump. After the United States army had come, these people flocked through their garbage too, seeking more scraps of food and shelter.

Sadness prevailed in this hamlet, and I observed it from my front porch swing, where I spent a lot of time. As a child, I cried when reprimanded by my mother. I cried for a long time, nonstop. I was the champion crier of my family. For this reason, my mom banished me to the swing where nobody could hear my bothersome cry. As soon as I left, everyone forgot about me and my crying. Sitting there outside on the swing, I could cry to my heart's content. I had a sustaining weak whimpering, which I promptly turned up to a full passionate wail when someone came near because I was too embarrassed to stop. I secretly hoped that someone would rescue me from this predicament, and eventually, someone would, to tell me that it was dinnertime. During these crying fits, I observed life as it played out on my rhythmic double swing, and I didn't always see pleasant things.

A boy under the age of ten managed to climb onto a moving American GMC truck carrying cargo. He was riding in the back of a motorcycle alongside this truck when he hung on to the side and climbed aboard. He probably wanted to steal something from the truck and throw it to the roadside. How he would escape, I had no idea. Everything happened so quickly I had no way of predicting what was going to happen next. In slow motion, I saw the boy losing his grasp, tumbling and spinning off the moving truck he once hung on so precariously. The truck moved on. The boy sprawled on the street motionless. He did not make it. The boy died instantly. I couldn't unsee what I witnessed. The accident occurred right in front of me, and it replayed in my mind again and again for weeks. I wished I could have turned my head more quickly and avoided seeing the whole accident, but it didn't work out that way.

I ran inside crying in hysteria. I stuttered in shock and couldn't tell my mother what had happened. Passersby stopped and gathered at the scene, forming a circle around his body. The Vietnamese and American Military Police arrived. The GMC truck driver had seen in his rear view mirror what had happened and returned to the scene, where he sat on his heels holding his head, crying. Needless to say, after this incident, I stayed inside and had nightmares for weeks.

Tết Mậu Thân ~ 1968

On an extremely rare occasion, my father got his military leave to celebrate the Lunar New Year in 1968, the Year of the Monkey, with his family. He dressed in his civilian clothes, bouncing Minh Châu on his knees, and relishing precious moments at home for Tết. We savored the fact that our large family could be together during this small window of time under one roof. Even brother Thảo, who attended college in Sài Gòn, made the long trek home for a holiday.

Whenever brother Thảo visited, we always circled him. "Tell us stories about Sài Gòn," we pleaded with him. He played the guitar and recorded us singing with his cassette tape recorder. And boy, oh, boy, did we all sing with gusto while he played. We giggled from the embarrassment of our recorded voices, but those singing sessions were some of my favorite memories. He told us stories of his college life, of renting a room from a family, and three meals delivered daily in a three-tier tin pail. He recounted numerous times, by popular demand, how he almost lost an eye from an ejected screw, while working on his moped.

Brother Thảo was the epitome of worldliness to us, and we were in awe of him. He entertained us, showed us love, and brought us laughter, but he could be very strict and paternal, as he was the oldest son in the family. When I was about three-years-old, and my mother was busy with guests, he was frustrated with my incessant crying and threatened to drop me down the well if I didn't stop. Nevertheless, we adored and worshiped him. I was heartbroken and hid my tears whenever he left for school in Sài Gòn. I always made my goodbye brief, as not to reveal my tears. I wanted that affection and attention to last because I frequently felt forgotten in such a large family, even though I knew my parents loved me in their traditional ways of providing for me and protecting me from harm.

We have one of the black and white photos that captured this moment when our whole family celebrated the most sacred holiday of our culture together. The carefree mood of the gathering was self-evident in the picture. We were giddy, with unbridled excitement, as we gathered around the oval dining table and made a toast for the camera. My parents and grandmother looked very young, and indeed they were in that picture. We smiled broadly and showed lots of white teeth. My mother and father were so young and beautiful; they made a very handsome couple. The older brothers stood in the back, and the younger kids sat around the table facing the camera. Above our heads was a small grandfather clock, with the pendulum swung to one side, marking ten to midnight.

*Tết 1968, Sơn Chà. Left to Right: Thọ, my Mother with Minh Châu,
Kim Chi, Thảo, Grandmother next to my Father, Bá (behind), Tâm,
Thông, Hoàng Chi*

I sat legs crossed, wearing a pleated dress like both of my sisters.
My mother was egalitarian in the way she dressed her children; we
wore identical outfits, just different sizes. "There was no squabbling
between you kids when I dressed you all the same way," she said.
"And besides, I could spot you a lot quicker when we were all out and
about!" All of the sisters wore braids, the result of a very painful hair
pulling and braiding session I endured each morning as a child. The
boys wore white short-sleeve button-down shirts, and dark slacks.
My grandmother wore her everyday-checkered turban, a muted color
cotton shirt, and black satin pants.

In the hours before New Year's Eve, my parents clutched three
incense each between their palms, standing side by side, eyes closed,

lips barely parted, uttering inaudible prayers in front of the ancestral altar that brimmed with offerings of food and cups with chrysanthemum tea. They prayed to our ancestors for their blessings, and continuing guidance in the New Year. The children stood around the strands of firecrackers, cracking and eating dyed-red watermelon seeds for good luck. We patiently waited for our parents to give us red pocket money, or tiền lì xì, at midnight. The excitement could compare to Christmas mornings when children open gifts from Santa and their parents.

A honey-colored, crisply roasted pig laid in front and center of an imposing table draped in cloth and lace. It was an offering table in front of the altar. A red apple propped the pig's mouth open, and a bleached-white, tripe veil draped over its head, like a bashful Western bride. Assorted candied fruit served in red lacquered trays flanked the centerpiece, showcasing my mother's endless hours of handiwork. For weeks leading up to New Year's, my mom sat on a small stool on the kitchen floor, in front of an earthen stove with glowing red coals, repeatedly ladling boiling syrup over thin slivers of coconut, wedges of winter melons, ginger, sweet potatoes, and lotus seeds. One of my most treasured scent memories is of the wafting scent of hot coal laced with caramelized fruit in the middle of winter. As a child, I savored and picked out the snow-white coconut slivers to eat first, and avoided the spicy, fibrous ginger I now love with my tea.

Promptly at midnight, brother Thảo lit strands of firecrackers as the younger kids scattered in the yard and squealed with delight and fright. The distant neighboring families synchronized their firecracker lighting, and the little hamlet came alive with the deafening explosion of gunpowder. After a long day of anticipation and staying up late, exhaustion came to the children. We acquiesced to my mother's announcement to eat our first New Year's meal of Bánh Tét, a sweet rice cake with seasoned pork and mung bean filling with the Dưa món and Củ kiệu, a dipping sauce of pickled scallions, daikon, and carrots in fish sauce. The red firecracker paper exploded into confetti bits and littered the front porch, much resembling the highly-esteemed plum blossom petals that bloomed this time of year. We learned the next day that it was the most massive massacre for Huế and its surrounding area, collectively scarring the people of the South. Ironically for our family, the Tết Offensive, a national tragedy, was the only occasion that our whole family celebrated the holiday together for the first time, and it was one of the happiest times of my childhood.

Tết 1968. Sơn Chà. Left to Right: Thông, Hoàng Chi, Kim Chi, Thọ,
Tâm holding Minh Châu, Thảo

CHAPTER 6

Back to Where We Started From

Shortly after the Tết Offensive, my father moved the family back to Đà Nẵng. Although we felt less removed from civilization than we did in Sơn Chà, I still didn't like Đà Nẵng. I felt disrupted and wanted to return home to Nha Trang. I liked nothing about it. The climate was harsh, either hot and humid, or wet and cold. The landscape was barren, with a hodgepodge of slums, incongruous storefronts, and buildings on one street, ranging from single-family dwellings to six-story buildings for rent, with stores on the ground floors. Clotheslines hung on the balconies like dingy and ragged flags. Dirty sidewalks with garbage filled gutters and flies abounded.

In the monsoon season, rainstorms filled the streets with filthy debris. One would wade in this torrent of unsanitary sludge to go to the marketplace in the rainy season. At least once a year we had weeklong storms with powerful winds peeling off sheets of corrugated tin roofs, sending them flying through the air, like magic carpets in waves of heavy rain. To hold the flooding water back, people placed sandbags, two or three high, at the doorsteps and perimeters of their homes.

Hoàng Chi on the front veranda of her home in Đà Nẵng, 1969

In Đà Nẵng, we lived with my two oldest brothers Tâm and Bá who were both younger than brother Thảo and whose mother was my father's first late wife. They shared an adjoining unit to our house that had a spacious living room with a dining table, a bedroom with two twin beds, and a bathroom. Tâm was an air force mechanic crew member, but he aspired to become a pilot. Even though Vietnam was a coffee culture, we would never find Bá congregating in cafes or anywhere else to discuss politics, as he was somewhat of an introvert. Unlike many young men who enjoyed hanging out at cafes, nursing their chicories and swirling their nicotine, Bá liked his swing on the verandah at home, where he talked to his imaginary friend about his views of the world. Bá was also a writer. He would write and toss and write and toss until he ran out of paper. He was judicious with his words. After we came to America, I realized how much I missed seeing Bá and having our daily chats and teasing. I missed his natural smile and innocent looking eyes.

Brother Tâm, younger than Bá, on the other hand, seemed strict and distant. Although he chatted and chuckled with older siblings, he seemed unreachable to me, perhaps because of our age and gender divide. My best connection with him was through music, when we listened for hours to his reel-to-reels, cassette tapes, and vinyl records of the popular American and French music that he brought home. Life is funny that way; I only remember the highs and lows of how someone made me feel. Once, I swallowed a piece of gum, and Brother Tâm told me that I would die within an hour. I took him seriously. I thought I would die as I stood there in the living room, watching the grandfather clock ticking away on the wall. Unfortunately and unbeknownst to me, he was only joking and didn't realize the impact his words had on me. As a child, I hung on to every word he uttered as he walked away, leaving me standing there in my fear and grief.

Both Tâm and Bá came from the generation of cigarette smoking. They always seemed to be in deep contemplation as they watched the cigarette smoke swirling out of their nostrils. I once asked what they thought of when they did that, and they smiled, saying that I was a child and wouldn't understand. And yet, I continued to follow Bá around, sometimes teasing him, at times pleading with him to tell stories because I loved to listen to my elders' real life stories, or far-fetched ghost stories and fairy tales. We came from a culture of oral history, passing down life lessons and advice, sometimes in truth and sometimes woven in embellishment to illustrate and emphasize a moral story.

Baby Sisters ~ Years of the Monkey & Rooster

In the Year of the Monkey, 1968, my lovely baby sister Mỹ Châu was born in Đà Nẵng. Minh Châu, now no longer the youngest in the family, at the age of four, joined the orbit of older siblings.

I recall the feeling of relief when my father brought Lanh and her mother, Bà Hai, home to help my mom with the new baby. They were a much needed help. At the end of my dad's battle in Khe Sanh, he found Lanh and her mother huddled in a cave and brought them back to the base where they underwent routine questioning and integration processing. Upon establishing that they were not working for the guerrillas, my father offered them room and board at our house with a salary as my mom's helpers. Lanh was sixteen years old. She had long, jet-black hair and a flattened moon face. They both loved salt and couldn't eat enough of it. "We didn't have any salt living in the cave, hiding from the VC." We never heard of anyone suffering a salt deficiency, and we told them that they could have as much as they wanted in their food.

Mỹ Châu was a year old when she fell and broke her arm. Our two in-home helpers, fearful of losing their jobs, kept it a secret. My sister cried nonstop that night. The next morning, Lanh and her mother confessed that Mỹ Châu fell, and they would quit for not doing their jobs. My mom promptly took Mỹ Châu to the hospital, and we learned that she broke her arm after the doctor examined the x-ray. My baby sister came home that day in a pitiful little white cast.

Upon arrival at the hospital, we walked through the hospital corridors and saw people on stretchers in the hallways. Some were bloody and bandaged up. I didn't like being there because I was squeamish at the sight of blood, and it brought back the memory of my brother Thi's last days.

I used to think that everyone had my same recurring dreams, but when I got older, I realized that wasn't the case. In these dreams, I walked through long, cold and dimly lit hospital corridors and saw many bloody and wounded soldiers lining the hallways. I sought my way back to my sister, where she waited for an x-ray, but the hall kept stretching longer. There were rows of beds full of wounded and dismembered soldiers, their white bandages blood-soaked, their hands reaching out, moaning for their mothers. I never saw their faces nor knew their names. The further I ran from them, the more wounded I encountered until I would throw up from seeing their protruding intestines and dismembered limbs.

Kim Chi and I took turns taking care of Mỹ Châu before we had our in-home helpers. Sometimes I babysat alone, as I did one summer morning while my mother went to the market. Without warning, Mỹ Châu convulsed, then stiffened in my arms. Her eyes rolled back, revealing only the whites, and her face and lips turned blue, drooling profusely. I did not know what was happening or what to do. It could not have lasted very long, but at the time it seemed an eternity. Then just as quickly, Mỹ Châu's color returned, and normal breathing resumed. When my mother came home, I recounted everything that had happened. I thought my sister had died in my arms. I told my mom I didn't want to be at home alone with my baby sister anymore because I didn't know how to save her, and didn't want to lose another sibling.

Our loyal driver, Uncle Lai, picked up our family doctor and delivered him to our house. The doctor consulted with my mother, and I had no idea what transpired because children weren't allowed to be present during adult visits unless we served tea. Much later, we received the diagnosis from our doctor; Mỹ Châu had epilepsy.

Naturally, my mother was upset by the news. Her knowledge of epilepsy was limited to the adult's epileptic seizures in the marketplace. These people walked around with heavily padded pillows behind their heads, in case their seizures wrestled them down on the hard asphalt. "They can't live independently and have to rely on the kindness of families and strangers to survive," my mother sadly explained to us. She struggled with the fact that Mỹ Châu had this terrible, life-long disease. We didn't know what to say or do to comfort her, so we only stood there watching her weep.

Before we had our helpers, my chores after school included changing Mỹ Châu's diapers, rocking her to sleep in the hammock, and spoon-feeding her baby food. She had big brown eyes and a cherubic face framed sweetly with a bobbed haircut. She had a pale pink complexion and looked quite like a doll. My mother explained almost seriously that my baby sister looked like the doll on her dresser because, "I admired her every day when I was pregnant with Mỹ Châu, and that's why she is so beautiful now, looking just like that doll." I continued to help my mother after Mỹ Châu's first epileptic seizure. At ten years old, I got used to saying "no" to playing with neighbor kids. Occasionally, when I couldn't bear it anymore, I'd straddle my sister on one hip to play hopscotch or jump rope.

A year later, in 1969, the Year of the Rooster, my sister Hồng Châu was born. We now had two babies, but we also had the extra help, and my mom spared me the night feedings and changing. Kim Chi slept in my mom's room, and she made a natural choice for the nightly chores.

Hồng Châu was the last baby born in Đà Nẵng, following her older sisters' footsteps to Sacred Heart. The school now had a grander façade and structures than when I had attended eight years earlier. They still had the same nuns, only older now, and hopefully more gentle to my sister than they were with me.

Good Cooks ~ Bad Cooks

Uncle Chiêu was our army cook at the time, whose integrity was called into question when Lanh accused him of peeping when she bathed. "He craned his neck to look into the window one late night when I was washing. Everyone was already in bed, and I couldn't call anyone for help." She explained to my mother that she had let it go that one time, not knowing if she saw things. "But it happened again and again, every time I bathed," she said. My mother had to be the facilitator and called them both in to enquire about the allegations.

Chiêu denied the charges and insisted that he was only collecting the clothes and hanging up wet ones. He continued, "The clothes line just happened to be next to the bathroom window." I believed and sided with Lanh and began avoiding Chiêu after that. I was eleven or twelve at the time, and this whole scandal gave me the creeps. I felt sick having such a perverted old man around; I stopped talking to him and kept my distance. I couldn't believe that this was the same man who taught me the children's Buddhist chants. He prided himself on being a good Buddhist, but I should have figured out that it was only a cover when I found him counting grocery money to the tape of Buddhist chants. I knew mindful meditation was what one did during chants, not counting money.

Every morning in the kitchen, our family sat down for breakfast. We huddled in front of a round table and ate what our cook served. Breakfasts ranged from Xôi Vò, or Mung-bean sweet rice sprinkled with salty sesame seeds to fresh baguettes purchased from the early morning market vendors. I preferred the homemade soups, made from scratch, such as minced chicken rice congee or the light fish broth soup with rice noodles. Our cook went to the fishing boats early in the morning and picked out the fish as they flopped about in the wet woven baskets. The silvery flat bodies were still firm, their gills blood red and their eyes clear like drinking water. The soup would be made early in the morning before any of us crawled out of bed.

The fish soup was made from a simple water-based broth with added pineapple chunks, tomato wedges, green onions, salt and lots of black pepper, brought to a churning boil. The small fish were gutted and left whole, and the larger ones cut in halves, then added to the boiling broth. A tiny bit of fish sauce could further complement the flavor and the broth simmered for a brief time before serving, to keep the fish firm and flavorful.

Freshly made noodles layered the bottom of each soup bowl submerged in the steamy, aromatic fish broth. Our cook painstakingly flaked the white tender fish into our bowls then topped them with delicately fresh strands of cilantro. I indulged in every bite of the sweet fish meat in the slightly tangy and salty broth. The green onions and cilantro freshened the taste of each bite of fish in firm white rice noodles. I wished that our cook would make this every day, but he reminded me that he would have to wake up at ungodly hours every day to buy fish as the fishing boats came in, then stop to buy fresh noodles and herbs, and cook it and serve it in time for us to make it to school.

Another cook, Uncle Tăng, took me shopping with him in the summer. We bought fresh rice noodles from the factory on the main street, its doors opened wide so you can see how the noodles were made. Uncle Tăng knew I would enjoy watching the process of noodle making, and he was right. I stood dwarfed beneath a steamy cascade of white rice noodles, extruding from a nozzle-like apparatus filled with holes the size of the noodles' diameter. The stream of noodles, from the height of about ten feet, continuously tumbled into a vat of cold water below, where workers scooped the noodles into large strainers. Street vendors bought basketfuls of the noodles for resale, but people like us could buy any amount we wanted.

Our driver brought us home for lunches. Hot and tired, we sat down to our four-course meal of rice, soup, vegetables, and fish. Rice was the main staple at most meals, and we had a stool designated for this family-size rice pot. We took turns tending the rice pot, which meant that the one who sat next to the rice pot had to serve rice to everyone else. We never passed food around the table. All the food dishes sat in a circle with the fish sauce bowl in the center. We had serving utensils for all the dishes, but we only used our personal chopsticks to get food from the communal serving dishes. There was an unwritten order in which we ate our food in my family. The server filled our individual rice bowls with rice; then we ladled the light broth soup on top to moisten it. We ate some of that, intermittently adding bite size morsels from the side dishes.

Our cooks were very resourceful and creative. They could prepare the same fish in a hundred and one ways; pan fried, deep fried, steamed, clay-pot, stuffed, grilled, fish cakes, fish soups, skewers, and the list went on because fish was on the menu every day. Our vegetable dish was usually stir fried and very saucy with seasonal produce. My mother and the gardener planted a vegetable garden of tomatoes, string beans, melons and a variety of squashes. My favorite vegetable dish was the stir fry of chayote, carrots, yellow onions, pineapples, and squid. My least favorite was the stuffed bitter melons, although I do confess selectively picking out the delicious stuffing of ground pork, black mushroom and cellophane noodles with lots of garlic and black pepper.

We had about three cooks throughout the years, and I liked Uncle Rỗ the best. He had terrible acne scars on his face, hence his name with a vague reference of pockmarks, my first visual image when I think of him. He taught me how to scale a fresh fish, remove the gills, and trim the fins and tail. "If you fried the fish whole," he said, "leave the head, otherwise cut it into sections like this," slicing the sharp knife in about an inch below the gill, another slice about two inches away, so there were equal parts of the fish, including the tail end.

I stayed home after lunch when I was in elementary school while my high school siblings returned for their second half. I followed my cook around when I didn't have homework, to see how he lit the cooking stoves, when to add more coals, or how to cut up vegetables in different ways for different dishes. He was kind and wasn't bothered by my shadowing.

In the summers, he even took me to the market to show me how to barter with the merchants. "Beware of the fish mongers. They are not afraid to rip your heart out with their sharp tongues," he said. "It's a fine line, though. You don't want to get taken, but if you offer too little, they will insult you and seven generations back." He leaned over and whispered, "Watch what I do." I stood behind him as he edged in next to another shopper. He watched and listened to their tennis-match-style bartering. The fish merchant never appeared interested. She would reply with her eyes, averting past you as if to say you are inconsequential and unimportant. The pair finally agreed on a price, and the fish vendor weighed two hundred grams of fresh blue shrimp on two sheets of newspaper and wrapped it up. My cook knew the acceptable price range of shrimp for the day and started low-balling ever so slightly. "If you don't barter, they will take you for a fool, and they'll remember who you are." I looked up at him and nodded, "I understand."

On the way home, Rổ told me that life would be so much easier if the price of fish stayed the same. He continued, "But it doesn't. Even in the same day, if their supply goes low early in the day, the same fish could demand a much higher price. Of course, the reverse can happen, and they may have to dump their surplus at a bargain at noon or lose the fish to spoilage. Does that make sense?" I hesitated but nodded again.

"Then there were the storms," he continued. "Fishermen can't get as many fish in bad weather. They spend less time out at sea and bring in less fish. That drives up the price too." He looked to see if I understood, then retreated. "I know that's a lot for you to learn in one day. You can watch me, and I'll let you practice after a while, alright?" I nodded and tried to remember what he said. I liked my cook very much. He didn't care if I messed something up. He didn't mind taking the time to fix it, and he showed me that making mistakes was how you learned. Besides cooking for our family, the cook also made rice gruel slop with livestock-grade vegetables for the pigs and fed grains to our feathered friends. We raised a few pigs, but every winter one or two got sick and died. We were better at raising chickens, ducks, and geese for their meat and eggs, and because I'd seen them in the yard and their coops, I often felt repulsed that we killed them for food, and usually didn't eat them.

CHAPTER 7
Social Challenges

I wanted to learn how to cook, but my mother wouldn't let me do many things in the kitchen because my work wouldn't be up to her standards. On special occasions when we had guests, or when we had ancestral mourning ceremonies, my mother single-handedly shopped and cooked because only she could cook to her liking. My mom knew how to butcher chickens, ducks, geese, and pigs. She was not squeamish, not even with eels.

I watched my mother butcher chickens on several occasions. She stood on a cement pad overlooking the yard, her eyes scanning the flock for a good-sized chicken, then marched in and grabbed one by its legs. I will spare the faint of heart and skip the gruesome details of killing a chicken. The chicken's blood was carefully saved in a bowl to make blood pudding. My mother had a large pot of boiling water ready to dunk the dead chicken. "This will make it easier for me to pluck the feathers," she explained.

As I shared earlier, I didn't eat poultry when I was young. My dislike for poultry was not because I was attached to these animals, they were food for my family. I didn't want to eat the chickens, ducks, and geese because the smell of boiled feathers reeked like wet dogs, especially the oily and fatty skins, which smelled even worse. Steam from the pot fogged up the kitchen windows, and the whole house reeked of boiled feathers and fats all day long.

Besides being an excellent cook, my mother was also a skilled knitter and embroider. Although she no longer did this professionally, she still made sweaters for her family. She helped me with my schoolwork in embroidery and taught me how to knit. She used to laugh and said that my knitting looked like a long strip of bacon because the stitches weren't consistent. They were wavy and curly. She occasionally helped me with arts and crafts homework, such as cutting out letters in different colored foil papers to improve my artistic and fine motor skills.

In those days, parents weren't directly involved and active in their children's school. My father hired two math tutors for us. They alternated teaching at our house two times a week in the evenings. The tutors had to contend with our wide range of math abilities. Third-grade math for me; advanced algebra for my oldest sister, Kim Chi; and everything in between for the others. The nights seemed long and arduous, but I had less homework and left before my older siblings. I could hear the tutor's voice and his squeaky chalk dragging across the board in the next room. They were still sitting around the long oval table solving their problems. Tutoring sessions were very stressful, and afterward, we made up songs about the tutors to liven things up. We needed the teachers' help, but at the same time, dreaded their arrivals.

In eighth grade, I had to join a mandatory math study group. Our teacher was adamant about having these groups to work on our algebra and geometry problems. We took turns and met in each other's homes. I enjoyed my math group, but my mother was not keen on the idea. She didn't like me to go to friends' houses, but gave in for school's sake. She disapproved of my having friends. It was alright as long as I kept them at school, as long as I didn't visit them at their houses, and they didn't visit me at ours. She didn't want me to be chatty or gossipy, and she discouraged me from having friends. It was okay for my older sister, Kim Chi, and my two older brothers to have friends, but I was too young for that. My mom was distrustful of people and wanted to be secluded. She may have had valid reasons to be this way, but I wanted to have friends. I wanted to live a normal life, with friends coming over to visit, but that was too exhausting for her. She said her life would be much simpler if she could just have all her kids at home where she knew where they were at all times.

Fifth grade school identification photo of Hoàng Chi

I still wanted to have real friends. Kids at school already drew a circle around me because I was the colonel's daughter. In their assumptions, I was privileged and had everything I wanted. I was consistently one of the top five in my class of fifty students, but they thought the teachers must be partial because I was the colonel's daughter. They believed I was only riding my father's coattail and my good grades were not my doing.

The last year of elementary school, in fifth grade, my classmates were convinced that I sang the best solo at our school's award ceremony. They propelled me to celebrity status. This reputation stayed with me through high school. The next year, the kids in my class expected me to continue singing and join dance troupes for my homeroom class.

High school began in sixth grade when I was assigned to a different group of students than I was with in fifth grade. A group of students from another elementary school decided they didn't like me. To them, I was an elitist because my father was a colonel, and I had good grades. I thought I was a quiet but nice person. If I could choose, I would rather have my dad be a civilian, a dentist or some respectable professional that wouldn't risk dying in battles. I doubted these kids would like me even if my dad wasn't a colonel, as they would find some other reason to hate me. I was not like them as I came from Nha Trang and didn't speak or act like they did.

I had two wishes then: I wanted a civilian, stay-at-home father; and to be a regular kid. I tried hard to be humble, to be accepted by them and be like them, just a normal kid. But in their eyes, I wasn't just a regular kid and would never be one of them.

English Lessons & Boys

A typical childhood was not possible for me, even away from my school and my neighborhood. The kids in my English night classes knew who I was, and one boy made sure I knew he didn't like me. My after-school English teacher held classes in his modest home behind a long alley. In a tiny living room, a cotton curtain partitioned "the class" from the rest of his private home. Ten students shared a long table in the middle of his makeshift classroom, five on each side. The students were mostly boys. As I'd attended all-girl schools all my life, I found this co-existence with boys very unnerving.

Our teacher was an English interpreter in the army. He had a Northern accent from Hà Nội, but was a pleasant person. Our class met three times a week in the evenings when aromatic and acoustic distractions of dinner preparations proved to be acutely challenging. Jasmine rice canvassed the air with wafts of pungent caramelized claypot fish, making me hungry.

The alternative to this unconventional classroom setup was the Vietnamese-American Association where American soldiers were teachers. It seemed logical to learn English from them, but my parents were fearful of exposing me to this environment. I was grateful they gave me the privilege of having extra English classes and didn't complain about the source of the lessons, as I wanted to be proficient in English so I could go to America as an exchange student one day.

The kids in my class were decent except for one smart but ornery, spiteful boy. He was the class clown who disrupted our lessons, and I did my best to ignore his disruptive behaviors. After class one night, as I walked through the narrow alleyway to be picked up, this boy turned the front wheel of his bike to stop my stride. I tripped forward and caught myself at the tire. Without much thought, I pushed his bike aside and strode forward. I was scared of what he would do next, but didn't have any choice. I prayed that my ride would be waiting at the end of the alleyway.

No ride. I stood on the sidewalk holding my leather book bag in a ready-to-strike position, just in case this boy harassed me again with his bike. I don't remember his name, but despised the way he paced back and forth in front of me, like a hyena waiting to outlast his prey. He murmured something inaudible under his breath. I held my striking stance with a brave face while desperately wishing for my ride.

This boy's detestable and neurotic behaviors concerned me, but failed to deter me from attending class. Instead, I asked the driver if he could please come early and protect me from this bully. In retrospect, I suspect he wished to be rid of me since we were competitive rivals in class. The next time class adjourned, he sat leaning back casually on his banana-seat bicycle, arms folded, eyes pierced my way. I passed him in the alley, but he gave me a wide berth. Then suddenly, he slowly rode up alongside me. How long would he do this? I could smell his sweaty, dirty hair and undoubtedly, his sweaty and dirty hands. I summoned up all my courage to ignore him. At the end of the alley, he threw a folded piece of paper my way. A reconciliatory note, no doubt, I thought. There was not a remote chance that I would pick up anything this boy threw my way. I ignored him and walked on. Just when I thought he was gone, the boy turned his bike around and caught up with me again then gravelly announced, "I'm sorry." That was the end of his outburst. After that, I never talked or looked at him again, and he left me alone.

I had a sweet and lovely childhood friend whom I could trust. We'd known each other since second grade, and her name was Hạnh Thi. She didn't care that my father was a colonel because her dad was also one. We adored each other. She had a charming face and sweet smiles. She had "toothpick" legs like mine, and we comforted each other that we'd wear pants as soon as we could. Hạnh Thi was a doll. She was sweet and innocent and had a Huế accent thicker than molasses. She came from a large family like mine, and we both loved to sing and draw paper dolls. We held hands everywhere and skipped ropes together. We were each other's first confidants and best friends. When I entered high school, Hạnh Thi was placed in a different class, and I lost my best friend.

From sixth through eighth grades, my best friend was Xuân Mỹ. She was an excellent student who spoke English with a French accent because she attended a French elementary school. Her mother was a pharmacist, and her father was a teacher. I was very envious of her family. They had a store in the front and lived in the back, right in the middle of town. I chiefly envied her civilian lifestyle. Her parents were scholarly and friendly towards other children and me. Xuân Mỹ embroidered a beautiful handkerchief for me for an end-of-school-year gift in seventh grade. I was not superstitious then, but I learned later that this gift brought bad luck because it would bring you many years of separation (hence the use of a hankie). I liked Xuân Mỹ but was not sad to lose her. I didn't pine for her, not the way I did for Hạnh Thi, when we were separated in sixth grade.

My limited experience with boys was a neighbor named Dzũng. He was a year older than me but at the same grade level. He attended the all-boy high school across the street from mine. My brothers and his were friends, and they started carpooling with us when I was in seventh grade. There were five boys in this family. Dzũng was the middle child like me, and his father was also a colonel, though not a commander. His parents were from the North, or at least their accent was. I never met his father, but I met his mother once when my brothers took me to their house. She was beautiful and lavished me with the compliments of how I would someday become a lovely lady. I was skeptical of her comment since my driver had once called me toothpick legs. This made me self-conscious and insecure about my image for years, but I doubt that my driver even remembered saying such thoughtless words.

Dzũng and I met while carpooling, and he started to come over to my house with one of his friends to collect insects and plants for our respective biology classes. I liked how we shared our collections and learned to press ferns while we ate wild fruit. We pulled the ferns carefully with all their roots then brush off the dirt or washed them with water. I pressed the warty underside fronds, and twine-like roots to a natural position as Dzũng helped me press down the top paper. We placed heavy books on top of each pressing and stashed them on top of our wardrobes.

Dragonflies were my favorite insect to catch and press since they were plentiful and easy to find, unlike butterflies and bees. I stared for a long time into their bubble glass eyes with emerald-green pupils. Their opulent bluish-green thorax and lacy wings were magical like fairies. I felt a twinge of remorse for suffocating them in the plastic bag and later pinning their wings and bodies to a stiffened stance. I believed, then, in reincarnation and worried briefly that I would fall a rung or two my next life to become an animal. Dzũng didn't tell me how he felt about killing these insects. He gave me a bagful of dragonflies once so that I could end up with one well-pinned specimen.

My brothers took me to the movies at their school one day. I can't remember what it was about, partly because the film broke about half an hour into the movie, and the students didn't know how to fix it. We left and met up with Dzũng and his brothers. I was thirteen then when I discovered that I was very fond of him. He began giving me flowers that he collected, as well as special insects and plants. Dzũng liked to bring berries in a bag so we could eat as we caught insects or worked on our presses.

We knew each other for about a year before I realized that he was quite handsome and sweet. I started to daydream about him, and it gave me a very unusual sensation, one I had never felt before. I wasn't comfortable catching bugs with him anymore. I felt a mixture of excitement and discomfort because I was not certain of how to behave around him all of a sudden. Either I had my first crush on Dzũng, or he was my first love. Neither of us spoke about our feelings, so I had no idea how he felt.

My older brother Thông knew something was changing and one day forbid me to talk to Dzũng. "You are too young to think about boys." It was a mixed blessing because it would take care of the problem of not knowing how to behave around him, but I was upset and sad that I could no longer be Dzũng's friend. I wondered if my brother spoke to Dzũng as well. He and his brothers continued to carpool with us, and under my brother's watchful eyes, I distanced myself from Dzũng. I felt awful about it. We stopped catching insects and collecting plants together.

Becoming a Young Lady

Seventh grade was memorable for me. I was twelve years old and wept when I first discovered my period. I knew my body was changing, but I was startled at my bleeding one afternoon before leaving for school. It wasn't at all exciting, as my classmates had said it would be. I was afraid and despised my new body. I did not welcome the bleeding. I wanted to remain a child.

I rehearsed how I would let my mother know about my period. I knew I would be late for school if I didn't act quickly, but I was afraid she would be angry with me. We had never talked about menstruation. I was tormented and couldn't go to my older sister either because I was afraid that somehow this was my fault and I would get into trouble.

I summoned my courage and approached my mother. "Mom, I'm bleeding...in my pantie and don't know what to do," I whispered, as if I'd just committed a crime. It was not earth shattering news to my mother. She simply took me to the bathroom with a piece of white chalk in hand. My mom learned the old wives tales and superstition that to shorten the length of a woman's periods, we needed to draw two and a half solid lines on the wall. "This," she said, "indicates that you only wish to bleed for two and a half days." I must have rolled my eyes in exasperation because that was how I felt. Never mind, I thought, of how many days I wished to bleed, I didn't want to bleed at all. I preferred to stay a child. I couldn't turn back time, so I only wished she would help me not hemorrhage to death. Though I didn't articulate my displeasure, I waited patiently for my mother to empower me with some sanitary napkins like she and my older sister used. Perhaps some motherly comfort and advice wouldn't hurt at this time of fear and uncertainty. I wanted to hear my mother say that it wasn't my fault and I wasn't a bad girl because this happened. I needed to know that I was still the same good kid.

To my dismay, my mother folded several layers of bathroom tissues, and then handed them to me. "Here, line your pantie with this and change them regularly." That was the last I heard from my mother about menstruation. She didn't expect a young girl my age to experience heavy flows. I went to school that afternoon in my white áo dài uniform. I wished I could have talked to my older sister about it and asked for help, but it was such a taboo.

I felt an unexplainable and sublime sadness that day. I grew up. I looked at Minh Châu differently now. She was just a sweet little girl, and I felt a hundred years older than my ten-year-old sister. My period had suddenly carried me to the far side of childhood where I felt separated from my younger sister and her innocence.

I told Xuân Mỹ the news when I arrived at school. We winced and exchanged our first horrifying discoveries. As uncertain and insecure as I was with my sister and mother, I was proud of my periods with my friends at school. I had finally achieved the status of a young woman. We vowed to look out for each other for any early signs of mishaps and thank goodness that we were at an all-girl school. Some allowed their students to wear black pants for uniforms when they menstruated, but ours didn't, and we lamented about that as well. After the initial period, I didn't have another one for a few months and felt relieved of not having to deal with the ordeal. I forgot all about menstruation and being a grown up. My life continued uneventfully, as though nothing had happened.

CHAPTER 8

The American GIs

My father worked with American advisors, and on occasion invited them to our home for dinner. They dressed in olive drab uniforms decorated with stripes, stars, and medals earned in that wretched war. They were big men who towered over my father, and when they walked through the front door, we were always in awe of their enormous stature. These men reeked of deodorant and after-shave. It was a joke amongst Vietnamese that we could smell an American before we could see them, and it was true in this case.

My mother and the cook prepared specialties and delicacies for the parties, crab farcies (stuffed and fried meat filling in crab shell), beef ragout, asparagus crab soup, steamed freshwater fish, jellyfish cucumber salad, and of course, the lovely, fragrant Jasmine rice. Our driver brought in crates of Tiger orange soda, and "33" beers. The American guests brought their gifts of Hennessy, Johnnie Walker, and other cognacs.

Sometimes we ate with the American guests. My father taught us to use knives and forks on steaks and how to break our bread to bite sized pieces, not to slurp soups or shovel rice from bowls to our mouths. We used plates, forks, and knives like the Westerners, not rice bowls and chopsticks. He taught us table manners like they taught him in the academy. Sometimes when my father had parties for his American friends, we ate separately, and we didn't mind that at all because we could talk, laugh and eat with our chopsticks and rice bowls. We didn't have to be stiff and wonder all the time if we behaved appropriately for our father and his friends.

From Left to Right – My father, Lieutenant Colonel working with his US counterpart, Lieutenant Colonel W. Ray Bradley, circa 1969 (General Bradley's son)

My limited experience with the Americans was also outside our home, away from my dad's parties. We often saw young soldiers with their bleached hair in the tropical sun. They complained that it was too hot and humid and rode in the back of their GMC trucks, the kind with long benches along both sides of the vehicle. It was indeed hot and humid, and the GIs devoured watermelons, riding shirtless, tan and muscular, for they were young men that had been through rigorous training. They flashed their white teeth and looked at us with their exotic colored eyes. I felt sorry that they had to leave their families to come here and fight in this wretched war. Unfortunately, so many died or were injured.

The Americans couldn't tell us apart. They thought we all wore pajamas on the streets and that's what the Việt Cộng also wore, except that they wore black pajamas and carried guns. This assumption proved to be problematic. It wasn't as simple as that, and many young GIs couldn't tell Việt Cộngs from innocent civilians. The young American soldiers were scared for their lives, and if they were in doubt, they would kill a peasant. Both Vietnamese and American soldiers had been sniped or maimed on minefields during their routine surveillance. I felt very guilty when I saw injured soldiers or those sent home in coffins, whether they were Vietnamese or Americans.

We also saw American GIs in their civilian clothes around town. They mainly went to bars and did whatever they did in them. Some women worked in those bars as waitresses or dancers, and they were frowned at and looked down upon by our society. These women made the American GIs forget their sorrow for a while with their drinks and their companionship. The young soldiers were very scared and confused. I assumed that they wanted to go home to their families, girlfriends, wives, and to their homes where rockets didn't launch at night. Some of the soldiers resorted to girls and drugs to make them feel "A-OK" momentarily. I felt sad for them because they were victims just like us.

Father's Home Visits

My father's visit home included his review of our grades. He stressed higher education and respect for our elders. "Discipline and perseverance will pave the way to success," he always said, and I strived to please my father. He told us stories about making good choices in friends and choosing our environment, for these decisions would impact our future.

When we did well in school, my father rewarded us with money. I spent my award as fast as my feet could carry me to the bookstores. I spent my summers reading a broad range of books, including *One Thousand and One Arabian Nights*; *The Good Earth,* by Pearl Buck; and Aesop's fables in Vietnamese versions. I immersed myself in young readers' literature, in foreign travels and exotic safari animals, and more childlike comic books of adventures of TinTin and the Smurfs. I read as many books as I could rent, borrow, or buy.

Our school library had a limited number of books and many restrictions on when and how many a student could check out. It also closed in the summer, and we didn't have a city library at our disposal, so my siblings and I rented volumes from the cheaper book shops to feed our hunger for entertainment. We also spent our reward money on sheet music and tapes because we loved to listen to them and practice singing for the annual school talent shows.

Besides checking our grades and rewarding us with good report card monies, my father held family meetings and reminded us what not to do. It was also about working on respect, perseverance, and hard work. We got reprimanded a lot, it seemed, for misbehaving and disrespecting our grandmother. She lived with us for a few months at a time, rotating between all of her children. She'd tell us stories as we swung her flabby triceps like pendulums of grandfather clocks. When we grew tired of this game, we plotted pranks on her. It was barely a month after Tết, or Vietnamese New Year's, and we had a few strands of firecrackers left over, the kind that looked like magazines of ammunitions for machine guns. The strings of these festive and loud firecrackers tempted us, and we couldn't wait to light them. Being restless and mischievous children, my brothers Thọ and Thông conspired to scare my grandmother with the firecrackers. We'd watched one too many episodes of *Mission Impossible* on American TV and had successfully poisoned our war-mongered brains. We wanted to apply some espionage techniques on our "oppressive villain," my grandmother.

Initially, Kim Chi and I had to reconnoiter my grandmother's site where she was sitting. Later, our brothers sent us as diversions to entertain her while they planted the firecrackers near her chair. The wick line was long enough to reach Thọ and Thông in another room where they lit the fuse. They signaled with a cough for us to evacuate. Our mission was to make sure the wick burned to some marked distance, and then flee. The tile floor had saved our house from being burned down on several occasions, and this was one of those times. My sister and I quickly and politely excused ourselves from the room, "so you can rest, grandmother!"

The firecrackers failed to go off, but the burned wick fumed the porch and my grandmother discovered our failed mission. She scolded us soundly and went straight to my mother, telling her to punish us for our unruly and disrespectful plot. We were all spanked, scolded and severely disciplined. In retrospect, we needed a reminder of our boundaries, and of what it is to be well-behaved children. The lesson learned was that we cannot disrespect and mistreat an elderly grandparent no matter how poorly she treated our mother.

My father lectured us on his home visits for these bad behaviors and some other reasons. In the seventies, the American's involvement in the war brought not only American television shows, music, magazines, but also the dreaded "hippie" flower decals. My father didn't want to see any more hippie flowers in our home, not on our book covers, not on our clothes, not on our reel-to-reel album covers. He said that we didn't understand the lyrics of these American anti-war songs. He was fighting the war against communism, and our generation could not be weak-minded and apathetic about it. He fought this war for us so we wouldn't end up dead or calling each other comrades. He didn't want his children to be the followers of Stalin or Marx, sitting high and mighty in Leningrad.

I didn't know hippie flowers were that wrong, but I peeled the evil flowers off of my book bag as he instructed. My father didn't want us to give in to the Westerner's way and lose our heritage. It was disrespectful to abandon our ancestry and become westernized, labeled as the "Lost roots" generation.

We loved our American and French music and still listened to them in secret, since we didn't understand the lyrics anyway, it was just the tunes that we liked. We secretly listened to Procol Harum's "A Whiter Shade of Pale", Three Dog Night, Creedence Clearwater Revival, The Doobie Brothers, The Beatles, and some other obscure groups that probably overdosed on LSD.

My father's visits made us fear him, but we also respected and believed what he said was genuine and meaningful. We never doubted our father's intellect and integrity, and most especially his patriotism.

While my dad was home visiting, I wandered around to see why he brought so many soldiers with him. There was a driver and two men in the back, armed with M16s, grenades, and army phones - the bulky block kind you had to turn the cranks to call.

The soldiers didn't mind me being around. I think I was invisible to them because they always cursed some rude sounding words. I knew they were bad words because I had never heard them from my mother, father, teachers or anyone else. I thought that since they fought in battles, it made them numb and callous, so they had to use expletives to feel better.

I saw their rifles, sometimes with bayonets. I watched them taking the guns apart, cleaning them with oily rags. The soldiers stuck their packs of Salem cigarettes in their netted helmets for that much-needed smoke after firing a shot at the Việt Cộng, who looked and talked just like them and had families who loved them very much. I would probably smoke something stronger than a Salem if I were a soldier who had to kill in a battle to preserve my life.

The soldiers were not discreet about their smokes, their guns, their language, or the girlie magazines they got from their American counterparts and posted the centerfolds inside their window shutters. These men guarded our house, kept us safe, and lived in the next quarters, a minimal facility with only cots, army blankets, and provisions. They ate what we ate, and kept our family safe, out of harm's way, around the clock.

These home guards still considered themselves lucky since they didn't have to go to the battlefront. Some Vietnamese soldiers came back from the battles missing legs and arms, and resorted to selling lottery tickets from wheelchairs or other odd jobs to make a living. Occasionally, I saw army trucks carrying coffins of dead soldiers to their loved ones, and one day, they delivered it to a family across the street from us. I didn't know them, but I felt anguish rising inside me. I couldn't help but cry, except I also felt an intense anger with this wretched war that took away too many lives.

CHAPTER 9

Last Night in Đà Nẵng ~ March 28, 1975

In late March 1975, after months of political unrest and instability in Đà Nẵng and Huế, the Việt Cộng advanced southward beyond the Demilitarized Zone, or DMZ. The guerrilla insurgencies also gained more momentum and footholds elsewhere in the Republic of South Vietnam. We spent a few days packing and getting boxes ready to ship to Nha Trang. I can't speak for my mother because she seemed pensive and secretive, but I was ecstatic that we would finally return to our beautiful hometown of Nha Trang. I was grateful that my family had the choice and means to evacuate from Đà Nẵng, but the empty shelves where the reel-to-reel music player and figurines used to be sent an alarming and chilling feeling down my spine. We emptied the contents of my parents' hard work and life's possessions into boxes and crates with the address labels for our home in Nha Trang

The influx of refugees from Northern cities like Huế and Quảng Trị, flooded the streets of Đà Nẵng for at least a week. Speculation and rumors grew from the masses that we would soon lose Đà Nẵng, especially since the ARVN troops withdrew yesterday from Huế per the President's order to minimize casualties. The Republic army had underestimated the large guerrilla front that joined forces with the VC troops advancing southward. Everyone grew uneasy as they listened to the BBC and packed for the inevitable.

My father called to inform my mother that his troops also retreated from Huế, and then we didn't hear from him for at least a day. When he came home to Đà Nẵng, his voice was hoarse, which I imagined was a result from shouting commands in battles. He arranged for us to be airlifted the next morning from Đà Nẵng to Tiên Sha, the shipyard near Sơn Chà.

That night, I lay in my bunk bed staring at the white acoustic tiles on the ceiling, the same ones I'd stared at for the last nine years of my life, but this was the first time I surveyed this room with such keen interest. My bedroom served as a bomb-shelter, its walls and ceiling reinforced with heavy-gauged steel and filled with sandbags. Looking around the room, I saw two sets of bunk beds flanking a small desk, a floor fan, a seashell night-light my brothers had made from a large chambered Nautilus they found on the beach, a turntable where we played the *Love Story* and *Romeo and Juliet* albums, The Beatles, and endless vinyl of the 70's. There were posters of performers on the walls, whose names I cannot recall.

Occasionally, we slept on the yellow tile floor because of the cool surface, and other times we hid under the bunk beds during air raids. I pressed my body down onto my twin-size mattress as though to imprint and capture all the memories of what I had experienced there, even though I thought I hated Đà Nẵng. Somehow that night, I had a premonition that my life would soon take a dramatic turn, but I didn't know just how extreme. I recall studying my room's every detail as to not forget any of it. I then closed my eyes tightly as if to seal shut everything in my memory. I wanted to get some sleep. I prayed that we weren't too late on the escape attempt and that there wouldn't be any shelling that night, so we could leave first thing in the morning.

The Việt Cộng target bombed Đà Nẵng's strategic infrastructures such as hospitals, army bases, airport, depots, and warehouses. We lived near an airport, and surprisingly, rockets always missed us while we lived there, although we frequently were woken up at night by the rockets and air raid sirens. Their deafening noises were disorienting and frightening. Every time I hit the floor during an air assault, I feared that our bomb shelter bedroom could only save us from shrapnel, not the bombs. Before my father had this bomb shelter constructed, we had to dash from our bedroom to my mother's bomb shelter room. When the bombing concluded, the siren also sounded, and we returned to our beds.

I had the top bunk where I had been conditioned to jump down to the floor during air raids and hide under the beds. We all threw our shocked and disoriented bodies on the cold tiles, hugging each other sometimes when the sounds of rockets grew louder, meaning they were nearer to us. I could hear myself whimpering, and my brother was comforting me, perhaps himself as well, with the hushing sounds. He rocked me back and forth, making "sh... sh... sh..." sounds, and he continued until my whimpering subsided. Sometimes the rockets sounded like thunder cracking overhead. Sometimes the deafening whistling sounds made me visualize the ravenous grim reaper cursing and spitting for missing us once more. I always prayed that it would spare us.

In the mornings after the air assaults, we surveyed the damages. Sometimes it happened to people we knew, sometimes it left buildings in ruins. At times people died, other times we all escaped unscathed. One never knew what to expect, and we went on with our lives knowing that next time it could hit us. One of my recurring nightmares was getting shot and not being able to pull the trigger to protect myself from the villains, the communists.

My Favorite Shoes

1975 was the year I lost my favorite shoes. Perhaps these were ordinary to most people, but not for me. They were a pair of pale, banana-yellow clogs that I finally persuaded my mother to buy for that school year. I knew that my mom no longer saw me as a child if she bought these for me, it was her nod to my becoming a lady. I felt mature and beautiful when I put on these clogs because they had chunky wooden heels. The soft leather felt luxurious on my bare feet, yet at the same time I had to press my soles on the wooden platform to stay on, so as not to slip back and gash the soft middle of my feet. The flower eyelet designs were die-punched along the edge of the upper leather, and a narrow strap trimmed the top daintily with a small metal buckle. I'd coveted these on the older girls for over a year, as I watched them fleeting about effortlessly.

My mother didn't take me shopping very often, so when she did, I felt very special and loved her undivided attention. I placed my newly acquired shoes by my bed where I could gaze at them at bedtime. I imagined what it would be like to wear them to school.

My last night at home in Đà Nẵng was a restless night. I woke up the next day to chaos and anarchism in the streets of our city. My parents had packed two bags for each of us for our immediate needs. Kim Chi was wise to pack some treasured photos and her piggy bank! Mỹ Châu and Hồng Châu were six and five years old, respectively. There were nine of us. My father, who would accompany us to the helipad, my mother, and all the siblings who were not in the armed forces. My mom also packed milk for my younger sisters and provisions for all of us.

On that fateful Friday morning, March 28, 1975, I put on my New Year's dress. It was a fashionable green dress with yellow trim and buttons. I wore my matching lovely yellow clogs, hardly worn since New Year's Day. I thought this homecoming trip would be an excellent occasion to wear my clogs, since, as it turned out, they were not sensible shoes and had been too uncomfortable to wear to school every day. I couldn't run and play jump rope with them as they would slip and hurt my feet. I didn't have the skills with these shoes like the older students and ended up saving these clogs for special occasions, like my homecoming trip to Nha Trang, and so I wore them.

In my new year's dress and favorite shoes. Huế, 1974.
From Left to Right, Hoàng Chi and Kim Chi

No one, not even my father, could have foretold the quick collapse of Đà Nẵng. We had lost Huế overnight. People now filled the streets with their worldly belongings, desperate to leave town and go southward. They pushed, shoved, and cried out for their families. There were few cars. Mostly mopeds, bikes, and motorcycles. And people everywhere. We were like the bruised salmon spawning upstream for our chance of survival.

Each person fought for himself, and some were armed. We saw the desperation and the selfishness of humanity in a state of anarchy. The traffic signals were blinking like Christmas lights, and no one paid attention to law and order. A child was playing in the traffic light control booth where an officer once operated with dignity. The traffic jam was unprecedented and nightmarish. Our Jeep finally reached the helipad, only to be further disappointed. People filled our private and designated helicopter. They didn't care where it was going as long as it was leaving Đà Nẵng.

Up until now, our parents sheltered us. We had never seen this face of humanity, nor faced any challenge like this before. We fought just as hard as the next family to get on the helicopter, our guards unable to reserve our transportation with the mobs occupying the aircraft. We pushed and shoved hard alongside the soldiers to climb to our seats. There were men, women, and children struggling to board. As the engine started and the propellers created a tornado of dust, people backed away and stumbled from the pad. I saw their angry and scared faces, their bodies soon became dots on the ground as the helicopter gained elevation. We were awestruck. This scenario must be a dream and couldn't be happening to us. The fear of all fears had finally materialized.

As a child, I envisioned the word "Communist" as a horrific entity. I thought that if I closed our shutters and doors, I could keep them out. But here I was, high above the ground in a "Huey," while I feared for my life and the lives of my family. I feared being shot down in flames. The chaos happened before my eyes. It wasn't a dream. I spotted the bridge that the US Corps of Engineers built joining Đà Nẵng and Sơn Chà. I saw the gray and choppy water below us, and in one quick moment, Đà Nẵng went out of sight.

When we landed in the harbor, we saw hundreds of thousands of people who arrived there before us. My father contacted the officers in charge at Camp Tiên Sha and learned that a Navy ship would come ashore that evening for evacuation. At this point, my dad told us to abandon one piece of luggage each because, judging from the crowded harbor, it would be a long and arduous journey. By late afternoon, we all felt the rug pulled from under our feet, our lives filled with uncertainties and unknowns. No one spoke about it, but the situation became increasingly dire because of this massive crowd on the dock who would fight to their deaths for a spot on the ship. Not only that, the streets clogged with thousands more arriving at the harbor by the minute, so when my father sent word to my brothers to join us, bringing more provisions, they got stuck and couldn't push their way to the Naval Base.

By nightfall, around nine o'clock, we moved closer to the office building where we could rest our backs, and shelter ourselves in the event of air bombardment and shelling. Hunger and exhaustion overwhelmed us. Mỹ Châu and Hồng Châu cried for food and milk, soon tiring and falling asleep on their blankets. I wondered uneasily what would become of us. All afternoon we sat on the ground outside an office building and waited along with hundreds of other families for the ship to arrive. We spoke to no one, and they did not talk to us. No one could afford idle and inconsequential small talk. We had to save our energy to claim our spot onboard that ship and stay alive, all nine of us.

CHAPTER 10

Exodus Begins ~ Đà Nẵng to Cam Ranh

On his own accord, a soldier came to tell us we should move into an empty office where we could comfortably wait for the ship to arrive and leave the harbor. As we settled in the room, rockets started to launch. We couldn't sleep for fear that we might miss the ship's departure. Adding to our fears and anxiety, we could hear the whistling sounds of the rockets piercing through the air, and the final deafening explosions when they hit a structure or the ground. Some rockets hit the water, and we could hear their impact, mixing with the sounds of people crying and screaming for their family. The rockets lit up the sky where they hit, and if it weren't for fear of dying, it would have been a spectacular nightscape.

Since I could hear the start of every rocket, I waited to hear the explosions when they landed. I found myself repeating the prayers to our ancestors, and to Buddha, to spare us the next time another rocket launched. I prayed that it wasn't our turn to die a fiery death. I hugged myself to control the involuntary shaking. Not having a proper bomb shelter, I only had the office building's roof and the desk above me for my "bomb shelter," and prayed we would come out alive. I even put the cookie tin from our provisions above my head for an added layer of protection.

The same soldier who informed us about the vacant office came back during the rocket attack to say that the ship had arrived for evacuation. We were all grateful for this guardian angel. Even as the rockets launched and lit up the sky, my family ran for the ship. "Stay together," my father and mother urged us. "Drop all your bags and keep moving," my dad told us. My sisters and I cried as we dropped our bags. I ran awkwardly in my beloved wooden clogs until my ankle twisted and one clog slipped out of my foot. "Run! Don't stop!" I heard my father say. "Don't go back; just keep moving." The rockets continued to rain overhead, and I didn't care if I lost one shoe, so I kicked off the other one and ran barefoot in my beautiful New Year's dress. It was dark and bodies crowded around us. We fought hard to stay together by listening for our parents' voice commands, as it was nearly impossible to move nine people in our family at the same speed through the chaos. I was stepped on, pushed, and shoved by the crowd. We couldn't see who was next to us. We kept calling each other's names to keep track of each other. I could hear the terrified screaming voices of my younger sisters as they cried hysterically because my father gripped their hands so hard, dragging them along. Hồng Châu cried loudly when the hardshell Samsonite briefcase on my dad's arm hit her head as they ran.

My parents herded us like ducks and called out our names as they counted our heads, making sure we were all there at the dock. We were all there. "Kim Chi, Thọ, Thông, you guys get in first then help your younger sisters." I watched them escape through the vast chasm between the ship and dock. If we missed our footings, we'd fall a long way into the ocean with no one to rescue us. I squeezed my head between the horizontal steel cable rails to reach the other side of the ship. Once I was in, I tried to help Minh Châu aboard. My youngest sister, Hồng Châu, was petrified and refused to squeeze her head and body through the rails. My mother climbed on and helped my dad push Hồng Châu through as she struggled. Sweat and tears drenched us. My father and mother counted all nine heads and fell flat to the deck with relief, grateful we all had made it this far.

While we thought we were waiting for a ship to evacuate us, it turned out to be a Sà lan (Cheland in French), or a tug and barge, and it was now moving slowly away from the dock once we boarded. Some families were separated, and parents and children might not see each other ever again. I could hear the fear, the grief, and the heightened sense of separation anxiety in their wailings, their last message to their family to meet again in the future at another destination.

In the course of one day, our lives took a sharp turn and changed forever. We were now refugees, fleeing for freedom. We left behind everything my parents had worked so hard for, but we didn't care about losing our home or belongings at this point. We cried tears of happiness and relief that we were alive and together.

The refugees crammed the barge, and there was standing room only. If you walked away, you'd lose your place. Since there were nine of us, we managed to stake out enough sitting room. We were tired, dirty, hungry and thirsty. The ship rocked rhythmically in the ocean and lulled some of us to sleep, sitting and leaning against each other. I heard and smelled humanity at its worst, sweat and vomit, greed and dishonesty.

I believed that heaven and our ancestors were looking down on us, blessing us with the brightness of a full moon so we could see our way to safety. For now, the rocket launching had ceased, and a sudden surreal calmness befell us, a collective exhalation punctuated sharply with occasional sobbing here and there. I leaned against my siblings, looking up at the sky, admiring the peaceful, bright moon that sailed through random wispy clouds alongside us. It was a calmness I've never felt as I sat among this vast sea of chaos. My feet were bare, cold, achy, and dirty. I saw my two younger sisters sleeping in my mother's arms. For now, it was all right. I was glad they found comfort in their slumber because no one knew what we would be facing tomorrow when the sun came up.

First daylight came shining on my closed eyelids. I had fallen into an exhausted sleep. Through the dash of madness, my mother miraculously hung onto her food and water provision. She cared for and protected us like a tiger and her cubs. We didn't have a lot of water so we rationed it, only wetting our mouths, not knowing how long it would be until we'd reach land. Later in the day, we received word that the Vietnamese Navy aircraft carrier would arrive and bring us ashore.

We watched our barge dock in tandem with the carrier. The large crow's nest rope ladders unrolled from the side of the ship onto the barge. We climbed to the ship as the waves swung the ladder about unpredictably and treacherously. I couldn't help but think it would be ironic to survive last night just to fall off the ladder into the ocean.

The move was much easier this time because of the daylight. People were helpful to each other. They held on to the rope ladders and assisted others onto the ship that would take us to Cam Ranh. The Navy commander had recognized my father as a colonel and provided our family a small, private room with two bunk beds and two porthole windows. The Navy officers gave us desalinated water that tasted slightly salty, but it was much more palatable than the seawater that we'd tried to drink out of desperation when we ran out of fresh water. They also brought us Meal Ready to Eat (MRE) canned meat and plastic packets of dehydrated rice.

People occupied every available square meter on the ship. They sat in the hallways, and we had to crawl over them to get to the bathroom. All nine of us fit in the room like packed sardines but looked more like wilted spinach. I felt nauseous and unsettled. I drew myself nearer the opened porthole window for some fresh air, but that only worsened my seasickness. The unstable horizon line upset my stomach and my balance. Nothing helped, so I resorted to closing my eyes and fell fast asleep. I dreamt that we were on the barge, rocking in the middle of the deep blue ocean, with absolutely nothing around as far as the eyes could see.

The ship commander only invited my father to dinner. It was just as well, we comforted ourselves, as we didn't have appropriate attire for dinner. For goodness sakes, I didn't even have my shoes! We were now refugees. For me, it was such a difficult notion. I felt like I didn't have my dignity since I'd lost my shoes. Being barefoot was never an option for me before. I tried to be brave. I told myself that I had my life and my family and that was a lot more than many people could say. I shook off the indignation of having bare feet and put on a brave face.

My father brought back some freshly prepared food from dinner, and fresh water. We were as grateful as if he had brought back a feast. I remember thinking that my father looked like a mother bird bringing some worms to her baby birds in a full nest. That's when we also learned that we lost Đà Nẵng. By March 29th, a day after we left, the Communists gained their foothold and complete control of Huế and Đà Nẵng, without any fighting. I was overwhelmed with mixed emotions. I was glad to be out of the Communist's control but was also worried for my two brothers, Bá and Tâm, and their safety, wondering if they'd escaped with their units like they'd said they would. Everything I knew from my childhood collapsed, like a burned home that one could never rebuild from the ashes. All my security, comfort, and identity had gone up in smoke.

By late afternoon the next day, March 30th, we arrived at Cam Ranh Bay. The vast sea of humanity pushed and shoved their way off the ship to walk on land, only to fight off eager vendors hawking water and food to the weary refugees. There were a lot of ramen noodle packets waved in the air by the vendors, something I wanted very badly on the ship, but now I just wanted to quench my thirst with fresh water, and we did. Peddlers sold food and drinks at extremely inflated prices, so we bought only water and walked on. I thought the end of my misery was near and immediately felt better. I looked forward to a real home cooked meal, fresh water, a bath, and getting some new clothes and shoes. As soon as we disembarked the Navy ship, I ran into our neighbors from Đà Nẵng. They leisurely strolled by with ice cream cones in their hands. They stopped and talked briefly to my brothers, explaining they had only disembarked the boat hours before us and cleaned up. Though Dzũng's mother was worried about her husband, who wasn't with them, she barely showed it in front of her children. We all knew that in her heart and soul, she was longing for him and quivering with fear.

I wished I could vanish when Dzũng saw me on the dock in my filthy dress with no shoes. I was humiliated and felt hot tears brimming up in my eyes, so I quickly brushed them away. He must have felt my shame and casually disappeared into the crowd. I started having recurring nightmares about being barefoot in public after that. It was as though I wore underwear in public. I have more than one pair of shoes now, and, to this day, I don't like to go barefoot. I'm still trying to comfort that small, frightened, and displaced teenager inside me, a girl falling like Alice in Wonderland, arms and legs flailing, long hair flying in my eyes and face, not knowing where I was going or what would become of me.

I promised myself I would not be defeated by this and followed my family to a Dodge truck that my father managed to get at the curbside which took us to Cam Ranh Naval Base. It was there that my dad borrowed the phone and finally got through to speak with my oldest brother Thảo at Phù Cát Air Base where he worked as a Financial Officer. That was the last communication they would ever have with each other.

That night we slept on wooden beds at the base in what looked like a guard checkpoint room, with large windows and doors, a structure you'd see at base entrances. We ate and drank the food and water we'd brought from the ship, and we slept, worrying about our brothers left behind. It was much more comfortable for us here than on the rocking ship that made most of us seasick. The wooden beds were hard, but nobody complained. It was peaceful here, there was fresh air, and we were grateful to have shelter for the night.

CHAPTER 11

March 31, 1975 ~ Our Brief Reunion with Nha Trang

March 31, 1975. Cam Ranh Naval Base. Since dawn, my father tried to hitch a ride for the family from the base, but had no luck until around noon, since transportation was in high demand and came at a premium price. Everyone wanted to evacuate southward, stricken with panic, retreating from the advancing tide of the communists. Since Huế and Đà Nẵng fell, the next strategic, vital city would be Nha Trang. Families packed up their few treasures and left on foot or crammed in cars, trucks, and buses, leaving their homes and other worldly belongings behind. Neighbors who stayed began looting their fleeing neighbors' homes.

Less than two hours later, we arrived at 15 Nguyễn Trung Trực Street, my parents' home, where my mom's brother, Uncle Cậu Nhượng's family lived. We took turns at the showers and went to the outdoor market to buy food and personal necessities. We also bought some shoes for me, though I borrowed my auntie's shoes so I wouldn't go barefoot.

It had been nine years since I lived in Nha Trang, and things weren't the way I remembered. The market seemed to be in a different location than I had visualized. I felt quite disoriented, out of place, and didn't feel as if I belonged, as I'd thought I would. After all, I had longed to return to my birthplace ever since I was four years old, fantasizing it was the most romantic place on earth. But this was no time to reminisce. Everyone stocked up provisions for their journeys, emptying out shelves and market stalls. Our family, along with many others, snapped up supplies in a frenzy for our respective voyages.

We kept our reunion in Nha Trang brief; our father said we were still in danger and allowed us only enough time to refuel and repack while he borrowed a car to pick up his mother and brother, Uncle Chú Sáu. We said our quick goodbyes to our relatives Cậu Mợ Nhượng then went to nearby Hòn Miễu island overnight, staying with my mom's relatives to dodge possible shelling. My father must have chosen this location for our safety, but possibly for its strategic proximity to Cầu Đá (Chutt, Nha Trang), where he rented a motor fishing boat for our sea trek that afternoon to Vũng Tàu (Cap St. Jacques).

On the way to the beach, heading to the island, my older siblings tried to cover my younger sisters' eyes and mine so we wouldn't see the corpses of children swept up on the shore, many covered by tatami mats. Did they drown from falling off the inner tubes on their way to sea to be picked up by larger boats? I didn't know. It could happen from anywhere up and down along the coast as families were scrambling to escape the impending takeover of the VC.

That night we stayed with my mother's relatives. Things did not change much since we'd been away. Time seemed to have stood still there. The house resided unpretentiously amongst the coconut palms. My ancestors lived there, and I felt a quiet calmness of a welcoming home. The large entrance led to the foreboding ancestral altar with a large brass urn for incense. Sandalwood perfumed the air, as three smoldering incense sticks glowed with embers. To either side of the urn were two tall brass candle holders with red candles recently snuffed, as I could smell the melted hot wax. I found much-needed comfort there and felt that my life still had some consistent stability among relatives whom I trusted.

Just as I'd experienced in my childhood, there was no electricity, running water, phones, nor paved roads. There were still relatives gathering in the evenings and talking on the front porch. And there were still toads blanketing the ground at dusk, like when I was four years old riding piggyback on my relatives because I was afraid of stepping on them.

The familiar waxy, sweet scent of flowers perfumed the moist countryside air, a smell I've yet to encounter anywhere else since. I knew we'd continue a long journey to freedom the next day. But that night, I immersed myself in the seemingly simple life my ancestors had lived. The large brown earthen water urn in the front entrance stood in the same spot since I was four. It caught rainwater and beckoned to quench your thirst with a ladle made of a coconut half-shell.

Now I returned as a teenager, sleeping on the wooden bed that was fresh and smooth to the touch. Its shiny lacquer had not worn through, and I pondered on the fact that my mother had also slept on the same bed when she was my age, yet we had led such different lives. Outside, the soothing sound of crickets and toads lulled me into a peaceful sleep, despite the worrisome murmurs of the adults in the main room. The oil lamp cast bent and elongated shadows of my parents as they devised a plan to escape to freedom safely.

Four Days and Nights at Sea

That next afternoon, on April 1ˢᵗ, our family boarded the fishing boat at Cầu Đá. We carefully stepped on board with one bag each, dodging the fishing nets and traps, and settled among the gears. It was a working boat, not a pleasure craft, and we definitely didn't find any pleasure on it, as the nine of us joined the owner and his one crew member.

We brought water, dehydrated rice, and canned meat. A crude stove was on board, and we boiled enough water to hydrate our rice. Eating at sea was humbling. The boat tossed about in the waves and wind. As I picked up the rice with my chopsticks or tried to shovel it in my mouth, the wicked gale promptly blew the grains away, like a cruel practical joke. I stopped eating because I was only thirsty, but tried not to drink too much because then I'd have to pee. When we needed to use the bathroom, we had to go toward the bow and hang on the nets, praying that a rogue wave wouldn't come along and wipe us off the boat.

The timing of my second period couldn't have been worse, arriving the day we started our journey on the vessel. I experienced cramps that I didn't know were supposed to happen. I curled up on the coiled ropes, but that was too uncomfortable, so I inched toward the nylon fishing net. I went to my sister, Kim Chi, for help. She was more sympathetic than I'd expected. "Here, we don't have any pads, but you can use these washcloths. We can get you some when we get there, hopefully, in a few days." I folded the cloth my sister gave me, then lined my pantie so I wouldn't hemorrhage all over the fisher-men's nets.

I looked for a flat surface to sleep on, but there was none. We all laid on the fishnets, trying to even out their lumpy knots as best as we could. I held on to some structures on the boat to keep from rolling right into the sea. I also held on to my sister's arm. We drifted into spurts of deep sleep while listening to the gusts, the putt-putt of the outboard motors, inhaling the pungent fishnets and diesel fumes infiltrating the salty sea air. My mouth tasted hunger, nausea, discomfort, and fear. I feared capsizing, running into pirates, and the uncertainties of tomorrow. I feared the communists capturing and killing us. Huế and Đà Nẵng had fallen, all in one week. It was inevitable that Sài Gòn would soon follow their demise.

I keenly felt the rocking rhythms of the boat, the salt sprays in my nostrils, my eyes and ears. When I was awake and stared up at the sky, it was poignantly peaceful. Black clouds were briefly silver lined as they passed the unaware and unconcerned waning moon. I felt disconsolately tiny and insignificant, though grateful that we were headed somewhere promising, away from this seemingly omnipotent and omnipresent ocean.

On the following days as we continued on our sea voyage, I daydreamed of warm and silky soy milk in a tall glass on the table of our veranda. I reminisced about my siblings, lying on cots in our garden courtyard on summer nights, listening to stories told by our old guards. I thought of my mother, perhaps working on her knitting inside or already sleeping, and my father away at his post in Huế, and I fell asleep in the late night breeze.

When I awoke, I thought of the last night we'd spent in our comfortable bedroom in Đà Nẵng, our belongings packed in crates and boxes bound for our home in Nha Trang. We'd been away for such a long time; I couldn't wait to get back home. We could walk or ride our bikes to the beach and would feel such belonging because everyone spoke like us.

For the time being, I lay there on the fishing boat, looking at the sky, listening to the occasional fish jumping out the waves, wiggling its tail and diving back into the deep, dark sea. I felt mocked by my miserable conditions. How was it that the fish could be so joyful and celebratory?!

Robberies on High Seas

Many years later, I learned of the secret my parents kept of how the boat owner tried to rob us on that fishing vessel. Luckily for our family, my dad was armed and able to stop him. After that incident, he shortened the trip to the nearest shore and stayed armed with vigilance. This incident was not the first time we were robbed or in danger of being robbed on a boat. My sister Kim Chi discovered that she had lost all the money from her piggy bank on the barge the first night we left Đà Nẵng. She had emptied all her savings into the outside pocket of her bag, and all of it was gone the next morning.

Before we left Đà Nẵng, my mother sewed a fabric pocket for each one of us to keep a thin leaf of one ounce of 99.99% gold on our clothing. If any one of us got lost, we would have emergency currency to find our parents. We were discreet about the hidden gold underneath our clothes, but when morning came on that barge leaving Đà Nẵng, every single one of our gold leaves had disappeared. Poof! All seven ounces of gold vanished into thin air while we slept. After that, we became more vigilant of our surroundings.

We spent four days at sea. On April 4th, we reached our nearest destination near Vũng Tàu. From there, we traveled in a series of trucks before reaching Sài Gòn in canvas-covered cargo trucks, safely hiding us in the back. My father took no chances of getting captured by the VC since no one could guess how quickly the rest of the country would fall. I couldn't see much through the cracks of the canvas cover except endless rubber plantations. Late that night, we slept on wooden beds at a "safe house," and would leave again in the same truck at first light.

The noise of a city was unmistakable when we reached Sài Gòn. When we opened the canvas curtains, we saw tall apartment buildings and a lot of people idling around the truck. They stopped and stared at us as we crawled out of the cargo truck. I heard someone whisper that we were refugees coming from Đà Nẵng. We were refugees even in our own country. Annoyed and embarrassed, I now walked in the shoes of those refugees who came to my mother for help in Sơn Chà and Đà Nẵng. We had only a few bags of belongings to carry up the flights of stairs to our relative's flat.

My sister-in-law's parents had a modest and tidy apartment. It resembled a little ship, and everyone on it had to keep things neat and immaculate. We ate dinner with them, then went to sleep at their friend's vacant apartment where I could see a few pairs of women's shoes under the armoire. It was a whirlwind of a stay, and I don't remember very much of Sài Gòn.

I tried to keep track of our journey though it was difficult with all the many detours my father took to avoid pirates and thieves. He continued to wear his sidearm and took no chance of being compromised. At this point, my dad's one goal was to get us out of the country. We bounced around and stayed at as many places as my dad saw fit for our safety along the most successful escape route from Vietnam.

After we left my sister-in-law's parents, we stayed with my paternal uncle Chú Bảy and his wife and infant child in Thị Nghè, a district of Sài Gòn, near the navigable Sài Gòn River, undoubtedly to plan for a boat escape overseas. I came down with the worst stomach flu, and my aunt used a coin dipped in Tiger Balm to massage the illness from my back. She convinced me to taste the green Menthol oil from a small vial and said I would feel better. I did get over my sickness just like she promised. My auntie gave me my first Eastern medicine treatment, and I just acquiesced to her wish. I became weary of being a vagabond, of sleeping in strange wooden beds, of being under someone else's roof, and the ground under my feet felt unsteady.

We next traveled back to Vũng Tàu Bay, planning to hire a boat that would take us to Hong Kong, by which we would make our way to America. But that plan also fell apart because my father learned of the many ruthless pirates at sea, so we returned to Sài Gòn and tried to leave the country via another route.

Shortly after our stint in Thị Nghè, my parents found a rental house on 363/83 Trương Minh Chiếu in Gia Định, a district of Sài Gòn, and we were glad to have our own place for a while, to no longer be an imposition to our in-laws or relatives. The landlord said this was a rental for the Americans, and it had all the conveniences of home. In the meantime, my father reported to work in Phước Long but he was determined to pursue an escape overseas and seek asylum status for our family.

CHAPTER 12

April 25, 1975 ~ Family Loyalty

I had complete confidence in my father. I knew that if anyone could get us out of a dire situation, it would be him. When we finally returned to Sài Gòn, my sister-in-law, Liên, her parents, and siblings were preparing to leave the country with the U.S. Embassy.

It took a lot of persuasion to convince Liên to leave as she didn't want to take her toddlers, who were two and three years old, without her husband, Thảo, who we still hadn't had contact with since my father had last spoke with him on March 30th. Her parents didn't want to leave either, as one of their sons was also missing. It was ironic that my father had been dragging his family to and fro, trying to figure out a safe route out of Vietnam to no avail, while Liên's family, with means of escape, refused to go because they didn't want to leave their missing loved ones behind.

We learned that David, an American embassy diplomat who had married Liên's sister, Tuyết, risked his life and career in Foreign Service in Japan to escort his wife's family to freedom in the United States. He had previously requested permission to offer his expertise to the U.S. embassy in Vietnam, where he'd served several years prior, but was denied because he was currently enrolled in an intensive language school in Japan. But he bought a one-way ticket for Sài Gòn to convince and evacuate his in-laws, compromising his career by leaving his post without permission. His wife, Tuyết, stayed in Japan with their nearly one-year-old daughter, where she lost touch with him for four agonizing days, fearing for his safety.

Upon landing at Tân Sơn Nhất, David took refuge at a safe house with his trusted embassy friend and sent a letter of instructions to Liên, who secretly met with him to plan the details for an evacuation of her parents' family. She refused, "I can't leave my husband behind, but please take my in-law's family. That would take care of one of my concerns."

Liên was reluctant; she didn't want to leave her husband, Thảo, at Phù Cát Air Base, where he had recently sent her and their two toddlers away to take refuge with her parents in Sài Gòn, escaping the danger of increasing shelling and bombardments.

David was equally unrelenting. "You have to think about your children and their future," he reasoned. "You must go to America and convince your parents as well. Your husband and brother will have a better chance of escaping without you and the kids."

He thought of another angle. "Besides, I have no way of taking the Trươngs, your in-laws, if they don't have you as their relation. They can go if you and your family agree to go." He had never met my family, all nine of us, and yet David would vouch for us at Liên's request.

Liên agreed reluctantly at David's continual persuasion, but she felt heartsick to leave Vietnam without her husband, wondering if he was alive or hurt. Her parents also decided to move with similar degrees of concern, as they hadn't seen their missing son in years.

My sister-in-law, Liên, delivered the good news to my father of David's agreement to take his family to America. We would leave Vietnam on his list of qualifying family members and under the protection of the United States embassy. Within hours, Liên's family and mine rode in a van that David had sent to Tân Sơn Nhất Airport.

We met David for the first time at Liên's parents' house. With compassion, he agreed to Liên's persuasive request to include our large family with his in-laws and claimed all of us as his family. We discovered that, because my father still served in the ARVN, we faced one major problem with bringing my whole family. My mother wouldn't go to America if my dad couldn't join us, but she insisted that the older siblings would leave, and I would stay with the young siblings and my parents. Nobody wanted this outcome, and we would have to devise a way out of this situation quickly, as time was running out before the last evacuation plane left Sài Gòn.

Tân Sơn Nhất Airport ~ Sài Gòn

We were among a sea of two thousand people, sitting and waiting in a bowling alley. We had never seen one before except on TV. The gleaming wooden floor now held the fleeing Vietnamese families and their expensive suitcases, not bowling pins and balls. Our family, by contrast, only carried a few soft bags since we'd lost everything the first time around in Đà Nẵng. We were seasoned refugees by now and were very agile. At a moment's notice, everyone in our family could pack our few items of clothing and be ready to move.

Most of the people on this floor were wealthy and connected "SàiGònese" who were experiencing mass evacuation for the first time. They were the first wave of elites who were well-dressed, well made-up and decked out with expensive jewelry, and undoubtedly stocked with gold in their suitcases. On the bowling alley floor, I sat with relief next to my family awaiting our fate. After a few agonizing hours, we moved on to the next waiting platform where all Embassy personnel and their families would board the bus to the Tân Sơn Nhất Airport in Sài Gòn.

We were almost home free, and if all went well, we would leave Vietnam in a matter of hours. Could we be that lucky? I sat there on the gleaming wooden floor watching a middle-aged woman sitting across from me who wore thick makeup and reeked of Chanel No. 5. Her gold bangles and jade bracelets clinked obnoxiously, colliding as she gestured while holding court with a group of women. I couldn't help but observe and compare the swarms of very wealthy women around me to my mother who rarely wore makeup, only wearing the beautiful pearl necklace that my father bought for her in Hong Kong for special occasions. She had only a few items of jewelry like her jade coin earrings, bracelet, and diamond rings, which paled in comparison with the blinding sparkles of diamonds and 24-karat gold bracelets, rings, and necklaces on the other women.

As I studied the heavily made-up and over-perfumed, middle-aged lady, I was glad my mother was not like that. This Chanel No. 5 woman shaved her eyebrows and penciled in thick and dark half-moon curves, punctuating permanent question marks on her face. She looked in constant bewilderment, as if to exclaim, "Really?"

We continued to wait anxiously in silence over the din of the excited crowd who would leave Vietnam in a few hours. We still didn't know our fate. Who would go to America, and who in our family would stay behind? Would my parents divide up the family? Discussions between my sister-in-law, David, and my father, then moments of David running back and forth with papers in hands. We sweated and feared the worst that we would not be allowed on David's list of family members. Finally, in an act of desperation, the "A-ha" moment and idea came to add my father as a "Retired" Colonel. We didn't know if this would work, but we had to try.

In line to the tarmac, everyone grew restless. We stood there waiting to board a C130 military transport. Up to this point, our family had been in all modes of transportation. We only wanted to leave Sài Gòn and never look back. The Việt Cộngs' southward advance was imponderable, but their victory was impending, and we could feel the collective urgency from the masses that day. It was a disquieting afternoon for us as we waited to leave Sài Gòn. We could see the army transporter only a hundred meters away.

The choppy sound of the aircraft's propellers was deafening. We leaned into the turbine's wind and ran forward to the gaping mouth of a metal ramp into the cavernous belly of the plane. I counted each joyous step to freedom, and my father walked as casually as he could in spite of his fear of being stopped and turned away. Nobody bothered to look at our faces or papers but only impatiently waved the crowd forward, gesturing us to sit down on the floor or on the sling-webbed seats along the sides of the plane. No one stopped my father at the gate or on the ramp. All nine of us safely climbed aboard, glancing at each of other and nodding to our success. The inside of this plane smelled like creosote, the familiar odor of army equipment that I'd experienced since childhood, and in an odd way, it gave me a sense of calm and protection.

Late that afternoon, on April 25th, the ramp gate pulled up and closed tightly. I took one last look at Sài Gòn. Profound sadness fell over me as I quietly said goodbye to my country. Vietnam would never be the same to my family, nor to me. We each said goodbye in our quiet ways. It was a sublime moment of relief yet with uncertainty, all mixed in one breath, in one heartbeat. We didn't speak to each other. I couldn't say this goodbye with words. We had been through so much since we'd left Đà Nẵng and finally escaped Communism, but at a high cost without our three brothers. We still didn't know their whereabouts or whether they were alive or dead.

David sat among us. His fate was almost as uncertain as ours since he'd abandoned his post to rescue our two families. I couldn't believe our luck, and that this happened to us. My brief morbid thought was if we got shot down and we never reached America, we would end up together in the end. I said "goodbye" to Vietnam because this was the end. We wouldn't be allowed to return home ever again.

Sunrise over Andersen Air Force Base

"Give me your tired, your poor,
Your huddled masses yearning to breathe free,
The wretched refuse of your teeming shore.
Send these, the homeless, tempest-tossed, to me:
I lift my lamp beside the golden door."

— Emma Lazarus

Upon entering international airspace, I knew I could no longer hold on to my Vietnamese citizenship. We didn't belong to Vietnam anymore, nor any other country. We'd chosen this option to stay alive and be free, to escape political persecution from the Communists.

I felt lucky but overwhelmingly guilty that my three older brothers didn't make it out with us. I would have a bright future of promised education and economic opportunities. My family would have food, shelter, and schooling without prejudice or persecution, but fear of the unknown made me incredibly anxious. I started to recite some English phrases and conjugated verb tenses in my head because it was never too soon to practice my language skills. In several hours, we would touch down on Andersen Air Force Base on Guam Island, and we would need to communicate in English with the Americans. I felt proud that I'd conscientiously studied English for three years.

With the constant hum of the plane, exhaustion, and relief, I fell into a deep sleep. There were only two occasions in my life when I wanted to kiss the ground, and once was the moment we landed and stepped off the plane on Guam. This moment presented our family with a new dawn, physically and metaphorically. At last, I didn't have to close my eyes and wish the communists away. I was safe and protected now with my family. The air was moist and warm, and the sky was glowing, just like home with the coconut palms swaying in the distance. I pinched myself on the forearm to make sure that I was, in fact, awake and walking on a free land.

The Red Cross had set up food stations to receive "your tired and your poor." We were introduced to lining up for meals and to our first McDonald's sandwiches. The Marines and Red Cross volunteers handed us hamburgers and cheeseburgers wrapped in waxed paper, something of a novelty for Vietnamese refugees. By now I accepted and wore the refugee label well. I became comfortable being called a refugee, though it didn't have the most pleasant sound to it.

We were the first wave of Vietnamese refugees on Guam, in what was only an empty field. We sat down away from the tarmac where it was safe from landing aircraft. US Marines walked around, greeting and handing out blankets and pillows to the weary people. They worked tirelessly to set up the "mess halls," showers, and big canvas tents. David lost no time pitching in. He also handed my dad a hammer to join others with the construction of the temporary housing for refugees, in anticipation of thousands to come.

The Red Cross medical tents took care of the sick refugees. There and then, I vowed to give back to the altruistic and selfless Americans who volunteered in my time of dire need. The iconic Red Cross symbol on a white circle background was clearly visible from a distance, and I was in awe of the humanitarians who served us tirelessly.

We stayed on Guam Island for ten days for orientation, health examinations, immunizations, and the processing of our immigration as resident aliens in the United States. Our next home on the US mainland would be Camp Pendleton in San Diego, California, where sponsors would help us start our new lives. We learned the routines of camp life very quickly. We washed up in the mornings inside the bathroom tents, then beelined for the ample breakfasts in the mess hall tents. Like clockwork, we returned to line up at noon for lunches, then at five for dinners. We were not left wanting for food.

There was plenty of time in between meals for us to ponder what the future would bring. I practiced my English on the canvas army cot in my tent. I lay there looking at the ceiling of the pitched tent and daydreamed about going to an American school. There would be the kids who spoke that beautiful language full of "esses" and they probably wouldn't be wearing uniforms like we did. They probably would be all lovely and friendly. For my daily practice, I focused on conjugating verbs and constructing sentences, making sure that the adjectives came before the nouns, then I posed random questions and provided a variety of answers, just in case anyone would approach me in English.

Our life was uneventful but restless on Guam. We ate, slept, and waited for our applications to process and for our turn to head for California, the mainland where fresh-faced boys and girls were playing safely on the front lawns as they did in the American TV shows we saw back home. In my seventh grade English class I had watched TV footage of California. I saw the mouth-watering oranges on lush green groves that went on for miles on the movie screen, the Golden Gate Bridge peeking through blankets of fog, and the stretches of sunny beaches with foreign-looking people whose hair was so blond and shiny, it looked like it belonged on a doll.

The Fall of Vietnam ~ April 30, 1975

On April 30, 1975, five days after we arrived on Guam, we received news that the old regime fell, and communists now ruled the country. We sighed, but it didn't come as a surprise. I cried because we'd lost the war and because I no longer had my country, but mostly because of my brothers, who were military personnel and would be captured as prisoners.

I said my farewell to Vietnam once and did not see any use for further extending my grief, but that quickly subsided. I felt guilty for leaving all others behind to suffer in my place. I even felt guilty for people who I did not know, the emaciated mothers and children without their fathers who had been hauled off to "re-education camp" or had been executed. I didn't know what to do or how to feel, so I went back to conjugating English verbs.

The Vietnamese at camp didn't say much about the fall of Vietnam. Everyone masked their feelings, moving forward with daily activities, grasping for some semblance of normalcy in their new life in America. David didn't stay around the sleeping tents. My father said he helped others around camp with setting up more tents, showers, and toilets, so we didn't see him very much.

From here, the refugees went to different Army and Marine bases all over the country where their future sponsors would help integrate them into the American mainstream. As for our family, we flew to San Diego, California, on board American Airlines. Liên with her two children and sister went on with us to America, while David and his wife in Japan sponsored her parents and siblings to live with them.

We enjoyed the cleanliness and comfort of the commercial airline. The seats were soft, and even the bathroom smelled like Camay soap and air freshener. It had been a long time since we'd last seen crispy clean clothes and nicely coiffed hair like that of the flight attendants. We didn't like the sandwiches filled with strange tasting mayonnaise and mustard or anything that was cheesy. Our diets had not consisted of dairy products, and they upset our stomachs, so we ate everything else and drank many cups of 7-Up, my new choice of beverage.

The patchwork of greens and browns below the scattered clouds became more detailed as the plane descended into Los Angeles International Airport. Sparkling blue pools randomly spotted the neighborhoods, and grids of roads dissected the cities here and there. Cars and trucks densely crawled on the geometric patterns of circles, oblique and straight roadways in some areas and at light-speed at others. Instead of seeing it on television, I now saw the highest concentration of vehicles and skylines I've ever seen anywhere before, and it was surreal. Was this still a dream, like the many dreams I'd had of coming to America? I'd dreamt of coming to America as a high school exchange student, of leaving home temporarily with a round-trip ticket securely tucked in my school bag. But this? It was surreal!

Upon descent, the cabin gradually filled with jittered excitement from the awakened yet groggy and disoriented passengers. Window shades went up one by one, the blinding sunlight streaming in as heads bobbed and crowded to see the cityscape below. As refugees, we learned to count only on the sure thing, and only acknowledge that we were safe and free when the plane touched the ground, taxiing on the runway.

After getting off the airplane, we boarded a Greyhound bus, and, though it seemed to take forever, we finally arrived at Camp Pendleton in San Diego. From the window I watched the scenes of urban and suburban America play out like a movie. Indeed, I saw miles of orange groves, and the fruits were plentiful. I saw many children riding their bikes on the neighborhood streets. The cityscapes became scarcer as the bus veered towards the hills to Camp Pendleton, a Marine base that had sacrificed some of its vast acreages for the refugee camp. There wasn't much to see in the countryside, and we all settled down in our seats like school children on a field trip, exhausted from the excitement of going someplace we'd never been.

Several hours later, the bus stopped at what appeared to be a military compound. The gate opened to let the buses inside. It was now late in May, and the hills smelled sweet and damp when we stepped off the bus. The evening was too chilly for my tropical self, and I got goosebumps on my bare arms and legs. Rows of army tents fit snuggly in the crooks of the hills beneath an elevated vista. The tents stood in perfect symmetry like subdivisions of green Monopoly houses. I stood still for a moment, behind a locked, guarded gate and high razor fence, inhaled one long, liberated breath, and felt secure and safe, finally in a place where the Communists couldn't hurt us. I grew very fond of the sweet, wet hay that perfumed the air and filled my lungs that whole summer, that was now our new home, though we didn't know for how many weeks or months to come. Slowly, this not-knowing feeling chipped away at our confidence and any sense of control we might have had about our destiny and security.

CHAPTER 13

Camp Pendleton ~ The Laundry Zen

I woke up to my mother's whispering to Kim Chi. My back was to them, and I remained quiet to make sure that I heard them correctly. "I'm pregnant." I thought I heard my mother softly confide. I mentally choked hard and pondered what life would be like with another sibling at this time of uncertainty. We had been here over a month, and the prospect of finding a sponsor for our large family was slim. I sighed quietly and wanted to fall back to sleep.

Later that morning when we bathed in the communal shower-tent, I secretly glanced in my mother's direction and saw that her belly was slightly swollen, a life already forming and growing inside her. I scrubbed my hair and rinsed every long black strand ever so slowly. The scent of green Prell and white Ivory soap mixed as they trickled and meandered down to my brown, pruney toes. I had time to soak as long as I wanted to. I'd had breakfast already, and lunch was the only thing I had to do. Even then, I didn't have to if I didn't have an appetite, and I didn't have one that morning. A feeling of resignation washed over me. I felt dread, boredom, insecurity, and mostly sadness. How would we survive after Camp Pendleton?

Would we go hungry and become homeless? No sponsors wanted our large family. They preferred those with the average two children and two parents. Our family had nine, with one on the way. We were looking for a financial sponsor, someone or some organization, which would pledge to the INS to assist us in starting our new life in America. This loosely entailed housing, food, medical care, job training, education and everything else in between and beyond.

"Hoàng Chi, meet me outside to do the wash," Kim Chi reminded me of our chore as she tucked her hair in a white cotton towel like a turban and walked away to dress. I felt a quick draft of cold air as the back door flap tore open. A stream of sunlight broke through, then a shocking chorus of shrieking, cackling, and giggling filled the tent.

"The... American is... look...ing!" An almost unintelligible, broken up voice was drowned out by the commotion and running water. I turned away as though able to cover my modest body, but simultaneously I wanted to look in the direction of the violator. He ducked away quickly. The backdoor flap fell closed again, and the tent resumed a shroud of fluorescent light and misty shower steam. I chuckled at the thought of the poor women who first saw the alleged peeping Tom. I felt lucky that the light-skinned man didn't poke his head in our area, or my reaction would have been markedly more theatrical than theirs. I listened to the exchange of accounts amongst the bathers, and the stories grew more embellished. Outside the shower tent, I heard a different and plausible version; a Marine worked on the plumbing and had to access a valve from inside the tent. Soon, the excitement died down, and everyone went about their regular washing chores.

I came and sat down next to my sister who had already started the wash. Our laundry facility consisted of a row of faucets of cold water only, lined up in front of a wooden-pallet-platform. Each family had two blue rectangular plastic washbasins as part of the camp supplies, and we used them for washing clothes. Detergent was handed out on a regular basis, as were other sundries, and we lined up for them. Every week we traded in our dirty sheets and pillowcases for crispy clean linens.

We now washed and hung dry our laundry, a chore that had been done for us most of our lives. I thought of the Chanel No. 5 lady on the bowling alley whose fingernails seemed too delicate and beautiful to soak in the harsh Tide detergent. I thought of the times my mother nimbly handled the tongs to put hot red lumps of coals into the cast iron contraption, called an iron, to press my father's Fruit of the Loom white undershirts and briefs when he was home. I convinced myself that I didn't have a privileged life and wasn't a spoiled child. Didn't I help hang the laundry squeezed dry between the rollers of our old washing machine?

The water was so cold that it stung my hands, but to get rid of the camp dirt, we had to continually submerge them in the sudsy wash water while scrubbing the clothes. Kim Chi and I each had a basin full of dirty clothes that ate up the soap bubbles and spewed out the brown water at each reciprocating motion of our arms and hands. After each article had been rubbed and punched, we wrung them and set them aside on the wooden pallets we sat on. We filled the basins full of water and added the clothes, keeping the water running as we punched the soap residue and dirt out of the garments. We talked idly in peaceful contentment, laughing as we washed our Salvation Army clothes, and a few items we'd brought from home.

"Well, we are safe here in America. We'll be able to work and go to school," we concurred, tucking our pride neatly away and accepting the handouts of food and clothes that were two sizes too big for us at the Salvation Army tent. We chose some items and brought them "home" only to find that most of the time, we needed to return them because they were too big.

Camp Pendleton never got warm that summer. Kim Chi and I squatted comfortably on the platform and washed our minimal wardrobes, and our hands would get tingly and slightly numbed from the cold water. The air was crisp and fresh as the gentle sun brushed our chapped and sun-freckled cheeks. It's difficult to say how or why I was content at moments like this. After so much loss, I was content to wash clothes, one item at a time, to make sure they were cleaned. At least I had control of something and contributed to my family; or perhaps it reminded me of when Kim Chi and I were young, sitting side by side, separated by a wall partition, doing our toilets as we talked.

One by one our clothes were rinsed and wrung as dry as we could get them with our hands. We collected them all and put them in the basins and walked, light-footed, back to our tent so as not to get dirt on our wet flip-flops. Behind our sleeping-tent strung a few clotheslines for our laundry. For a while, I had completely forgotten about my mother's news. I went back to my canvas cot, laid down on my back and looked at the ceiling again, forming more English sentences in my head.

All Nine of Us

All the tents were large and tall, which allowed even the tallest of the Americans to walk inside with extra headroom. Our family of nine shared the tent with another family. They were seven very decent and well-mannered people. Both parents were pharmacists from Sài Gòn who brought their grandmother and four children. The two oldest children were girls of my age and Minh Châu's. They also had two young boys. Our neighbors strung a line across the tent between our family's rows of cots and theirs and hung up the horse-dung colored wool blankets as a privacy partition. The separation line dissected our large tent in halves. The mothers seemed to enjoy each other's companionship. We compared our evacuation stories until we were too sad to continue with our family losses.

The pharmacists were in their mid-thirties, whereas my mother was thirty-nine and father was forty-nine. Together, the parents went to the sponsor bulletin-board to peruse the availability of sponsorships. Sponsors posted information such as their locations, biographical or organizational background, the maximum number of people sponsored, etc. After breakfast, this was the men's daily work. Usually, my father came back without leads, since our family exceeded the number of people most sponsors could financially afford. Every day, it was harder to feel hopeful, as our tent mates left for their San Diego sponsors and as other neighbors waved goodbye.

My father filled out many forms. Some were Immigration and Naturalization Services (INS) forms, and some were for sponsorships. The newest lead he brought home was a couple from Pinedale, Wyoming. They owned a resort that consisted of cabins, a lodge, a restaurant, a gas station, and a gift shop. Occasionally, the postcard read, their resort might have horse rides for vacationers. The owners were looking for a large family to help with all aspects of their operations. This lead sounded very promising to my father since it spelled job opportunities for all of us. We were hopeful and delighted to know that there was a sponsor for everyone, even a large family like ours.

We'd been there at least two months, and it took another month to process our files before we finally received acknowledgments from the INS and our Wyoming sponsors. There were more correspondence and meetings between my father and the officials at the camp to expedite the sponsorship process. There were glitches, more immunizations, and more requests for additional information of some form or another. We grew discouraged, but we continued to wait patiently. It appeared as though we were the only people left from the first wave of refugees to Camp Pendleton. It must be, to some degree, what it felt like for orphans who waited for new adoptive parents, but remained unchosen for their apparent lack of desirable attributes. I overheard my father contemplate splitting up our family so we could have a better chance of getting sponsors.

"We could send the older kids off together to one sponsor where they could work if they had to, and I could stay with you and the younger ones." My father strained his voice to explain the rationale of his thinking.

"But we've come this far together. Do you think we need to split up now?" My mother's eyes searched deep into her husband's heavy-hearted eyes. I could see that neither one of them was willing to pursue this option. My father certainly didn't consult or confer with any of his children on his decision, and I remained tormented over-hearing this contemplation. In his many hours of filling out forms, he might have tried both options, or perhaps not, though I would never know if he did.

Our family was larger than the average family, all nine of us, making it difficult to find a sponsor. I started to feel unwanted and terribly rejected and thought our family would never get out of Camp Pendleton. I imagined us being the last residents who were forgotten by the officials. I imagined seeing cobwebs spun in corners of the tent where our tent mates used to be, and the Marines would gasp in awe when they yanked the front door flap open to find us in there. Still more trucks full of new fresh-faced refugees arrived, and more eager faces pulled out every week to start their new lives with their sponsors.

CHAPTER 14

U.S. Marines & Supply Trailers

In their clean, pressed uniforms and shiny black boots, the young and fresh-faced Marines made our camp life orderly, comfortable, clean, safe, and predictable for us. They worked tirelessly everyday to maintain a high-level of sanitation for thousands of refugees.

From an aerial view, you'd see grids of tents separated by light gray ribbons of gravel roads dividing the "tent city" into columns and rows of tents. When you opened the tent's front door flap, you'd see a lime green porta-potty designated for the occupants of that tent backed up to another one, facing the opposite direction for another row of tents. Each tent's occupants would share the porta-potty closest to them, but they could use any available units. At the back of each the tent, a door flap opened to a cold-water spigot standing in drainage gravel. Back along the side of the tent, the Marines also strung up some clotheslines for us to dry our hand-washed clothes.

During the day, we tied back our tent's "doors" to get the circulation of fresh air and lighting, still leaving the netted door in place to cut down on the bugs and dust. At dusk, we plugged in a long cord with a thirty watt bulb so we could see our way in the tent.

My father bought a portable broadband radio so we could listen to the Vietnamese broadcast of the BBC and Voice of America. It was our one item of luxury purchased at the Camp's PX from the meager eighty US dollars he had exchanged at the last hour in Sài Gòn.

I became quite fond of the Marines because, contrary to rumors that American GIs were gruff, uncivilized, and demeaning to the Vietnamese, they seemed to be mostly very civilized and gentle. I still couldn't believe that I was safe here in America and felt immensely grateful every day for their service. At the same time, I was deathly afraid of them. If I was by myself around camp, usually coming or going to the bathroom, the "library" or the supply tents and saw a Marine, I'd cross the road as discreetly as I could to avoid walking near them. They mesmerized me from a distance, but I didn't want to acknowledge them with eye contact. That I wasn't ready to do. In their presence I was paralyzed, so frozen with teenage insecurity and shyness I'd be flustered and turn beet-red. In retrospect, I avoided them because I wouldn't know what to do if they asked me a question. I didn't want to appear stupid and tongue-tied, admitting that my years of English didn't prove useful.

Our camp life consisted of going to meals, taking showers, and lining up for supplies. Even when we didn't know what supplies the GIs were handing out, we figured that if they were handing them out, then it must be something we'd need. On our way back from break-fast one morning, Kim Chi and I spotted a long line. It captured our attention, and drew us like a magnet. We walked up to the end of the line and asked the last person if she knew what was being given out. She shook her head and said she didn't know, but that it didn't matter. Of course, she and the rest of the refugees had nothing but time until lunch and didn't mind lining up. We wished that we had Vietnamese books to read or paper and pencils to write and draw to pass the time, but those were luxury items. We had a few magazines from Sài Gòn, but we had read, reread, memorized and tucked them away in our bags under the cots. We lined up behind this woman, and soon more people came to line up behind us, asking us the same question, and we all shared an embarrassed chuckle that we didn't know.

By the time we were closer to the supply trailer, we could see the items that people had walked away with, and my legs went weak. They were feminine napkins, pads, tampons; all embarrassing womanly stuff! Of course, we needed them, but they were being handed out by a very handsome young Marine whose face was angular and whose teeth were unnaturally white. The olive drab, crew-neck T-shirt peeked above his uniform shirt, and his shirtsleeves were rolled up slightly above the middle of his forearms, where I could see the light copper color hair against his brown arms. I admired how beautiful he looked.

Kim Chi, standing behind me, probably embarrassed and awestruck as well, shoved me ahead of her. My face felt hot. I wished I could slither away without being noticed by this Marine, but it was too late. I saw his hands above me on the window ledge of the supply trailer. Each hand had a box of a different brand, and he gestured to ask me which one I needed. By then I could not care less which one, but pointed to one of them so I could quickly disappear. My sister nudged me and said no, that I didn't want that one. We only used the pads and not the stick kind.

Right, of course, you are right, dear sister. I gave the Marine a quick, grimacing smile that said I was sorry. I pointed to the other one instead and picked up the cardboard box of Kotex. I knew it was rude in America not to have eye contact, but I didn't even look at his beautiful face, only able to look past his direction. It was all I could do to not hyperventilate and black out in front of the line. Fortunately, not all Marines had that effect on me, only the handsome ones. Lately, I'd noticed that I wasn't so queasy in the mess hall with the ones dishing out the food, or with the ones at the soap and detergent supply trailer. My embarrassment that day mostly had to do with the taboo feminine products, highly personal items.

Porta-Potties & Bleachers

The Marines served and maintained the tent cities, barracks, and dormitories around Camp Pendleton. They worked on plumbing and installed showers, emptied trashcans, and porta-potties. It was just another morning when I came back from breakfast and went straight to the toilet with my personal roll of paper, as we all did. The walls were painted a nauseating lime green inside and out. I sat down and locked the door. The sunlight streamed through the horizontal vents on top, and the back side's screen was up high enough for privacy but allowed fresh air to flow through. I sat there and studied the white quilted toilet paper and wondered why imprints of daisies were even necessary on this perfectly soft paper. I looked around and spotted the white chunk of air freshener hung on the wall, and there on the floor, the paint had been worn off by people's shoes to reveal the metal diamond plate floor. I thought to myself how lucky we all were and was so appreciative of a clean bathroom. The ones on Guam were constructed out of plywood and started out just okay, then quickly degraded to nightmarish outhouses.

I was lost in my daydream, as I often was, when someone rapped on the door firmly enough to shake the structure. I was about to say in Vietnamese, "occupied," when, to my deepest fear, a tenor American voice boomed with some degree of urgency. I didn't understand what he said and became transfixed with confusion, fear, and indecision. I didn't know what to say because I didn't understand what he'd said. A moment later there was only silence, and I breathed a sigh of relief, just in time to hear a thunderous roar of heavy machinery outside my porta-potty. I dismissed it and went back to my thoughts, when a very sudden and sharp jolt rocked my buttocks off to one side, the whole structure lifting up slowly.

"Trời Đất ơi!" I screamed, an involuntary exclamation of shock, and banged both fists hard on the walls and door. I wanted to be put back on the ground, and in record time I stood up and pulled up my pants. Someone must have heard my screaming and banging, lowered the porta-potty, and killed the engine, because there was dead silence. I wanted to disappear, almost forgetting how to walk out of the porta-potty that morning. I didn't know how to act, what to say, or what I should do. I didn't have the luxury of time and had to move fast before they hauled me up and away again.

Begrudgingly, I unlocked the door and put one foot in front of another to march away with dignity. I imagined other residents must have gathered outside the toilet after hearing such commotion, but I didn't want their rubbernecking. I headed straight to my tent and disappeared behind the door flap. I broke down hysterically on my cot. I laughed so hard that my stomach muscles ached, and my diaphragm felt like it went into a spasmodic seizure. My siblings told me later that they had stopped the forklift driver because they saw me go in earlier; otherwise, he would haul me away because nobody could hear my scream with the forklift engine revving loudly.

My older brothers Thọ and Thông, on the other hand, were on the other extreme. They were not the least bit shy. Quite the contrary. They conjured up scenarios of setting up traps for the Marines to stop and question them for not following camp's rules. They weren't malicious traps, just mischievous behavior, as you would expect from restless teenage boys. Camp rules were few, but one of them was that all food must be eaten at the mess hall to prevent rodents, food waste, and trash. No one could take any food back to the tent, except for maybe an orange or an apple. Knowing how strictly enforced the rule was, my brothers were dying to agitate and test the boundaries with the Marines. After a lunch of fried chicken, mashed potatoes and gravy, Thọ saved a chicken bone and put it strategically between two styrofoam cups, with only a glimpse of the knobby bone sticking out, for the appearance of food taken away from the mess hall.

Instead of taking a hidden and less traveled route to conceal the supposed crime, my brother paraded in front of the guards and put on a guilty and mischievous look. He wanted to be caught for breaking the rules. He wanted the Marines' attention. He planned to throw his head back, maniacally laughing, if they stopped him. But no one inspected the cups. The guard just gestured to my brother to throw the cups away as he saw us coming from the mess hall. Thọ was very disappointed, but he smiled broadly with his usual resigned smile and a slight shrug. He asked me to walk with him toward the guard to reveal that it was just a bone, but the Marine dryly smiled and waved us away. He looked like he was a big kid himself and was not amused.

The Marines also set up bleachers for an outdoor amphitheater and showed movies a few nights a week. I didn't get to go because my parents said I couldn't stay out that late at night, but they let me attend the daytime shows from local high school bands and cheer-leading groups. The students, who seemed much older and bigger than me, put on rock-and-roll music and invited the audience to come down and dance with them on stage. I sat high on the bleacher, and there was no chance of their asking me to join. I wondered what I would do if they reached for my hand. I wanted to join in and dance because it looked so carefree and fun. I wished I were confident and self-assured, and that I could just take their offered hand and walk down to the stage and dance with them. Instead, I sat amongst my fellow shy refugees, all strangers to me, and watched. I wanted their self-assured attitude, their seemingly middle-class and comfortable lifestyle with no insecurity in their future. For one short moment, I experienced what it might be like to be at school with them. I once had a life similar to theirs, taking school and friendship for granted, not having many concerns about what the future might bring. I realized then that they were seemingly innocent compared to how much I'd learned about life and survival in the past four months.

The exuberant atmosphere with music and dancing suddenly made me plunge deeper into my dark and melancholic self, where I could only focus on our homelessness and having no country to call home. I reached over and stroked my younger sister Mỹ Châu's silky hair as she leaned against me to hide from the potential reach of the high school students. I felt fantastically regretful that I had spanked her earlier in line for being cranky or whiny. She certainly did not deserve that kind of treatment, especially not in public. I was frustrated, but then we were all frustrated for the uncertainty and the insecurity of our future. I went from self-loathing to self-pity, then to boredom and hopelessness. All I could think of, sitting there in the grandstand, was that we still hadn't heard news from our sponsors.

It was August, and school would start soon. I very much wanted to go back to school and wondered what would happen if we were still in the camp come September. If we were in Vietnam without the regime change, we would be shopping for school supplies and choosing fabrics for our school uniforms. Clothes were customarily tailor-made for the Vietnamese. We seldom purchased ready-to-wear garments. Most people bought their fabric at the ubiquitous fabric stores and market stalls where an on-site seamstress measured customers and fashioned their clothes to order, who would then return for a final fitting and pick up.

Dressmakers in these shops or market stalls would take our measurements and listen as we drew and described the styles of clothes that we wanted. Some nicer stores would have pictures and catalogs from which we could choose the styles for our uniforms. I imagined that these seamstresses stayed up late into the night at their drawing tables, running the sliver of tailor's chalk on the cloth, then standing back to squint at it, the soft measuring tape draped around their necks, as they tucked the pencil behind their ears. They would keep on working, pinning and cutting the fabric, ironing, machine sewing, as well as hand-stitching, to meet their many deadlines of back-to-school orders.

One of my favorite tailored items was a fuchsia colored muslin dress. The muslin was sheer with large magnolia floral prints. The bodice and arms were lined with white material that felt soft, cool and slightly slippery against my skin. Kim Chi designed the dress for me after Juliet's dress from the movie *Romeo and Juliet*. The sleeves were puffy at the shoulders and tapered to almost an uncomfortable tightness on the arms. A band of dark crimson velvet trimmed at the transition between the puffy shoulder sleeves to the tight fitting arms. It was a one-of-a-kind dress, even within my family, since we only had a small amount of this fabric, only enough for my size. It was quite a regal yet feminine looking dress, and I loved it. Unfortunately, I only wore it a few times before it shrunk too small for me, and I put it away in my wardrobe for my younger sister.

Sitting there on the bleachers watching the show at Camp Pendleton, I looked at what I was wearing now: some oversized Salvation Army pants and shirt. I almost felt sorry for myself, but quickly snapped to the reality that I now lived in America with my family, and not so long ago, before the Fall of Vietnam, that was all we'd ever wanted. I could not dwell on what I'd lost but instead on what I would gain. I took my little sisters home when the show ended and helped them brush their teeth at the faucet near our tent. We sat up in our cots and chatted with my parents for a brief time, then unplugged the string of light bulbs. My father and mother slept on the other side of the aisle from my younger sisters and me. I felt safe there, knowing that I would never have to hear the rocket warning sirens again, or crawl under the bunk bed in our bomb-shelter-bedroom to dodge shrapnel. I pulled up the horse-dung color wool blanket to cover my face, and tucked it under my head tightly to form a tent, as that was how I liked to sleep at Camp Pendleton, where it got uncomfortably cold. The clean white sheet slightly rustled when it shifted over the air mattress on my canvas army cot. I heard others in my family move around to get comfortable before they settled down and fell fast asleep. I could hear everyone's soft breathing and snoring. I also heard my beating heart harmonizing with the crickets outside. We were all alive and well sleeping under the same roof, and that was just enough for me.

CHAPTER 15

We meet again!

Dawn came, and I could hear old folks coughing and hacking, moaning and groaning of arthritic and rheumatic pains. Babies cried their colicky cries and shrieked for their early feedings or the changing of soggy diapers before falling back to sleep. If my grandmother were here, she would brush her thin gray hair back into a little quail-egg-size bun, then tuck it under a checkered-cloth turban. She would lament about the lack of betel-nuts and other ingredients to make her daily supply. She would stroll the "neighborhood," chatting and socializing with old folks. But she wasn't with us. My father couldn't persuade her to come to America. She was in her early sixties but said that she was too old to leave Vietnam. She'd rather die and be buried in her homeland with our ancestors because that was our culture and traditions.

My parents woke up early and listened to the broadband radio, but I resumed my fetal position and surrendered to the urge of sleeping in because I needed it, though there were times I stayed in bed out of boredom or refusal to face the day. My parents didn't let us sleep past eight. They made us get up and make our beds, such as they were. If we used the mosquito netting, we had to tie it up tidily. We all went to meals and sat together, though my older siblings would have preferred to sit with their friends.

Shortly after eight, we strolled to the mess hall for breakfast. Several hundred meals were served each day in this screened-in and plywood-floor tent. Shiny stainless steel, rectangular pans of steamy scrambled eggs, grits, boiled eggs, crispy bacon, applesauce, and toast lined up on the long tables on one side. Orange juice, apple juice, milk, coffee, tea dispensers, and condiments were on the opposite side. Marines, donning their white chef's hats and wearing their food-stained white aprons, stood behind the food table to scoop up the wet soft eggs, and grits, deftly transferring the wriggling strips of bacon to our metal trays.

The menu sometimes varied to offer oatmeal or pancakes, which, like grits, took us some getting used to because of their textures and tastes. We'd never had bacon, toast, or applesauce before either, but they were tasty and didn't take much coaxing. We didn't use ketchup on our scrambled eggs, or mayonnaise and mustard on our sandwiches. Since we didn't have these products back home, they gave us digestive issues, and we preferred not to suffer after the initial discovery.

Our camp was number eight at Camp Pendleton. Camp one, where my sister-in-law, Liên and her two babies ended up, was the permanent base with rows of red brick buildings and was a bus ride away. Since all the camps were temporary like ours, the food must have been cooked there at these permanent buildings and trucked to the surrounding camps for every meal, but I don't remember for sure.

Lunch and dinner were equally plentiful and as delicious as the Marines could concoct. They served up a large selection of hamburgers, hot dogs, sandwiches, and fruit, along with beverages. Just as quickly as the cooks could clear off our metal trays, wash the tables, empty the garbage and put away the food tubs, it was time to set up dinner, and the routines repeated like clockwork every day.

The older folks had the hardest time with the new American camp food. They missed white rice and fish sauce. They longed for the fresh greens and spicy herbs. They dreamt of fresh catfish in their sour soup, an imagined whiff at the caramelized egg and pork stew, and the indelibly pungent, salty shrimp paste in the hot and spicy beef soup mixed with shredded red cabbage and mint. It was hard for them to endure the lack of their native food, and they said so in their not-so-stoic way. The new food, tasty or not, made their stomachs a little queasy.

The Vietnamese younger adults and children were most malleable. Not yet set in their ways, they enthusiastically consumed the new American food in great portions. One could make a case for the refugees here that, like in the wild kingdom, we had the propensity to gorge when food was plentiful for our survival because we didn't know when our next meals would be available.

Dinner menus varied from delectable and savory to not-so-tasty dishes. We could tell when our favorite meals were served from how long the line grew outside the mess hall. Meatloaf, spaghetti, lasagna, and chop-suey were foreign to us. Sauerkraut, hot dogs, and hamburgers still took some getting used to, especially the kraut. The Marines undoubtedly enjoyed our facial reactions when we tasted the pickled cabbage, or as we first saw the revolting shape of over-boiled and shriveled hot dogs lying between the white seeded buns. An American advisor friend of my father's told him the history of how the hot dog was named, and it made it even less palatable when these were served for dinner.

Almost every day, canned fruit in thick syrup, boiled green beans and carrots were on the menu. I liked how the peach halves always looked perfect. They were skinless and slicked smooth in a viscous syrup. They were always cheerful and bright as the promising sun, or looking like farm fresh egg yolks. I wondered how the Americans made their canned peaches perfectly flawless that way. I pictured women and men sitting at a table, in front of a peach skin mound, carefully peeling each fruit as not to mar or damage any of them.

Back home on my front porch swing, I had watched the American cooks in their barracks. Here, I looked at the dining hall Marines clobbering around in their chunky steel-toed boots, smacking flies with damp white towels in mid-air—on the screens, on the tables, anywhere flies buzzed around. For the first time I saw the use of a mop bucket, the kind that squeezed the stringy, cotton-wig kind of mop with one move of a handle, then the Marines plopped the sopping cotton mop on the wooden floor and smeared it around.

I'd first seen black Americans at the height of the war back home. At camp, there were more ethnic Americans, if that's the proper word to use. I even saw Asian-looking Marines who spoke English, and acted so very American with their loud laughs and wildly waving arms. I wondered if I could ever become proficient at this complicated, yet pretty-sounding language, and some day give new immigrants pause. But here they were, working hard to serve our meals and happily cleaning up after us. They were polite, and no one ever made faces or ridiculed us for our cultural differences. We were the first wave of Vietnamese refugees, and we were a novelty for the Marines, as they were for us.

My older brothers roamed the camp looking for old friends and making new ones. Kim Chi and I limited ourselves to home except for the regular meals and chores because my mother didn't want us to be loitering about unchaperoned. Minh Châu had always been the outgoing type. She joined the Girl Scout Brownies, attended their meetings, and participated in various activities led by American leaders. She looked adorable in her green uniform with her hat and scarf. My siblings and I took turns taking Mỹ Châu and Hồng Châu to the library tent where they had a limited selection of well-used and well-loved American picture books. I worried about my three younger sisters who had never had English classes, and wondered how they would get along in school.

My family went to the Red Cross tent on one occasion when my father was interviewed by what must have been a radio reporter. After they conversed, my dad brought the reporter over to sit down on a folding chair next to my cot where I sat with my younger sisters. I didn't understand their conversation, but my father asked me to sing for her recorder. "What song?" I asked, eagerly naming a list of songs in my repertoire, "A love song, a war song, a patriotic marching song, a sad song, a funny song— what song do you want me to sing?"

"Sing something youthful," my father diplomatically suggested.

It was September and back-to-school was on my mind, so without trepidation, I sentimentally swooned a nostalgic and bitter-sweet song, longing for an alma mater. The tiny microphone placed not too far from my lips made me feel slightly staged. A rush of singing endorphin surged in my body, and for one moment I felt so alive and happy, reliving the glory of my fifth-grade solo performance at school.

I felt giddy when I got to wander around camp with my older siblings. I wanted to know if there was more to this camp besides what I saw from the routes to my usual destinations like the mess hall, bathroom, and showers. I grew tired of the same scenery. I wanted to see what was beyond those blonde hills, but my brothers said they had already explored and saw nothing, except more panorama of endless hills. They reported that they had found a few of their old friends from Đà Nẵng, including Dzũng and his brothers.

This news filled me with mixed emotions, dread, and excitement. On the one hand, I was pleased to hear that Dzũng's family made it here, yet I felt quite confused about how to feel about him. Our circumstances had changed so much since we collected bugs and plants, except for my brothers' surveillance of me around boys and Thông's particular order to sever my association with Dzũng.

Our inevitable and eventual meeting didn't go well. I first saw Dzũng near the bleachers with his throng of new and old peers. I stood in line, luckily a safe distance away, where I could assess his new look. His hair slightly longer and tousled unruly, perhaps by default because of our exodus. I'd always loved the way his mouth curled at the corners when he smiled, and the way he devilishly winked for emphasis in our private conversations. He held court with his flock of admirers, gregariously center-staged, talking and shrugging animatedly in a very American way. He wore a short-sleeved, button-down shirt and bell-bottomed jeans. And not just any bell-bottomed jeans. I saw that he must have had his mother sew a triangular colored swatch at the seams to make the pant legs wider. How quickly he had adapted to American ways, I thought.

I looked at him in a slightly different perspective now. He was no longer a neighborhood boy with whom I'd once collected dragonflies and plants. I appreciated his physical attributes now, and distractedly felt a sense of longing for his company. Surprisingly, I felt a sense of excitement seeing Dzũng. But, too bad, I was only thirteen, a mere baby, and my brother Thông already told me not to talk to him anymore. I looked away from his direction, hoping to avoid him. I was not allowed to be his friend, so meeting him would be pointless. When I looked up, Dzũng had caught my eyes, and I saw that he was happy to see me, as I was to see him. I smiled heartily with my eyes but didn't want to get caught and reprimanded by my brothers, so I looked away. I felt bad doing this to him because he had no idea that I was forbidden to talk to him. My impulse was to walk up to him and ask how he'd been, but instead, I looked away. He must have thought I was heartless and had changed.

After our brief encounter, I seldom saw Dzũng again because I couldn't stroll around unchaperoned. But whenever I did, he was always the center of attention in an entourage of guys and girls who seemed to have acculturated quite well. They seemed at ease, striking up conversations with the Marines, no doubt trying to practice their English. I liked Dzũng's Hà Nội accent and wondered how that transferred into his English voice. Gradually, we avoided each other. He must have grown tired of my outward indifference and lack of communication. His brothers frequently visited my brothers at our tent, but Dzũng never came around after our first encounter.

PART TWO

CHAPTER 16

Our Wyoming Sponsors

August 8th, 1975 was the day we'd been longing for, the day of departure from Camp Pendleton. I would miss some things about this place, like the predictability and familiarity of routines. I was delighted at the prospect of seeing civilians, residential and commercial buildings, roads and cars, and all things representative of normalcy for middle America, as I'd seen in films during English class back home. I wondered if the interned Japanese in World War II had similar feelings; the yearning to see the outside world again and to have actual walls, doors, and windows with all the comfort of home where, when we stepped outside, we wouldn't see the windy, desolate landscape of a God forsaken countryside.

Finally, it was our turn to be the envy of our tent mates and surrounding camp neighbors. Similar to the experience of orphans whose newly adoptive parents came to take them away, we were ready for our new and fresh start and to integrate into mainstream society. I took a last look around the tent. We folded up our blankets, stripped our sheets and pillowcases, and folded the deflated air mattresses into flat rectangles.

There was no fanfare, hugs, or tears. Off we went, riding high on our adrenaline rush. We followed my father's footsteps like ducklings, to and fro, stopping and waiting for him to look up at the overhead signs, trying to decipher which way to go to the right terminal gates and planes. All nine of us made our way from Los Angeles International Airport to Colorado, and then to Jackson Hole, Wyoming. Dizzy with an excitement of the unknown and travel weariness, we stumbled off the plane at dusk, walking off the puddle hopper and into the building, anxious to meet our sponsors, Curly and Peggy Brooks.

We scanned the crowd, looking to match their faces to the Polaroid self-portrait they'd sent us a few weeks ago. There was a sea of faces staring back at us, actually staring like they had never seen anyone like us before. It dawned on us that, indeed, they hadn't seen Asians here, except for on television. There were some signs, "Wilsons," "Marshalls," "Lowells," and then we saw it, a cardboard sign with scrawny, shaky cursive that spelled, "Brooks/Truongs," their family name and ours.

No, Curly didn't look anything like Curly of the Three Stooges. He was barrel-chested, and his short black curls peeked out from under the Wrangler's plaid shirt collar. The pearl snap buttons stretched to the point of almost popping at his oversized belly, which spilled over the dark blue Levi's jeans. I believe he got his nickname from his very curly hair, even though he was slightly balding now. His skin was darkened and weathered by long hours of outdoor work, and his beady eyes were too small for his huge, bulldog-like face. His neck was massive and almost as wide as his head, and his fingers were shockingly large and thick like bananas, disproportionate to his hands. Mr. Brooks didn't have any facial hair, but he had black curls crawling out of his small red ears. I was scared of him. His voice didn't soothe me either. It was raspy, like he had smoked all his life, although he wasn't smoking now.

His wife Peggy was rail thin, frail, and almost invisible behind his large build. She came to his armpits in height, was considerably older than Curly, and wore the smoker's wrinkles, but was very pale. She wore a floral triangle scarf that tied in the back of her head, draping over her short gray hair, and topped off with a pair of silver cat-eye bifocals. When I came up to greet Peggy, I could see the blue veins under her thin, translucent, white skin. Dark age spots randomly filled her small face. She reminded me of my grandmother. Peggy moved in a smooth gait in her plain leather moccasins, alongside her lumbering husband in his well-worn work boots.

It was late at night, around eight-thirty, and they appeared tired and slightly put out. We rode in silence in the station wagon for almost the entire time, so afraid to talk amongst ourselves, only daring to exchange knowing looks of mutual discomfort. Darkness enveloped us, and we could only see what the headlights illuminated. I was getting hungry now. It was past our camp's dinnertime, and I hoped it wouldn't be long before we reached our new home.

We had no idea what to expect for our living situation because we had limited information on the Brooks. We only knew that we had a place for us to live and work, so we were anxious to find out what our new home would look like for our family. In the darkness, we could see a warming red glow in the distance that slowly grew brighter as the car lurched ahead.

At last, we saw a red neon sign reading "Vacancy." It was the first sign of life we'd seen in a while, maybe an hour, and one-by-one, more fluorescent lights gradually appeared, and then we saw a gas station with two pumps on a concrete pad. Their station wagon pulled into the half-circle gravel driveway and parked at the entrance of a two-story log cabin. To the left stood a string of cottages, possibly unoccupied because there were no cars in sight. A low wattage light bulb dimly lit the front of each log cabin door, but we saw no sign of life. When the station wagons stopped, only a few words exchanged between my father and the Brooks as they opened up the rear doors so we could fetch our luggage. Our arrival could be described as anti-climactic, unwelcoming and very unlike what we had dreamt it would be. We tiptoed and whispered to one another. "Is this it?" we inquired softly of one another, as though the Brooks could understand us.

Rookies Lodge

We walked through the lodge's dining room to the back kitchen and settled our bags on the floor as Peggy turned on the range light and gas burner to heat up a big pot of soup. She gestured for us to follow her through a small door, like a pantry door, but it opened up to a steep staircase. She flipped the light switch and pointed at the low ceiling ahead with a nonverbal warning not to bump our heads.

"Thank you," we all said to Peggy as she turned to descend to the kitchen. The Brooks said goodnight and left us to eat our first dinner alone. After a bit of rummaging around, we found bowls in the cupboard, and my mother served the vegetable beef soup. Kim Chi sliced a loaf of bread that Peggy had left on the counter for us, and placed the slices on a large plate for all to share.

"Maybe things will look better in the morning," my father optimistically suggested. We desperately wanted to believe him and nodded in unison as we ate our soup and bread at the dark wood kitchen table. We were tired from traveling, intensely disappointed, and wondered what tomorrow would bring. I hoped that my father was right, that morning's sunlight would bring renewed hope and energy to deal with our new situation. My sisters and I hand-washed the dirty bowls and plates. We placed them on the dish rack, and then everyone piled upstairs to figure out who would sleep where that night and from then on.

The attic two-bedroom accommodations were cramped but adequate, and, most importantly, well sanitized. My parents shared one bedroom with the two youngest sisters on their queen and two twin beds, respectively. In the second bedroom, Kim Chi and I shared one queen, and Minh Châu slept in the twin bed. There wasn't room for much else except for a couple of wicker armchairs along one wall. On the other side of the narrow hallway was a low-ceilinged loft with a sloping floor where my brothers had to stoop to crawl into their fold-out couch in the space of about fifty square feet.

My parents rose before dawn, and through the walls, I heard them talking in their whispering voices. They showered and tiptoed downstairs so as not to wake the youngest kids. Kim Chi, Thọ and Thông woke as well and dressed for work downstairs. My mother came to tell me that she would have breakfast for us when we got dressed, and not to sleep past eight. I agreed and went back to sleep.

My younger sisters slept deeply as the room stayed dark with the curtains closed. I woke up to the buttery aroma of fluffy buttermilk pancakes, sumptuously fried eggs, ham and bacon, and slightly burnt, coffee-shop coffee. As soon as we woke up, my sisters and I rushed to the windows to see our new surroundings. We couldn't see any neighbors out of the south window, just an open field that ended abruptly at the border of dense pines. In the front and side of the lodge, we saw parked trucks with dogs in the back barking at passersby, cars, and people idling about, laughing, and chatting with one another.

We saw our father a hundred feet or so to the right of the lodge's front entrance, standing at the gas station with a red shop towel hanging from his back pocket. He wore a red plaid flannel cap with faux fur earflaps, something he'd been wearing since Camp Pendleton, but now it seemed to be more fitting because it was colder with the high elevation pine trees backdrop. My two brothers were washing the windshields, arching and reaching with their wipers while the drivers stared at them from behind their steering wheels.

My father signaled to one of the drivers to pop his hood then knelt slightly under the hood to unlatch and raise it up to check the oil.

My three sisters and I watched our father and brothers already at work. I could see my brothers pause after each task for further instructions from my dad. We glanced at each other at the windowsill unbelievingly witnessing our family's first day working in America. In bewildered silence, we got dressed and padded lightly downstairs to breakfast.

My mother and oldest sister alternately oiled the large griddle for pancakes, eggs, ham and bacon. They deftly poured the pancake batter from the large spouted plastic cup onto the hot griddle surface, as if they'd done this every day of their lives. I could see visible droplets of sweat on their foreheads and necks, but this didn't break their stride and didn't seem to faze them. I could almost feel their pride as they earned their first U.S. dollars, their compelling self-argument that the steep fall from the privileged class wasn't so hard to swallow. We all grew tired of the idling boredom and felt the increased anxiety about our future in the refugee camp.

We had always been a proud family, and were determined to rebuild our lives from scratch. The phoenix rose from the ashes, and so would we. I was accustomed to being in the privileged class, to instant resentment from friends and neighbors because of my father's position, regardless of how hard he had worked all his life and the many sacrifices he'd made personally and for his country. His many scars and war injuries were not visible to everyone, some not even to his children and wife. There was so much we didn't know, nor had the right to know about my dad. We had lived in safety and comfort, and that was the life my father wanted to provide for us.

Instead of feeling sad watching my father working as a gas station attendant, after a lifetime of being a commanding officer, or of my mother, who had not worked since she was a teenager, now pregnant and slaving away over the hot grills, I was eternally grateful because they were here in America working. It meant that they were alive and we were together as a family. I reasoned that this was only a temporary situation, a new chapter of our lives, our new humble but proud beginning. I was young and malleable and knew I could adapt and survive the new set of challenges.

My mother and sister were in the middle of their busy breakfast rush and said we could get our cereal and juice. I told my sisters to take their seats, filled up their cereal bowls, and sat down to join them, unsuccessful at making casual conversation this morning. My mother said we could go outside and play afterward, but cautioned us to stay out of trouble. I told her I was old enough to help, but she wanted me to watch the younger kids.

Everyone kept a stiff upper lip as we left my mother working at the kitchen counter. Peggy handed them a new order for two over-easy eggs with sausages and coffee. Kim Chi explained to my mom what that meant and turned to grab a cup and saucer for the coffee. The dining room beyond the wrap-around bar counter looked crowded with ranchers in their cowboy hats, smoking, and drinking their brown cups of fresh brew. I couldn't tell if the smoke came from the hot beverage or the cigarettes. It could also have been from the grease of splattering bacon and sausages on the kitchen grill.

I had long been a devoted fan of Westerns. Now I had a live performance of real-life cowboys who spoke just as they should, with deep, twangy voices. They all, without exception, had triangular bandanas that creased in several half-moon folds beneath their stubbly chins. They all wore plaid shirts of different colors and well-worn blue jeans which bore evidence of field work. Some had black suede vests on, and some were camel color with well-worn darker patches. A few women, also in western looking shirts, accompanied the men at the booths. Most everyone had light color hair, with curiously white blond lashes as well. Without being rude, I studied their peculiar, almost invisible eyebrows and eyelashes upon their fair skin,

141

sprinkled with freckles, and they innocently stared back at us, because, as we soon learned, there were no Asians in Pinedale, Wyoming.

My sisters tugged at my shirt, interrupting my observation of the dining room. They wanted to play outside, so we cleaned up our bowls, and I told my mom we would be right back. The screen door snapped closed with a loud bang behind us. I didn't think it was from our being hasty or abrupt with closing the door but I thought I should be gentler next time. Soon after we went outside, we were surrounded by mosquitoes. They were giant, piercing us painfully with their thirsty nozzles. We swatted them with furious futility, but it became apparent that we must at once seek refuge. Our stint outdoors was shockingly short, and we didn't get to see anything but a blur of our collective swatting against the bloodthirsty beasts. We ran back to the lodge for cover and understood fully why the screen door snapped shut so quickly behind us to keep the mosquitoes out.

We didn't have permission to be anywhere besides our loft or outside. We had no other place at our disposal, which meant back upstairs we went, confined to a space of less than four hundred square feet. That was our routine for the first few days. Except for breakfast, lunch, and dinner, we would retreat upstairs where we wouldn't be eaten by mosquitoes. Since I was the oldest of the four, I made sure to keep an eye on them and kept the morale up. We relied on each other for entertainment, as we didn't have any books, toys, or television.

A few days later, my father gave us mosquito repellent so we could go outside to play. It wasn't something we were used to and found it very troublesome to apply. It wasn't entirely effective, but at least we could stay out a bit longer. With our newfound freedom, we wandered the perimeter of the premises and saw more of the grounds each day. A row of cabins faced the long gravel driveway that buffered us from the main thoroughfare, a two-lane road where trucks roared past mercilessly, leaving trails of diesel fumes and particulates assaulting the pristine mountain air.

My sisters and I met a young family with a couple of bright blond-haired kids under five. They liked to play with Mỹ Châu and Hồng Châu, despite the age gap. Minh Châu and I sat on the logs on the perimeter of the lawn and watched them exploring their cultural differences. Neither group understood the other's language, but they managed playing ball and chasing each other on the vast lush lawn. I wished the family could stay longer, but after a few days, they continued with their vacation.

Several days later, my mother and sister brought me along to help them clean the guest rooms upstairs in the lodge. I welcomed the change, even though I wasn't particularly fond of the hotel rooms. I felt sorry for my younger siblings who were stuck behind in the same tight space upstairs, or the limited activities they could engage in outdoors without my being there to chaperone.

My mother and Kim Chi counted the rooms that had checked out from the guest book and brought enough sheets and pillowcases for replacements. I didn't have to do very much except for a few things here and there when they asked me to pitch in. They didn't need me to work yet. I watched them strip the sheets and pillowcases, empty the garbage, vacuum the bedroom floor, clean the bathtubs, sinks, toilets, and mop the bathroom tile floors. All I had to do was learn how to tuck in the sheets so they would stay securely in place, stuff the pillows into new cases, and fill the bathrooms with new shampoo bottles and soap. I also wrapped the drinking water glasses in crisp, waxy paper bags and placed them on the tables in the rooms. In the bathrooms, it was my job to make sure there were enough disposal bags for feminine napkins on the toilet water tanks. I didn't think they needed my help. I figured they felt sorry for me and rescued me from cabin fever by giving me something different to do. Whatever the reason, I had a glimpse into what they had to do daily after cooking for, serving, and cleaning up after the breakfast crowd. I was grateful for the lessons in hotel housekeeping because it was fascinating to see what it took to keep a lodge clean. I understood my family was working hard to earn our first dollars in the United States.

It had been two weeks since we'd arrived at Rookies Lodge, Curly and Peggy's resort. My parents and siblings worked six days a week from dawn to dusk and went straight to bed after dinner. My father didn't like our working and living conditions. He saw no future for us here. The workload the Brooks imposed on my siblings would compromise their schooling. They had to work every day after school, and there was no college within driving distance for Kim Chi to attend. We had no car, no money and felt trapped in this small Wyoming town, a family of nine living in this cramped, upstairs maid's quarters.

Without our sponsors' knowledge, my father called the same INS caseworker to explain our predicament and requested new sponsorship. Knowing that it took a long time for us to find a sponsor in the camp, my father was quite discouraged but prepared himself to wait it out, or return to Camp Pendleton if permitted, rather than staying here. He was our hero. We had no idea how to navigate the immigration and naturalization system.

Tensions increased between the Brooks and my family. Peggy and Curly tallied up everything consumed by us, such as groceries, incidentals, energy used from our living quarters, phone bills, and every conceivable expenditure. At the end of almost a couple weeks of working at the lodge, the Brooks charged us ninety dollars, claiming the wages earned from five adults didn't cover the rent of the rooms, food, and miscellaneous. This net charge for our labor was the final blow for my father and Curly. My dad told him that his accounting of our labor and living costs was inequitable.

To strengthen his case, my father sent a photocopy of this settlement from Curly to the caseworker in San Diego. A week later, my dad received a letter from a pastor of a Lutheran Church in California, stating that his congregation would help us settle there, and they were working on getting plane tickets to get us out of Pinedale. The last ten days there were difficult for all of us. The children were deathly afraid of Curly and what he might do to prevent our leaving his establishment. We didn't know what he was capable of doing and worried that if he had no misgivings in exploiting our labor, that he might somehow trap us here. We avoided him at all costs and stayed in our rooms except for being in the dining room at mealtimes.

A Superb Rancher Family

As dismal and challenging as it was for our first month working and living in America, I held on to one good memory of a good-hearted ranching family in Wyoming and what they'd done for us. It was a Sunday, my family's only day off, and it was a day I had been looking forward to for a few weeks. A rancher had befriended my father at the lodge and invited us to meet his family and spend a day with them. My parents didn't want all of us to go, but, for reasons unknown to me, they sent Kim Chi and me. I wished that my three younger sisters could come, but perhaps they were too young, or my parents didn't want to burden Mr. Thomas's family with so many of us. They must have had a good and trusting relationship to earn my father's confidence to take us to meet his family.

I took an immediate liking to Mr. Thomas, who had a kind face and gestures. He was one of the people with such light blond eyebrows and lashes that they almost seemed invisible. He came to meet us early in the morning, and we climbed into his raised pickup truck. It was clear that it was a work truck; some tools were on the floor with a coil of rope. In one swift move, he gathered them up and threw them in the truck bed. He tipped his slightly stained felt hat, clucked his tongue, and threw a thumbs up sign at us. We took it that this was a good gesture since he exuded genuine friendliness.

Both sides attempted to rally a conversation, but we didn't know how much we understood each other. Kim Chi and I both had some years of English, but it proved grossly insufficient to communicate with Mr. Thomas. This trip was the first time I'd left the lodge since our arrival three weeks before. Different members of my family might have gone to the grocery store and post office, but this was my first trip away from "home."

"The Rockies, right there," Mr. Thomas said, pointing ahead to the impressive white-capped range. We mimicked his words, "Rockies?" And he nodded, "Yes, the Rockies." Then he gave us another thumbs up. We asked him what it meant when he showed his thumb, just to be sure we understood him correctly.

"Excellent," he confirmed. "It means very good. Also, this...is very good," gesturing an A-OK sign with his thumb and index finger forming a big fat zero. We nodded at this new non-verbal communication lesson and waited for this to sink in while watching the scenery out the windows. Mr. Thomas rested his left arm on the door and lightly leaned that way as he tapped his thumb on the leather-wrapped steering wheel.

"I have to stop here girls. My engine is overheating, and I think I'll need to top off my radiator." I hadn't realized that we had been ascending the mountains and his truck was overworking. After crossing a bridge, the truck rolled slowly to a safe stop. Our new friend popped the hood to check his engine and poked his head in to say he would fetch some water from the river below to cool his radiator. Before he left, he put on his emergency brake and said we must stay in the truck for safety reasons. He threw a fatherly wink at us then grabbed a canteen out from the back of his truck.

Occasionally cars and trucks passed by, but none stopped to see if we needed help. Oddly, I felt safe and had confidence that Mr.

Thomas could get us out of there even though we'd just met and knew nothing about him. The air was crisp and clean. A mosquito was getting big sucking on my arm and spilled blood when I swatted it. I realized that at the lodge, mosquitoes would be feasting on me without repellent. Kim Chi and I watched Mr. Thomas stumble as he lost his balance on the rocks while descending to the riverbank below. The swift clear water rushed past the rocks, the Poplar, and the Aspen trees, like it had an important agenda of its own. Mr. Thomas knelt unsteadily at the water's edge and dipped his canteen into the rushing current. It was a surreal and picture-perfect moment of a cattle rancher in his element, with the Rockies for a backdrop. I consciously etched this still frame in my mind for memory's sake, something I always did to preserve the moments of significance, if the luxury of time permitted.

"I have two daughters at your same ages," Mr. Thomas later told us as we resumed our journey. "I'd like you to meet them, and we'll go to the auction together. I have to get some calves today." He glanced discreetly at his temperature gauge on the instrument panel and continued. "Later on, the girls can show you two around the ranch, and we'll have supper together, then I'll take you back to the lodge." Mr. Thomas leaned comfortably against his door again and looked at us for signs of acknowledgment. We both said our obedient and eager yes, and that was when I realized the reason we were picked for a visit, to meet his daughters who were our same ages.

"My wife and the girls will meet us at the auction, and they'll take you back to the ranch. I gotta stay and take care of my business. Okay?" How I wished then that he was our sponsor. He was kind, thoughtful, and was always making sure we were okay with every-thing. I shivered at the thought of Curly. He was scary and scruffy looking even when he shaved and groomed. He lumbered around the house in his heavy work boots shifting his excess fifty pounds of weight as he walked. He watched us like a hawk, as though we would steal from him or eat too much food that we bought against our wages. He and Peggy peered suspiciously at us and acted as though we'd taken up too much space in their kitchen when we sat down to eat. We never once had dinner with Curly and Peggy, not one single time. We always sat down as a family for meals after my mother and Kim Chi finished their workdays and cooked simple dinners for all of us. Minh Châu and I washed and put away the dishes, while the Brooks slinked around, sulking, keeping their hawk eyes on us.

Unlike Curly, Mr. Thomas was eager to teach us English, American English, and its nonverbal gestures. We barely understood each other but felt comfortable around him because he was relaxed and jolly. Our host wore the Wyoming rancher's uniform, with a leather pouch for his pocket knife on his belt loop, and kept a pair of well-worn work gloves on the dashboard of his truck. I wondered how he had such light skin since he was an outdoorsman, a rancher, but I didn't doubt his work ethic, because clearly his hands on the steering wheel were large, rough, callous, cut, and belonged to a hard-working man.

I tried not to stare at Mr. Thomas, or at any American I saw. I tried to be discreet as I studied their features, which were utterly and vastly different than mine. The patrons at the Rookies lodge always did their double takes or stared at us, although with innocence, it soon became annoying and uncomfortable to endure. From this experience, I learned what not to do, and how not to become an annoyance for others.

Although Mrs. Thomas and her daughters were gracious and friendly to us, the crowd at the auction made me slightly uneasy. People stared at us from the minute we hopped out of the truck. I felt as though the crowd parted as we walked through, but they stood transfixed in their path. I tried to imagine what my sister and I looked like to them. We both wore pigtails, long pants, and long-sleeved shirts to fend off the mosquitoes. None of our clothing matched. I wore plaid pants, a lightweight jacket of a mismatched pattern and color, all items donated to us by the Salvation Army. Kim Chi also wore mismatched clothes. I concluded that it wasn't our clothes that warranted their stares, it was our ethnicity, our Asian appearance, and physiques. We were the only Asians they'd seen outside of the television screen, and ironically, we felt the same way about them.

I wanted to disappear, or to be a chameleon in this grandstand, and not be treated as a spectacle. But soon the auction started, and people grew so engrossed in their livestock viewing and bidding that they finally left us alone. The gate opened to let out a herd of calves, and the auctioneer started singing his fascinating bidding voice. His amplified announcements echoed around the arena, drowning the crowd's indistinguishable din. I finally reclined and observed the people around us. Some had mouthfuls of hot dogs dripping of ketchup and yellow dyed mustard, others had popcorn, and still others had pink, fluffy cotton candies.

Mrs. Thomas extracted us from the auction before it adjourned. We said goodbye to her husband and followed our new acquaintances to their station wagon. Lisa, the girl most near my age, stood significantly taller than me, and must have weighed at least twenty pounds heavier. I was five foot two and barely reached ninety-two pounds. Lisa looked well-proportioned and had a healthy glow to her slightly tanned and freckled skin. Her blonde hair draped slightly over her broad shoulders. She too had the junior rancher uniform on; cotton Wrangler western shirt, and bootcut blue jeans. Her belt buckle was an oversized oval of polished silver engraved design.

Lisa's sister and mother were bigger boned and dressed similarly to her. They chirped joyously the whole drive home, most of which we didn't understand. The open, two-lane road widened up our view in the valley where their ranch sprawled on our left, the white wooden horse fence esthetically and functionally defining its boundary.

They had a welcoming home, just like they were as people, and the buttery baking aroma comforted me when we walked in. The kitchen was bright and homey with a colander full of inviting dark red cherries.

"We'll have a roast for supper," Lisa's mother said. "That's what I usually cook on Sundays. I hope you girls will like it, Kim and Gigi." That's what Curly and Peggy called us because they couldn't pronounce our names correctly. We ate a handful of cherries each and followed Lisa outside to see some of their new calves, with their light color lashes and soft patches of fur. She filled a large bottle of milk that looked like a large baby bottle and let us feed the calves. Lisa also brought a camera and took a picture of Kim Chi and me feeding the animals. We were delighted that Lisa wrote on the picture and gave it to us as a souvenir. She asked us to fill in our names because she wasn't sure how to write them correctly. She wrote on the back of the picture, "These are our Bum Calves Chi and Kim are feeding. We enjoyed them and hoped they could come again to our house. Lisa and Joslyn Thomas." Lisa explained that "Bum Calves" were what they called calves whose mothers died, which was why they needed bottle-feeding.

Lisa and her older sister, Joslyn, took us on a John Deere golf cart ride around their ranch to show us their cattle and horses. I was flattered when Lisa asked if I wanted to drive the rig but happily declined the generous offer. I was content with being a passenger taking in the view. We came back to their house to a nice glass of cold lemonade, and Lisa showed me her room with her large collections of dolls and Breyer horses.

Kim Chi spent time with Mrs. Thomas while I was with Lisa. Soon Mr. Thomas came home to have supper with us. They were a lovely family who cared about other people who did not look like them and spoke a different language than their own. They didn't treat us like we were inferior to them. They didn't want to exploit us. They only wanted to extend their friendship and show us a fun time and slice of western America. I never saw the Thomases again after that day, but we left their house with a warm and fuzzy feeling and a renewal of faith in humanity.

CHAPTER 17

Bethel Lutheran Church & Congregation

On August 28th, twenty days after arriving at our sponsor's lodge, we thanked the heavens above and boarded the plane out of Wyoming. A van came to pick us up that morning. Our parents said good-bye and thank-you to the Brooks, and sorry that it hadn't worked out for us. We kept our distance from Curly and Peggy and waved good-bye.

We felt no love lost when we left the Brooks and their lodge. We made sure not to celebrate our good fortune prematurely until we could successfully leave their god-forsaken, miserable, money-losing so-called resort. How could we be sure that our next sponsors would be better than the Brooks? We wanted to make sure that we weren't getting out of a pot and into the frying pan, and anxiously waited and prayed that there would be a better home for us in California, a destination for our new promising life.

On the descent, we looked from the plane's windows to see if Fresno was going to be another desolate town like Pinedale. We prayed that it wouldn't be. The suspense was the hardest for us because we had one more connection in San Francisco with a two-hour layover. Again, we followed my father, marching like ducklings between terminals, and found the correct departure terminal with no time to spare, as they closed the gate right behind us.

On the way to our gate, a Hare Krishna man in loose-fitting clothing with very long flowing hair offered my brothers a small paper flower with a tiny slip of paper and a message on it. My brothers took it, and the man immediately jingled and thrust a can with some change at my brothers. Thọ and Thông looked into the can and called out to my father. He briefly looked back with slight annoyance and waved the man off. "Keep walking!" he commanded, and marched on. We later figured out that this peace-loving man wanted donations for his cause.

We were very restless on the plane. I drank more than my share of 7-Up and looked for the first sight of land. My father told us our new sponsor was in a very fertile agricultural valley. From thousands of feet above the Central Valley I only saw patches of land, not cities, and started to worry. We all did, but tried to stay calm and upbeat.

At last, we landed. The pastor and several members of his congregation greeted us warmly with their held up sign "The Trươngs," as soon as we entered the terminal gate. The pastor looked dignified, like the image I had in my mind of a preacher. He wore the black suit with the "pastor" collar and black tie, the uniform I was used to from my days of Catholic school, even though they were of different denominations. Older women and men, dressed in their Sunday's best, shook my father's hand and nodded lightly at my demure mother.

"Hello, Mr. and Mrs. Trương. Welcome to Fresno." The pastor said in his sincere but proper East Coast voice, adding that he was glad we'd made it safely. The rest of the people took turns shaking hands and nodding at my parents and seemed jubilant to see us. They didn't look or sound disingenuous. They looked like God-fearing individuals who had never tried to bend the rules, whose lives were spent helping other people, like us.

My father, in turn, introduced his seven tired but excited children, oldest to youngest. I felt warm energy radiating from this group of people. They vowed to help us and give us another chance at a good life in America. I thought of Mr. Thomas as I looked at our new Pastor Johnson and felt secure that this was our hope for a new life.

They said our house wasn't ready for us yet, since the sponsorship happened more quickly than expected. Mrs. Lambretch, a member of the congregation, would let us stay at her house in Coarsegold, a small foothill town outside of Fresno. She would live with her daughter, Karen, while our house was getting set up. I'd never experienced this kind of generosity from strangers and was astounded. We all were so surprised to see her rambling and luxurious home tucked in the oak studded lot. We savored our freedom and the vastness of our host's home, quite a welcome change from the Rookies lodge. Mrs. Lambretch worked as a butcher at a Coarsegold grocery store and volunteered to take us shopping there during the week. With a beautiful and genuine smile, she checked in on us every few days to make sure we were getting along alright.

We received the good news of our move-in date that weekend, in less than two days. We wasted no time in splitting up the chores of cleaning Mrs. Lambretch's house. We scrubbed the floors, vacuumed the carpets, dusted the furniture, and cleaned the bathrooms and kitchen. We longed to settle down in our own place, a place we could finally call home since our departure from Đà Nẵng five months ago.

On September 4th, it was love at first sight as we saw our first home in America on North Park Street. It was a lovely, white stucco Craftsman bungalow with a porch, and an old-fashioned driveway, one with two long cement paths leading to the carriage-style garage in back. The pastor and another church member drove us in two separate cars, and we chatted happily as Pastor Johnson pointed at the house.

"Here we go. Let's go inside, shall we?" His proper, well punctuated and projected voice sounded like he was giving a sermon. Judging from the look on everyone's face, we were all ecstatic. My family was happy for obvious reasons, but the pastor and the church member seemed overjoyed, seeing that we were tearful with happiness. We thanked them profusely, showing our appreciation and sincere excitement for their hard work. We would be very comfortable here!

We walked up several steps onto the modestly sized, gray, wooden-floored porch with two large windows in symmetry with the front door. The white Venetian blinds for the front windows were tightly shut to keep the house cool and the sun out, but the inside was fresh and bright with filtered light as we delightedly entered. The living room and adjoining dining room had green shag carpet. They furnished the house with an older mid-century chrome and shiny vinyl dining set, dark green upholstered couches with wood frames, and matching colored drapes covering the three windows. The house looked spotless, right down to the sparkling leaded glass-paned hutch against one wall.

My parents' room was to the right of the living room, with a white matelassé covered queen size bed and an adjoining green-tiled, shotgun bathroom with another door on the opposite side of a large dressing room. This room was Kim Chi's bedroom where a twin bed wedged against a maze of painted plumbing. She had a closet in her room and a swamp cooler unit that fit in the window, one of two in the house; the other one was in my parents' bedroom.

The four younger girls, myself included, shared the last bedroom that tightly housed four twin beds, although it was a bright and cheerful room with white ruffle curtains. We had access to the bathroom through Kim Chi's bedroom. Our room opened up to the kitchen with its scallop-edged cabinets and gas range. The whole house was fully furnished, with large appliances, down to the tiniest details like the salt and pepper shakers in the kitchen. It looked as though someone had just recently cleaned the house then handed us the keys.

Thọ and Thông, again, didn't have a proper bedroom and slept on a pullout sofa bed in the kitchen's dining area. It was now neatly made up with blankets and linens, but folded away with two crispy fresh pillows stacked on top of the sofa cushions when we arrived. Again, they didn't mind and said they might just sleep in the granny's unit with a private bathroom when it wasn't too cold or hot. They did eventually try in earnest, but gave up because it didn't have heat or air conditioning. We used it as a spare half bathroom and it came in very handy for getting ready for school in the mornings.

Pastor Johnson pointed out that we had telephone service and gave us the phone list of the church members along with the big thick Yellow Pages phone book. He apologized for the lack of a dishwasher and a dryer, but my father waved his hand dismissively to reiterate how grateful we already were for everything. Both men smiled in agreement, and the pastor continued to say that garbage pickup was on Tuesdays and church was on Sundays. Church? I hadn't thought about that, although in retrospect it seemed like a natural course of events. We would come and respectfully pay a visit and express our utmost gratitude. I looked forward to meeting our givers, and yet, I felt nervous. I didn't do well meeting and speaking a few words of pleasantry to one American, let alone the whole congregation.

The pastor and his congregation left us alone for the first time in America, in our home, and we knew we should be happy, but a new sense of insecurity set in quickly. What if we didn't adapt well? I didn't want to disappoint these Samaritans after all their hard work, devotion and sincere Christian generosity. What if someone came to the door or called on the telephone, what then? I had always been a "what-if" kind of person, constantly thinking of all the potential scenarios that might happen.

My father couldn't afford to be the theorist that I was. He had to enroll his children in school, study for the California driver's license, look for work, apply for medical assistance and find an OB-GYN for my mother, along with other tasks on his agenda that weren't obvious to us. He spent a lot of time on the phone, for the most part, trying to learn where everything was with a map of Fresno in hand. The church secretary helped him find schools, the DMV, and the doctor's office.

I mostly stayed out of my father's way and watched him only when I didn't have anything else to do. He was still the figure I feared, and I didn't know how to behave having him around twenty-four hours a day. My mother was happy to have her kitchen to prepare meals for us, and she improvised excellently in the kitchen. In 1975, the Vietnamese were the newest wave of immigrants in America. We had nowhere to shop for our ethnic grocery items. My mother bought spaghetti noodles to make Phở or Bún Bò Huế, which took an enormous amount of imagination to pretend that it was somewhat like the authentic rice noodles we used back home, but we were so grateful to freely sprawl about and eat our mother's cooking in our own home. My mom lovingly made these so-called Vietnamese dishes for us, with the wrong ingredients, and we devoured them nonetheless like they were the most authentic food ever.

I was thirteen that fall and would have attended ninth grade in Vietnam. Instead, I lined up to join a sixth-grade class at Lowell Elementary School, on whose decision it remained unknown to me. My knees barely fit under the desk, and every time I moved to prevent cramps, it would rise with me. My legs went numb by lunchtime, as I hobbled out of my chair to line up for the cafeteria.

I barely drank the waxy smelling milk from a carton, but gladly ate the Sloppy Joe on my metal cafeteria tray. Most of these kids were

Minh Châu's age, where she well ought to be. I had been in advanced algebra and geometry in March that year, and yet now I was adding fractions. I was bored and discouraged to have snot-nosed children as classmates, and endured their silly grade school ways. It tested my now short supply of patience. My father explained that I needed to be here to improve my language skills before advancing to the Junior High School. "Be patient," he said. After my repeated complaints, my dad agreed to enroll me in seventh grade at Tehipite Junior High, where I was still grossly placed under my grade level, but I was satisfied with steps in the right direction.

With the rationale that Thọ and Thông were more advanced in English than me, they enrolled in Fresno High School, right at their proper grade levels. Kim Chi, however, decided to defer college for the time being. She, being the oldest, volunteered to work full-time to help my parents and family. I didn't know how her decision came about, but I knew the deferral surely wasn't a happy decision for my parents or Kim Chi. My parents valued education first and foremost, but family loyalty and devotion were ingrained in all of us who followed the teachings of Confucianism.

CHAPTER 18

Tehipite Junior High School

There was nothing that could have prepared me for my first day at an American junior high school. The modern and blocky buildings with large smoked glass windows stared down through the intense sun onto the concrete sidewalks where shade was in short supply. Dwarfish newly planted trees eked out small puddles of shade almost like dabbles of dark paint on the lawn. Early September's heat created shimmering mirages on rows of tennis courts and smoldering steamy curtains off the rooftops.

Tehipite Jr. High's student body surprised me the most. I was too old at Lowell Elementary School, and yet I seemed to be too young to fit in here. Many girls, who were supposedly my same age, were wearing skin-tight and low-cut tops, only suitable for nightclubs on the undesirable sort of women back home, revealing their full-figured bodies at thirteen or fourteen. Their faces were made up, caked on with foundation and two distinct smudges of cheek's rouge, their eyebrows were shaved, and then penciled in with dark colors. Their lips were also penned in with colored liners, and then covered with very dark brown, almost black lipstick. It was more like the color of old dried-up blood. Their hair was big, full, and black in the "feathered-back Farrah Fawcett" style, plastered with hairspray.

These girls hung around in packs and wore blue denim jeans as tight as their shirts, which seemed to be very uncomfortable and restricted movement. The jeans looked like they would take hours to put on and take off. To be fair to the student body, not everyone dressed provocatively like these girls, but they made such a big impression on me that it gave me a wrong view of the school. The boys wore big wavy hair, "feathered" on the top and sides and slicked back. They wore white tank tops with low-slung, baggy, black or khaki pants. Many of them wore a chain that looped from their belt loops to their front pockets. These boys had a rather streetwise and intimidating appearance to me. They looked older than high school age, and nobody seemed to carry books around campus.

Weeks later, I discovered that these kids belonged to the Mexican-American gang, "The F-14ers," which reigned in South Fresno, a predominantly poor neighborhood marked by drugs and gangs. The minority of the student body was made up of "white" Americans whose families lived in the area until they could afford to move north of town, as was the economic migration trend in Fresno. That was the first clue that we lived on the "wrong" side of the city. Otherwise, our elderly neighbors to our right, albeit aloof to us, were quiet and tidy, just like the others in the neighborhood. They must have bought their homes decades ago when this was a nice neighborhood and couldn't afford to move as the area declined. I figured that our moving in must have had the older residents mumbling "There goes the neighborhood with the foreigners," which might explain their silence and coolness to us.

The second clue I got that we lived in the wrong neighborhood came the first Friday night after we moved in. North Park, the street we lived on, dead-ended into a major thoroughfare called Belmont Boulevard, a long, straight stretch of four-lane street, metered by traffic lights, designed to encourage thirty-three miles-an-hour driving if you wanted to continuously hit all green lights, something all drivers in Fresno eventually figured out. When the city planners created the grids of roads north of downtown, they didn't factor in the youth cruising scene going east to west. Belmont became a beautiful drag strip for high school and college age groups to cruise on Friday nights. Later, someone explained to me that this was the cruising and "pick-up" scene in Fresno. On weekends, cruisers would pull over and park on the side streets or empty fields, such as one next to our house, where they could sit and watch the crowd, drink concealed beers, make-out or hang out there.

On these weekend nights, we could hear people honking and yelling from their cars while their music was blasting from their radios. Occasionally, the sound of bottles smashed against something hard like the wall on the other side of the street. Cars revved their engines in place, and when they did move, they moved at a crawl. People got out of their cars freely and ran up to other vehicles. It was one big chaotic party amongst people who didn't know each other, from what I could gather.

My parents didn't let us watch from the front porch, so we peeked through our side bedroom windows. Soon we lost interest in the chaos and found it annoying and disruptive to our otherwise peaceful Friday night. We distracted ourselves by watching television with the sound turned up, and went to bed trying to block out noise from the street with cotton balls in our ears. It was warm, and we wanted to open the windows, but resorted to turning on the swamp coolers instead to drown out the cruising mob scene. This new American phenomenon went on until early morning, and daylight found the street filled with litter and broken glass from the drunken activities of the night before.

I used to walk to school about two miles each way until the church congregation donated two bikes to our family, one larger bike for my two brothers to share riding to school (one riding on the crossbar!) and a blue Schwinn banana seat bike for me. I distinctly remember the miles I peddled to school on that small boy's bike. One morning I was running late and locked my bike to the fence, and when I returned at the end of the day, the bike was gone. I walked the length of the chain link fence a few times, praying that I must have forgotten where I parked it and looked again and again for that blue bike. I wanted to be sure I hadn't missed it somehow, but it was not there. I wanted to blink to wake up from a nightmare, but I couldn't. My throat tightened up with grief and anger, my head throbbed in the afternoon sun, and my eyes teared up, admitting to the conclusion that someone had stolen my bike. I was back to walking the four-mile round trip each day. Who would have taken it?

I went to the office and talked to the secretary. "I lost my bike. I think someone stole it." After some discussion with the rest of the office staff, she called and reported it to the police and to my parents. I waited for over half an hour for the police to show up and answered their questions as they filed the report. They said they would call if they recovered it, but I somehow knew I would never see it again.

During my first semester, even with my language deficiency, I managed to make a friend, Martha, a girl in my history and P.E. classes. She wore a reasonable amount of makeup and somewhat normal clothes. She was moderately respectful to the teachers, unlike the mobs who vomited their comments and questions then laughed like a pack of vicious hyenas. They paid no attention in class, splayed their legs under their desks, and slumped sloppily in their seats. Most kids didn't listen to the teachers or take notes from lectures. Most didn't even bring a pencil or notebook. What was even more astonishing to me was that the teachers did nothing about the students' unacceptable behavior. The worst punishment was sending the juvenile delinquents to the principal, someone who could do something about it, like sending them home or letting them sit it out until the next period.

Martha and I had lunch with her friend, Terri, who was slightly smaller than me and had long black hair. She also wore makeup and wore slightly tight black jeans. I was entitled to free school lunches and sat in the cafeteria eating with my two new friends. The food wasn't too bad. I liked it because it was a hot meal, cooked that day by a large kitchen staff in a full-blown industrial kitchen. I thought lunchtime was too long since I didn't have much to talk about, or know exactly how to say anything if I did. I'd noticed that their version of English had a Mexican pronunciation and inflections, and they liked saying "ay" at the end of their sentences. Overall, they were much nicer to me than other Mexican kids who would glare at me with intimidation.

P.E. was hard for me to get used to, and, by far, was my least favorite class every day. I didn't mind running around the field with bigger kids than me in ugly gym uniforms of blue polyester shorts and red jerseys. I didn't mind being in class with disgusting boys who spat and strutted in the field in their equally ugly gym shorts with no shirts. I could even endure the coaches who favored the jocks and cheerleaders. What I despised the most about P.E. was having to shower en-masse, with no curtains, and dress in front of my peers. The water was either too cold or too hot, shooting at us sharply out of the pinhole shower nozzles. And the women coaches paced back and forth on the elevated ramp, watching us like hawks to make sure everyone got wet and soaped up. They whistled shrilly like prison wardens when it was time for us to leave the showers and queue up for towels. The coarse and dried yellow towels smelled like powdered milk, not too objectionable, but they scraped the skin to the degree of finer grade sandpaper.

Adding to my distaste for P.E., I had body insecurities since most of the girls were more developed than me. They wore bras, and I didn't. I escaped embarrassment on the days I was on my period and didn't have to shower. At least this wasn't my first shocking initiation to public showers, since I'd already learned about it in Camp Pendleton, but now with classmates, I felt an added layer of insecurity.

My course work that year included electives of wood shop and homemaking, math, history, P.E., English as Second Language (ESL), and mainstream English. In ESL, I discovered I wasn't the only Vietnamese in Fresno or at Tehipite. A young Vietnamese boy was also in this class, and we shared Mrs. Valdez, whose language specialty was Spanish, not Vietnamese. Since she was the only language resource the school had, they assigned her to us. We sat at our partitioned desks, listening to words on headphones and practiced pronouncing them. We listened to stories as we followed along the written text in the book, and then took comprehension tests at the end. We kept a log of new English vocabulary with their definitions in Vietnamese from these stories, and, unannounced, our teacher quizzed us every week.

At the end of the school year, Mrs. Valdez invited the boy, Phụng, and me to her home for board games and lunch. She was an attentive teacher who cared for us above and beyond what a teacher was responsible for providing. My new favorite teacher was in her forties, a woman who had a flair for acquiring beautiful things for her home, included her two Siamese cats. I think Phụng and I were her mission that year, and I hoped that I lived up to her expectations of progress and assimilation.

I learned more than words, grammar, and pronunciation from Mrs. Valdez. I asked her when I had questions about how things worked in the classrooms; why kids behaved so poorly yet weren't reprimanded; why girls wore tight, revealing clothes; and why boys strutted the way they did. I asked her why the girls teased me with my name, and passed my wallet around in Homemaking class then got mad when I reported them to the teacher, Mrs. Rice. But I was too embarrassed to tell Mrs. Valdez that I lied to the girls who threatened to beat me up after school when they circled me in the hallway. For self-preservation, I blurted out, "I know Karate!" Miraculously it worked, and the girls never threaten nor bother me again after that.

I learned from my Homemaking incident that American kids frowned upon tattle telling, and I decided not to tell Mrs. Valdez about what happened. She was mostly helpful although didn't always have all the answers; I was happy that she was there for me every day. She had a pageboy haircut and wore proper attire for a teacher, sweater-set and straight skirt and low-heel shoes. Her small mouth was lightly applied with lipstick and it rounded slowly with each word she pronounced for me to copy and repeat. Mrs. Valdez described that the tip of her tongue was placed at the back of her top front teeth when she uttered the word "the," which I had trouble enunciating correctly.

On Mondays, we usually spent a few minutes talking about what we had done over the weekend. She genuinely wanted to know how things were for me as she assessed the progress of my language skills. I knew when she was pleased, and when she was displeased, by the slight nuances of her gestures and by her non-verbal communications. I liked and respected her so much that I wanted to do well in class, to please her and thank her for what she did for me, even though I was sure she did that for all of her students.

My math class was in a lab setting. The classroom opened up to help sections where students reported as needed for individual one-on-one assistance. I was in algebra, not yet caught up at the math level where I'd left off in Vietnam, but this was an improvement from doing sixth-grade math at Lowell Elementary School. Phụng, the other Vietnamese student, showed up in my math class. He was younger than me by a few years, short, chubby, sloppy and clownish. I was embarrassed that he was the only other Vietnamese student in the school, and wasn't a good example of excellent Vietnamese students, so I stayed away from him. I knew it was harsh, but I felt that being his language buddy would impede my acculturation progress, and I needed to be free to explore and learn.

I met Randy in math class. He seemed to be one of the only few decent students who respected the teachers and didn't slouch in his seat. When Phụng introduced us, I understood only a bit of what he said and only when he spoke slowly. Sometimes I'd ask people to write down what they'd said, in hopes that I would understand the written words better than the quickly spoken words.

Randy was the first American boy I'd met since coming to America. He had blond curls, blue eyes, and lightly freckled skin. He lumbered clumsily like John Travolta in the *Welcome Back Kotter* TV show, but was not quite as tall. He wore a striped polo shirt, Levi's jeans, and sneakers. He wanted to talk, but my English was rather limited, so all I could do was smile, and I smiled very often.

After we had moved to California, one of the first things my father did was study for and get a driver's license, then he looked for a used station wagon to lessen our dependence on our sponsors for transportation. My father bought a used car with the help of the church's co-signed loan. He now took the kids to school in the mornings, and we walked home, rain or shine. I didn't mind the heat as much as I did the rain, especially when it was unexpected. I'd steeled myself to hardship since leaving Đà Nẵng, but buckled while walking home drenched in the chilly winter rain. I was alone, cold, wet, tired, hungry, and felt profoundly homesick and lost in a newly adopted country.

Every time I felt sad, defeated, and discouraged in learning how to live and thrive in America, I immediately reminded myself that we were free and alive, and rebuilding our lives from a humble beginning. I told myself to toughen up and smile. After all, it was just the rain, but my being unsheltered and vulnerable represented a bigger picture of the insecurities and uncertainties of our lives ahead.

I was a teenager who narrowly escaped death, and was the luckiest girl on earth to be alive. So what if I just skipped adolescence and moved right into early adulthood?

I felt immature and selfish to feel sorry for myself. I heard a rumor that when the Việt Cộng seized Huế, they stormed the General's house, my father's superior, to capture him and his family. If we had not managed to escape, that would have been our fate as well. I knew my older siblings suffered worse losses than I did, leaving all their friends in the prime of their high school and college years. Every time I felt discouraged on my daily work to become a U.S. citizen, I reminded myself that I owed it to my parents who sacrificed so much and worked hard jobs so we could get our education and economic opportunity in our new country. I also reminded myself that I owed David and his wife Tuyết, who had risked their career and life to bring us to America, and that I must continue forward with one courageous step in front of another.

Our First Months in Fresno

The church had given us a new start and the least we could do was go to church and thank them, and that we did the first Sunday after settling in at our new house on North Park Avenue. My Sunday best was less than best. It was the same green and yellow dress I wore the day we left Đà Nẵng. It was now out of fashion, a little too short and out of season now that it was autumn. Minh Châu wore her matching dress. Mỹ Châu and Hồng Châu also had matching dresses. We were called to line up in front of the Church as the pastor introduced each of us. It was the first time I had heard our family name grossly butchered, and in turn, we each had our names mispronounced to the point of no recognition, so Pastor Johnson took the liberty of nicknaming all of us so everyone could pronounce our names. He called me Chee-Chee! How did this happen? Losing everything wasn't bad enough. Now I had to lose my name too?

My sister Kim Chi became Kimmy, Thọ became Joe, Thông to Tom, Minh Châu was mispronounced and they didn't have a nickname for her yet, Mỹ Châu was Mimi, and Hồng Châu was also a mysterious sounding name without a substitute. My family name sounded very dignified in Vietnamese and now became something like "throng." I thought of Mrs. Valdez and how, if she could teach me how to say the word "the" the correct way, she could probably teach them to enunciate our names correctly.

Every Sunday after that we attended church for several hours. My father spared us from Sunday school. We only had to be polite and quiet in our pews, then smile at the adults and other children afterward. My dad seemed to listen very intently to the sermons, and we tried extremely hard to be respectful and quiet even though it was exceedingly difficult for us to endure two hours of something of which we had no comprehension. It was the least we could do to show our respect and gratitude to our sponsors.

My mother's pregnant belly started to show slightly, and my parents finally told us she was expecting. None of us were surprised. Maybe my siblings had also overheard my mother, or had speculated, or maybe we were all just used to having a new sibling every few years. We just wondered what it would be like to have an American citizen for a baby sibling.

Besides taking us to school, and mom to the doctor and grocery shopping, my father looked for work. When nothing availed, the congregation offered him a job as the church custodian, and he accepted. Kim Chi took a job at an industrial laundromat, the kind specializing in commercial accounts like restaurants and hospitals. Her job was to sort and fold, and to do other miscellaneous tasks. It was hot and hard physical labor, but she felt lucky to have it, and for the time being, happy to lessen the burden for my father and the church. They had been so kind to us; we had almost forgotten about the unscrupulous sponsors Curly and Peggy.

My sister was proud to give all her pay to my father. In our culture, children are forever indebted to their parents, and we could never do enough to show our gratitude. We could not act in any way as ingrates and must always do what is deemed best for the family.

We loved our new home and everything in it. The congregation stocked it well, and everything was clean and in good working conditions. On the weekends, my father used the old push mower to cut the grass in front and back. It took him maybe half an hour at most, and that included the edging with the old hand edger.

My father was always busy with projects. He didn't like to have idle time. Before he was employed, he brought out the giant Fresno phone book and started looking up last names. He looked for common Vietnamese names to see if, in fact, anyone we had known had moved here before us. He systematically went from the A's to the Z's under residential listings and finally found a family named Trần. He phoned them up.

"Aloh, Mr. Trần? This is Mr. Trương." My father spoke so loudly that everyone could hear him in the kitchen. He was hard of hearing from years of heavy artillery and now not only could he not hear very well on the phone, but he also couldn't hear himself talk. He would pause a great deal as he spoke, with a habitual hesitation of "ahs" between words that made a conversation with him very suspenseful.

My father cupped his free ear to focus on his hearing of the other end and returned his account of how he got here and when. It sounded like the two men had connected and exchanged their horror stories of the exodus from Vietnam. The Trần had lived in Sài Gòn and didn't have as long a journey as we'd had, but their journey was no less harrowing than ours. They'd been here almost seven months before Mr. Trần had found a job working on the assembly line at American Safety where they made car seat belts. He had been a captain in the South Vietnamese Air Force before 1975, and had a wife and five children, one of whom was my brother Thọ's age, and Hằng, who was my age but went to a junior high school on the far side of town.

"My family and I would be delighted to have dinner with yours. Let me get some directions from you. Yes, this Saturday would be very nice."

My father scribbled down the directions and asked Mr. Trần to wait while he grabbed the map. They confirmed where their house was, and my dad highlighted and red marked the route when he got off the phone. He was as thorough about the directions to the Trần's as he was a battle's location. He couldn't help being methodical and orderly. It was the only way he knew.

That Saturday we went to our new friends' house in the morning, with a plate of assorted fruit and a tin of Jasmine tea bought at Cost Plus. Their sponsor rented a lovely house for them on the east side of town where Hằng went to Hamilton Junior High. She took me to her room right away, which she shared with her younger sister. It was a cute room with dolls lined up on one bed and pin-ups of teen heart-throbs over the other.

"Your parents don't mind? About the pictures of those guys?" I blurted out, unchecked.

"Sorry, we've just met." I realized my recent blunder.

Hằng waved a dismissive hand and showed me her stack of Tiger-beats, the teenage idol magazines. "Oh, that's nothing. Look at these," she insisted.

"Wow," was all I could say. The magazines didn't do anything for me, and I thought of how quickly Hằng was Americanized. I didn't watch TV and didn't know any of these people who were the flavor of the month.

"Want some gum?" Hằng offered courteously with her hand spread out. The green Wrigley spearmint gum sticks smelled sweet as they protruded from their sleeve. I thanked her and took one to unwrap, the scent an overwhelming memory of being back home. Gum was such a coveted item, because it was the epitome of Americans, of white toothed, American GIs smiling as they gave pieces to the pestering kids who trailed them. I was lucky to have my father hand them to me when he came home to visit, and I coveted them no less than those pesky kids in the streets.

Thái, my brothers' new friend, worked nights and weekends at a Chinese restaurant named Tangs, a fifteen-minute drive northwest from us. My brothers applied for dishwashing jobs there, and were hired on the recommendations of Thái. Three nights each week, my brothers rode their one bike to work and back, one peddled and the other sat side-saddle style on the cross bar. They precariously carried take-out cartons of delicious food every night after work, and when their paychecks came, they handed them over to my father. Each Saturday, my brothers mowed the lawn for an elderly couple from the church. Sometimes Joe and his wife gave them lunch and lemonade and drove them home with their bike in the trunk, but most of the time they would ride their bike home.

A month had passed, and we still felt intimidated by the outside world. When the phone rang, we looked at each other and said, "You answer it," to each other. We could construct a sentence or two, but our comprehension of light-speed English was an entirely different matter. In the meantime, the phone continued to ring and we all gawked at it in immobile silence until my father picked it up or it stopped ringing altogether.

If we were in the living room when our doorbell rang, we'd freeze for a moment, then run to the back of the house, because nobody wanted to answer the door. Whoever was on the other side surely would have heard the thundering of our running steps, wondering what on earth was going on inside, but honestly, we were still afraid of the American adults. They were so tall and broad-shouldered, and what would we do when they spoke to us? When my father wasn't around, the oldest one of us had to step up and take a message or a contact phone number from the visitors. At this stage, communication was the most difficult thing for us and continued to be for quite some time.

My First Letter to a Boy

I started to write my diary in an old, red, cashier book that Peggy Brooks had given me, one she wasn't using anymore. In the beginning I wrote about our departure from Đà Nẵng and how I felt, but that only lasted for a few pages. I wanted to write about my daily events, like the sewing machine the church ladies brought over for us that week. I wrote in my journal about getting a letter from Dzũng from Omaha, Nebraska. His older brothers and mine had been corresponding, and he took a chance of writing me, wanting to know why I'd acted coldly towards him in the camp and if he could keep writing me.

It was a pleasant surprise to receive a letter from Dzũng. I hadn't thought of him since we'd left San Diego. I couldn't afford to reminisce about old times in my new life in Fresno. I had my assimilation work cut out for myself. When I sat down to write Dzũng, I realized I was rather upset with him for cavorting around the camp with a lot of girls my age. I was jealous that it wasn't me, even though I didn't have permission to be his friend anyway. My brothers repeatedly told me I couldn't have anything to do with boys.

Writing a letter to Dzũng proved to be easier than talking to him. I wasn't tongue-tied or embarrassed by the deafening silence in between dialogues. Still, it took several tries before I was satisfied with my letter. I wanted to sound proper, yet friendly, not too anxious, or with too much zeal.

Fresno, October 5th, 1975

Dear Dzũng,

> I'm pleased to hear from you. What is Omaha like, and how
> do you like living there? How did you end up in Nebraska? I
> hope you heard from your father.
> It's been an eventful first few months for us in the U.S. We
> lived in Wyoming for less than two months and had to
> change sponsors, but we're OK now with a church congre-
> gation sponsoring us. I'm in seventh grade. I know, I should
> be a freshman this year, but things didn't quite work out that
> way. I hate my junior high. Do you like your school?
> I'm sorry that I snubbed you in the camp. My family didn't
> want me to talk to boys. I wish we could have been friendlier.
> Do write and tell me how you are doing.

Your friend,
Hoàng Chi

This letter was my first one written to a boy. I sealed the envelope
with trepidation. Would my parents be upset if they knew I'd written
Dzũng? I didn't try to hide the fact that I was writing to him, but I
didn't ask for permission either. I used one of my father's postage
stamps and dropped the letter in our neighborhood mailbox. I went
home with great excitement that I would be getting a letter back from
him soon.

When I returned, Kim Chi said she would take me to the fabric
store, and I jumped for joy. She had a lot of sewing experience and
made alterations with Salvation Army clothes, turning them into a
bag or vest. Sometimes, she took up the hemline, or cinched the
waistband of a pair of jeans. That weekend we walked to the nearby
Beverly's Fabric Store and bought different selections of cotton to
make pants and dresses for our younger sisters. The coordinating

flower prints and solid brick color for our youngest sisters' dresses and blouses, and a yard and a half of white fabric for my pants.

During the school days, when I wore my new sewn clothes, I thought of Kim Chi working at the laundromat, handling the hospital white towels and sheets to help our family with living expenses. I thought of my father cleaning the church and its grounds; of my mother trying to cook with unfamiliar ingredients, making do with what she had; of her being homebound without any friends; and of my siblings treading for dear life at school. Everyone worked hard at assimilation, but we didn't talk about the life change in our family. We just soldiered on every day.

I struggled to understand the teenagers at school. I tried to sort out their hostility, angst, hormones, racial, and individual identity. I didn't know how I fit into this chaotic and fractious puzzle, or how to develop new friendships. Their behaviors mystified me. I didn't understand why girls my age wore makeup and shiny lipgloss, why boys looked so grown up with their slicked back hair and gold chains above their white tank tops. The glossy-lips girls coupled with the slicked-back hair boys in the hallways between classes and at lunch-times, arms hugging waists, making out whenever they could.

I ate lunch with Martha and Terri for the rest of the school year because I didn't want to sit alone. I wanted to fit in, not stand out as the "fresh off the boat" Asian girl, as they called me. The other two American-born Chinese students, Jane and Lily, seemed to navigate their social scenes with ease. We became acquaintances from being in the same few classes, but we didn't get to know each other beyond the superficial greetings and small talk. I felt discouraged by the seeming-ly insurmountable obstacles. This academic environment didn't match what I had envisioned for myself in America. I'd expected a place that offered me more, not the raw immaturity of this place called school.

I thought about my father now taking his lunch of a fried egg sandwich and a slice of pound cake, sipping Lipton tea from the thermos under the shade of the elm tree at the church. Soon he'd return to shine the social hall with the rotating waxing machine. He'd arrange rows of folding chairs for an event that weekend, and put out two long tables for the buffet. He'd clean the bathrooms, stock up the toilet paper, and shine the mirrors. He'd polish the pews with lemony Pledge until they squeaked when the parishioners sat down on Sunday. I imagined that his new job was more carefree and uncomplicated. He didn't have to strategize or struggle with the consequences of his battlefield decisions. The cleaning business was cut and dry, black and white, and it didn't keep him awake at night.

Instead, what kept him up was his recurring war nightmares. He woke up screaming or saying incoherent things. I heard frighteningly primal sounds that I'd never heard before. I didn't know my father did all these things in his sleep. I didn't know a million things about him, some of which I didn't want to know, like what he'd done with prisoners and what swift decisions he'd had to make on the battlefields. I didn't want to judge his actions. After all, I wasn't qualified to judge.

After work, my father sat at the dining room table to do his bookkeeping. He kept his paperwork and stationery in the vintage, lead-pane hutch. For him, everything had its place. The little stapler sat next to the box of Bank of America checkbooks. Its top lid held pens and paperclips, rubber bands, and a roll of stamps, a habit I got from him; I still use my checkbook boxes to keep the same contents today. A couple of dictionaries leaned against the wall of the hutch and the thick Yellow Pages phone book next to them.

My parents went to bed like clockwork at ten and woke up at six every morning. My mother made Folgers coffee for my father. He had two eggs with Maggi steak sauce and white toast. We had cereal and sometimes eggs. We grudgingly poured milk into our Corn

Flakes and suffered lactose intolerance symptoms of severe flatulence, but the option of no milk made the cereal taste like sawdust or a soggy mess with water.

My dream of having a stay-at-home dad came true, but instead of being happy I didn't know how to behave around him. We all tiptoed around the house so we wouldn't disturb or annoy him. He remained silent and preoccupied with matters unknown to us, perhaps raising a family of seven kids in a foreign land had that effect on a person. He didn't play with the younger siblings, nor read to them, and he didn't have casual conversations with us either.

I was scared of my father. I could smell his aftershave and hair-dressing. He smoked Winston's cigarettes and flicked the gray columns of ash into the rectangular glass tray. His serious intro-spection and contemplation mystified me. I knew practically nothing about his past or his experience, besides what he had told us. I cannot pretend I knew anything about his feelings of leaving his mother, sister, brothers, and sons behind. Did he have regrets that he couldn't bring our older brothers and grandmother to America? Even then I knew that as human beings, we sometimes have regrets about what we could have done better, or said more nicely to someone while we had the chance. But I struggled to understand my survivor's guilt, so I could hardly project my feelings on anyone else, least of all my father.

Making Difficult Adjustments

We still hadn't heard anything from our three oldest brothers in Vietnam. We had completely lost touch with them. After moving out of Camp Pendleton, Liên and her two kids moved to San Francisco to live with the rest of her family. She worked at Bank of America in downtown San Francisco while raising her children in the comfort of familiarity, leaning on parents and siblings for support in the absence of her husband. She rode the Greyhound bus about once a month to

Fresno to visit us. I wondered how Liên could endure this pain of not knowing and the long separation from Thảo and not break down in front of us.

She told us about her dream of welcoming a flock of descending white cranes where her husband appeared for a visit. They talked like they used to, with ease and no mention of the war or of her leaving the country without him. He didn't say whether he was alive or dead. Liên told us she prayed to God for a sign or news of Thảo, and this dream might be that message. Whatever the pain I felt, it must be insignificant to that of Liên's and my father's. I tucked my pain aside. There were other immediate concerns to address, like how to survive my new life and how to best support my parents in their difficult times.

Seventh grade at Tehipite was an easy school year academically, but it was a difficult transition socially. I'd learned that kids got new clothes at Easter, costumes and candies at Halloween, sweetheart candies and cards on Valentine's, loads of gifts at Christmas, and kids my age "went together" and "made out" shamelessly in the hallways, some even got pregnant and dropped out of school. There were many at-risk kids in our social and economically challenged area of town.

My father wanted to take us away from the bad influences in this part of the city and looked to move the family to North Fresno, an improved school district. He searched the ads in the newspaper for a house to rent so we can attend better schools with lower dropout rates and better test scores. I didn't know how my father knew to find out about such things, but it was paramount that we went to the best public school possible.

The Trầns introduced us to another Vietnamese family they'd met at the Chinese grocery store downtown. The Lês lived in the Manchester neighborhood, a quiet area with middle-class homes and no cruising boulevards. The residents were elderly and liked to fuss over their lawns, like the rest of the residents we knew thus far. The

Lês had two older daughters Kim Chi's age. They worked at their sponsor's restaurant, the Lauck's, and asked Kim Chi to join them. Soon, my sister took a full-time job there as a prep-cook, chopping and dicing every vegetable imaginable. She sometimes got tips, and the working conditions were an improvement over the laundromat job.

We became friends with the sisters and spent our weekends at each other's houses. Their mother and ours became fast friends, so did our fathers. Loan, the younger sister, was more my age and would go to McLane High School the following year. I wanted to join her there, but my father bought a house in the Hoover School District, a better district, and insisted that I attend Hoover. For the first time since we came to America, I was extremely upset with my father. He excitedly told me, "Get dressed, and I'll take you to meet your principal at the new school. You finally get to be at the right grade, and your brother Thông will be there to watch over you."

I didn't like the prospect of not attending McLane with Loan and being best friends. I didn't want to be lonely again. My father didn't budge. We went to Hoover, and he parked the station wagon in the visitor's parking lot. The school year hadn't started, but the staff was there. The secretary said that the principal was busy, but we could see Mr. Philips, the vice principal.

He was a handsome, well-mannered man who dressed professionally in a tie and slacks. He had lightly colored hair, almost graying, and a similar nicely trimmed mustache. He extended a hand to my father and gestured for us to sit down on the wooden chairs facing his expansive desk. He said many things to my dad and me, but one thing I remembered clearly. He said I would soon forget the pain of losing my friend at McLane. He said most students would make new friends here and I'd be glad that I came to Hoover. Mr. Philips had no idea what I'd had to endure, and I loathed his insensitive and dismissive ways because he had no idea how much I'd lost.

I sat there in his office chair feeling glum. I resented his wisdom but stayed quiet, polite and obedient so that I wouldn't embarrass my father. I swallowed my anger. We left the vice principal's office that day with a stack of paperwork. My dad talked to me on the way home about how deeply he cared about his children getting the best education at an excellent school.

I didn't have much to say on the matter. I sat like a big silly-putty blob next to my father on the passenger side's vinyl seat, absolutely dreading the first day of school. I felt deflated and unmotivated. I would be lonely like I was at Tehipite because I would know no one there and had no friends.

CHAPTER 19

Home on Anna Street

We moved to our new home on Anna Street in Fresno in May 1976, at the beginning of our summer vacation, a year after entering the U.S. mainland. The Huberts, a prosperous farming family from Bethel Lutheran Church, loaned us twenty-two hundred dollars with zero interest for the ten percent down payment on our new home. It was a four bedroom, two bath, tract home in a working-class neighborhood near Ashland and Fresno streets. My father immediately went to work partitioning and insulating the long, shotgun, one-car garage into another bedroom, leaving about ten feet as garage storage. In several runs and on many weekends, he hauled the lumber, insulation materials, and sheetrock from Osh Hardware, in his station wagon.

The man at Osh suggested my father look to the Ortho book on remodeling and advised him on what tools to buy or rent. My dad spent many hours hammering and sawing, something he hadn't done in his military life. I didn't think he'd touched a nail since he became an officer, but there he was nailing sheetrock to the studs of the garage, painting the walls, running electric wires through conduits, laying linoleum floor over the concrete floor, and building our bedroom.

Finally, we moved into the finished, sheet-rocked, spackled, and brightly painted bedroom with a single square glass light fixture. Kim Chi sewed sheer yellow and white dotted curtains for the tall windows and bought yellow quilted bedspreads for the two twin beds. She also bought two framed pictures of daisies and a lamp with some money from her paycheck. I felt grateful having a selfless sister like her. If it had been up to my parents, I probably would have slept on old bed sheets and worn secondhand clothes forever. It wasn't that they didn't care, it was because they had higher priorities than cosmetic things like home decor. They had priorities like making the 30-year house payments, something completely foreign to us, but it allowed refugees like us to own a home in America.

By now, if one only looked at a photo of us, we could pass for Americans. We did an extreme makeover with new clothes and hair to blend in, and in an instant, voilà, we were the Americans next door, or at least the Asian Americans who had been here for generations. It was deceptively simple to Americanize ourselves physically. The tricky part of acculturation took a painfully long time to accomplish because we not only had to be fluent in the language and know the customs, we needed to find a comfortable place in our hearts and minds to settle in between two starkly different cultures.

I wasn't American enough at school, and I wasn't exactly all Vietnamese at home either. What was emphatically correct at school wasn't at all correct at home. It was okay to discuss things with teachers and asked questions there, but it was impolite and disrespectful to ask questions or for explanations at home. I didn't dare ask our parents why I must do something once they told me to. That was considered disrespectful and disobedient.

My mother and Kim Chi still hadn't offered me any guidance on menstruation. I used the supplies in the bathroom when I needed them. By now, after months of using Camp Pendleton's feminine products, my mother must have known that I had regular periods. Neither of them had offered to buy bras for me even though I had turned fourteen and was a sophomore in high school. I was too embarrassed to ask my mother for them and still wore camisoles until I bought some bras myself with my first paying job, which was cleaning house for a lady from church.

Mrs. Jacobsen was my savior. She first hired Kim Chi, and then me, to clean her house every Friday. She drove her luxurious white Continental to Hoover High School and parked at the corners of Barstow and First streets, where the "stoners" smoked pot freely on the lawn in front of other kids at the bus stop. Some girls wore skin-tight jeans with brass zippers that went from the front of the inseam to the back, and if they were zipped off, there would be two separate pant legs. The girls had feathered-back, 'Farrah Fawcett' hairdos, and the boys wore big, wavy hair and shirts that were unbuttoned down to the hollowed indentations of their chest bones. Many of the boys wore big "fros," hairstyles that resembled miniature tumbleweeds into which they stuck big black plastic picks. Some of them kept large, colored combs with long curvy handles in their back pockets. Their fashion statement looked uncomfortable, sticking straight out of their jeans pockets when the boys sat down in the classroom chairs.

On Fridays, Mrs. Jacobsen picked me up at three o'clock and drove me to her house on Platt Avenue, on the south side of town near Roosevelt High School, where residents maintained their beautiful old homes with pride. She was in her late fifties and always looked well groomed and dressed. Mrs. Jacobsen's signature scent was her Wrigley's spearmint gum, her oral fixation, and her Estee Lauder fragrance. She had aged gracefully, and I was sure that she was very charming and beautiful in her youth.

She suffered from a bad hip that made her gait uneven, but that wasn't the reason she hired us to help her clean house. Mrs. Jacobsen wanted to help us and befriended us "girls," as she used to call Kim Chi and me. She liked talking to us and taught us things in her subtle ways. I had a dream job for a teenager. Mrs. Jacobsen had a routine for me. In three hours I dusted all her wood furniture in the living room and dining room with a Pledge-oiled cloth, fluffed up the cushions of the sofas, made the guest room beds, cleaned the spotless bathroom, and vacuumed the floors. I also helped empty the dishwasher and mop the kitchen. Then it was time for her to take me home. She generously spared me her bedroom and bathroom and paid me two dollars an hour. The extra bonus was that my father didn't have to pick me up at school and take me to her house, which was clear across town, nor pick me up when I finished my work.

In the summer and on holidays Mrs. Jacobsen had both Kim Chi and I working together on big projects like cleaning the attics in the granny unit, or bringing out decorations for Valentine's, Easter, Halloween, or Christmas. She had ornaments for every season and holiday, and they were neatly packed away in labeled bank record boxes. As we worked alongside each other, she talked to us about her family. We were more like companions to her and gradually got to know every detail about her two grown children, Jim and Laura, and their spouses and kids. We learned of her sisters and their weekend trips to their house in Morro Bay, their coast house, as she always called it.

We knew about Jim, her oldest son, who was in Vietnam for over a year and was now in management for a construction firm. His daughter was Tara. She sometimes spent weekends at grandma's, in the guest bedroom. We learned that they were second generation Danish and had gone to Denmark a few times to visit relatives there, a lovely country, she reminisced. They brought back mementos from Copenhagen and trinkets with the white and blue flags for friends.

Mrs. Jacobsen was gregarious but genuine, sweet, lovely, kind, and never raised her voice at us. She laughed easily and must have had a charmed life judging from the gentle touch she had with people around her. I loved her dearly and regretted that I hadn't thought it important enough to tell her this.

Mrs. Jacobsen met her husband after the war, and they married young. Neither of them went to college, and they started running a Hofbrau called the Oak Leaf after he got out of the service. They'd been living in Fresno, in the same lovely craftsmanship Tudor house, ever since they'd married.

Their restaurant catered to the neighborhood folks and vicinity. They made the most mouth-watering meatloaf and mashed potatoes, roasts and steaks, French onion soup, and even egg salad sandwiches. The lounge was where they drew the neighborhood's working class for happy hours and dinners.

Mr. Jacobsen worked very hard. He woke up at five o'clock every morning to get the kitchen staff started, then sometimes came home for lunch with his wife. He'd return to work to close down the restaurant, coming home around ten or eleven at night. We were very fond of Mr. Jacobsen, but felt bad for him and his wife. He was so tired that one day he fell asleep over his soup at lunch with us. Mrs. Jacobsen wasn't embarrassed about it, so I deduced it must happen frequently. Without missing a heartbeat, she woke her husband up and led him to bed, then returned to finish her lunch with us.

Henry, as he had us call him, was a good match for his wife. He was also a gentle and sweet-natured man. Mr. Jacobsen wore a cherubic face on a large-framed body. He always seemed calm and happy with his life and family, but we couldn't be sure if he'd had an uneventful life. He'd been in WWII, so who was to say he didn't suffer a lot in his younger days. They were both Christians and went to Bethel Lutheran Church most Sundays, except when they were away visiting family or friends. Once in awhile we got to see him at the Oak Leaf Restaurant, and he served us plates of sliced roast beef and mashed potatoes. When we left, Mrs. Jacobsen told him what to bring home that night, and he grinned his most affectionate grin for his wife.

Awkward Teenage Moments

Since I didn't have an allowance, my earnings from housecleaning for the Jacobsens were mine to spend as I wished. I felt grateful for the work, as it allowed me to buy personal items and clothes with my money. I was most thankful that I didn't burden my father for spending money. On weekends my sisters and I went to the fabric store and bought patterns and fabric for clothes we couldn't afford to buy but were easy to sew, like ruffled skirts and simple vests. My homemaking elective at Tehipite, where I learned how to sew from patterns, paid off handsomely. Kim Chi and I walked everywhere and had to think carefully about what we had to carry home on our shopping trips.

My father and Kim Chi both worked full-time now on the assembly line at the American Safety company, where they had coffee and lunch breaks with Mr. and Mrs. Trần. After graduating from high school, Thọ soon joined them for a year before he started college. We paid our home mortgage with income from the three full-time jobs and Thông's part-time job at the car wash where he worked after Tang's Restaurant had closed from a kitchen fire. Instead of coming home with Chinese food at the end of his shifts, he now came back every day with wet and soggy shoes.

We met another Vietnamese Family who eventually bought a house near us, on the corner of Anna and Willis. They were a well-educated family whose parents had been teachers in Sài Gòn. They had five children ranging from college age to sixth grade. Gradually, the Vietnamese community increased to four, then five families, and soon there were many others whom we'd never met until the older Vietnamese generation formed a Vietnamese Association and brought everyone together. The teenagers and college-aged kids went on outings, formed choirs and practiced traditional dances for the annual New Year's celebration.

The Lunar calendar that year occurred in February, and we put on a show for our community. In my fibers and textiles class at Hoover, I silk screened the sheet music folders for the choir members, and we rehearsed on weekends for our performance. About a hundred people showed up at Washington High School where they graciously allowed us the use of the auditorium. The girls wore the traditional áo dài, and I wore makeup for the first time, courtesy of older girls in our choir.

I didn't perform a solo and thank goodness for that, because, somewhere along the line, I'd lost my nerve and confidence. I felt my voice cracking, my body shaking on stage, and I hoped that my loose-fitting dress didn't reveal my nervousness. I stood on the stage, peered out to the crowd and saw my parents with their friends. For the first time in my life, my parents attended an event that I participated in, and it wasn't even my best performance! I felt proud but was overwhelmed with fear of disappointing them, of not being good enough.

I scanned the crowd, looking for friends I knew who would help boost my confidence, but immediately realized they were all on stage with me. Instead, I saw Randy lumbering awkwardly into the auditorium with his Vietnamese buddy, Phụng, from Tehipite. He was the only non-Asian here and looked like a lone black sheep. I was happy to see him, and my heart thumped right out of my chest, but I hoped that he wouldn't blow my cover by saying "Hi" to me. The Vietnamese guests would not take kindly of me having a white friend, who was also a boy.

Randy once walked home from Tehipite with me, right to the front door, and my mother didn't get mad at me for this. I thought she even smiled at him. That was the only time we'd talked to each other, which wasn't significant, except to say I liked him enough to be with him for two miles. I felt uncomfortable afterward and avoided him at school. I didn't know what to do around Randy, so I just ignored him and hoped the awkwardness would go away. When we moved to our new house on Anna Street and I went to Hoover High School, I forgot all about Randy, until now.

Our performance went poorly, and I thought we sounded horrible. We could have used more practice, but we were the blind leading the blind for not having an experienced music teacher to guide us. I was so embarrassed and disappointed that I didn't want to see Randy or talk to him, even though I wished I could. Besides, there were a hundred pairs of judgmental Vietnamese eyes that would scrutinize me if I had anything to do with an American boy. I didn't want to cause a scandal by foolishly talking with him in front of that audience. I wanted to do the honorable thing by my parents, so I shunned Randy. I didn't even acknowledge him being there, or even smile and say hello. What was wrong with me? What happened to my sense of decency? How could I have ignored him? I was ashamed of myself for doing this to the poor guy who came to see me, but I quickly rationalized that he'd just come to watch the show and to have some great homemade Vietnamese food with his buddy. That was it, end of the story. It wasn't about me at all.

I had chosen to be good to my parents and bad to my friend. It felt both absurd and unfair that the traditions which dictated being faithful to my parents, which was right, also forced me to be unkind to my friend, which was wrong. Randy hadn't done anything to deserve my poor treatment, and he left shortly after the show. He didn't even hang out for the delicious food. I regretted my childish and awkward behavior because, in my mind, I wouldn't have another chance to set it right with Randy.

High School is Hard Work

Hoover High School was an affluent school district, unlike that of Tehipite. Its student body was more ethnically diversified, and no one picked on me or stole things from my purse. Maybe the bullies had a bigger population to choose their victims from on this crowded campus of over two thousand students. The senior graduating class had over seven hundred students, plus similar amounts of juniors and sophomores.

Mr. Bacome was my homeroom teacher. He briefed us on our routines, schedules, rules, and the school administrators. He taught biology and I greatly admired his disciplines of punctuality, civility, and fairness. My electives were typing, textile, and French for the first semester. P.E. was equally dreadful here, as it was at my old junior high. We had to shower and dress in the same district-wide polyester shirts and tacky, clingy shorts.

Again, P.E. was co-ed, and the coaches gave the jocks, female athletes, and cheerleaders preferential treatment, as though they got their training from the same boot camps. It seemed that only the juvenile and bullying boys got all the attention in P.E. class. Keith was one of them, and he was an ornery, loud-mouthed kid who bullied other boys in hopes that the beautiful girls would notice him. On the field the guys strutted for the girls attention. They stripped off their t-shirts and smacked each other on the rear. They head-locked each other and wrestled on the grass where another boy had spat just a minute ago.

On the other hand, French class was about civility and good manners and taught by Monsieur Proudian, one of my all-time favorite teachers. He was born in Prussia and moved to America when he was young. He spoke French beautifully, from the moment we walked through the door. He would disapprovingly tsk-tsk at us to show his displeasure when we misbehaved and said, "Alors, acutez-moi!"

Typing was just a class of practicing muscle memory skills. In the beginning we just click-clacked our way through the keys, a, s, d, f and j, k, l, semicolon. By the end of the semester, our room was deafening with keystrokes like the old office from hell. That's when I knew I didn't want to be a typist for a living, because I made so many mistakes per minute, and was always stopping and backing up with white erasing tape to correct the misspelled words.

Biology intellectually challenged me in my sophomore year. I had a lab partner named Sue. She played on the girls varsity volleyball team, and the teacher talked sports with her before class every day. Sue was a friendly person and a good partner who never missed a day of school, and we worked very well together.

I liked biology and desperately wanted an "A" in this class and used to work for extra credit whenever allowed. That was when I discovered that I thoroughly enjoyed drawing cut-away views of plants and animals. I thought I might pursue a career in medical illustration or biological science one day. I studied hard for this class and read the chapters over and over until I thought I understood the material. I looked up words I didn't know, which were many, and often went to get help from Mr. Bacome at lunchtime. I managed to get an "A" in biology, and wanted to take more science courses.

Ms. White was our reading class teacher, who didn't bother to engage us in English. She sat knitting at warp speed behind her desk as the class read silently. I'd signed up for this reading class because I thought it would improve my language skills, but it turned out to be a mistake and a waste of time. It was independent reading, and there were no lectures or tests. Our grades reflected the pages we'd read, and, since it was an honor system, we'd sign out at the end of the period with the book's title and amount read. To my horror she singled me out for reading Nancy Drew from the book bins. She said to the whole class that this was too easy for a sophomore. I peered past her black horn-rimmed glasses to see if she was serious, but there she sat, ignoring me, knitting away in her matching cardigan set and plaid skirt.

I played freely and creatively in my fibers and textile class. I don't think there were many boys in class, and I felt very comfortable with this. We wove with wool yarn on looms, batiked and tie-dyed t-shirts, socks, or fabric, made twine macramé pot hangers, and silk-screened our designs on fabric or papers. I met several seniors whom I wanted to be friends with, and we had fun chatting during class. They silk-screened the Who's record label and talked about rock concerts they went to on weekends. I brought home my woven and batiked pillow-cases and Christmas ornaments, which only I appreciated. My father, however, did like the beaded macramé pot hangers and hung his spider plants in the corners of the living room.

Mr. Phillips was right when he said I would soon forget the pain of not going to McLane High School. My friendship with Loan took an awkward turn. She was at least three years older than me, and was more of Kim Chi's peer than mine, as it turned out. Then one day they quarreled, which subsequently spilled over to me, and gradually we grew apart. By the end of my sophomore year, I saw the wisdom of my father and Mr. Phillips. McLane turned out to be another Tehipite, just larger, or so I heard.

I had more choices for friends at Hoover High School than I would have had at Tehipite. However, it seemed as though everyone knew each other, and they already had enough friends. I was still shy, and my improvement in English didn't ease the pain of making new friends. Social structures were similar to those back home; birds of feathers did flock together. For someone new and a foreigner like me, I pretty much flew solo and perched alone. Liz was my friend from

French class, but she hung out with someone else, and I ended up eating lunch with another shy sophomore named Jackie. It was an odd kind of comfort because we both were quiet and only spoke when we had something to say.

The quad was an active social scene at lunchtime. Groups of different sizes gathered on benches and picnic tables by the cafeteria, with throngs leaving campus to smoke or get Chinese food at Wah's restaurant near Foodland Supermarket. The exuberant green and white uniformed cheerleaders rehearsed their routines on the lawn. The jocks in their lettered jackets bantered light-heartedly with each other in front of their lockers and within the proximity of their cute cheerleader friends. Scheduled events to promote school spirit were led by the energetic pep girls squad or cheerleading teams, and sometimes they dressed up like clowns in mismatched clothing and socks, with the football players cross-dressing, using balloons under their football jerseys as fake breasts. Needless to say, I never understood these pep rallies or their promotions.

Jackie and I watched and offered our view of the antics before us. There were kids with whom I would like to be friends, kids who seemed decent and sincere, but I didn't know how to do this, even though they were in the same class. I didn't know that making friends required the skill and nerve to strike a conversation, to risk rejection, to ask and listen to the students around me as if to say, "I'm interested in being your friend, to learn what you are about, and this is who I am." I didn't know it was okay to make small talk, and that it was not disingenuous because this was how people got to know one another. But this took nerve and self-confidence which I didn't have at this stage.

For much of my sophomore year, I felt mostly invisible as I walked down the corridors to classes, listening to lockers click open and slam shut, and thought that this was hard work. I didn't know anything about American schools or how to make friends. I felt alone and longed to be one of them so I could know what it felt like to be a part of something and to be with friends in classes and at lunch. This realization made me determined to master the language so I could have the confidence to make friends, be gregarious and well-liked.

Our Vietnamese Identity

Our new house didn't have a laundry room, and the washer was in the kitchen where the dishwasher should have been. My mother thought that having a dishwasher was a luxury anyway, but a clothes washer, now that was something we had to have with such a large family like ours. We took turns hand-washing dishes, and my job was to sweep the kitchen floor after each meal and hang up laundry every morning before school.

My father changed jobs and now worked as a press operator at Vendo, a company that manufactured vending machines. His job description included operating the die cutting press, that weighed over a thousand pounds, safely and efficiently. These vending machines dispensed soft drinks and snacks, and my father worked as another cog in the wheel to produce hundreds of these each month for worldwide sales. He worked swing shift from four in the afternoon until two the next morning. He preferred this schedule because it paid more, and allowed him to run errands during the days.

Instead of taking us to school in the mornings, he told us to take the busses. My father woke up and listened to the BBC in Vietnamese, drinking Folger's coffee and smoking a Winston cigarette. After my morning chore, I walked about a quarter of a mile to the bus stop on Fresno Street to school, which cost twenty-five cents, and rode the same bus home, ignoring the stoners who smoked pot on the lawn in the afternoons. My friend Liz and I found out that we lived nearby each other one day when she saw me at the neighborhood bus stop. She and her generous mom offered me rides both ways for most of my sophomore year, and this was how our friendship got started.

Preparing meals was my mother's responsibility. She still didn't have the patience to teach me how to cook. I could peel potatoes and carrots and wash the dirty pots and pans, but cooking was too easy to mess up, so she kept me at arm's length. I could help her with the new baby, though. Thomas, or Tommy as we called him, was born in November of 1975 while we still lived on the cruising side of town. The church ladies gave my mother a lovely white bassinet with christening-like lace and ruffles. Tommy was adorable, lovable, and the most undemanding baby we'd ever had, so we all doted on him. If I ever felt invisible at school or unloved at home when my mother was mad at me, Tommy's innocence and his baby-sweetness would make me feel whole and needed again. We'd stack blocks on the floor, then knock them over and he shrieked and cackled with delight and bewilderment. Again and again we repeated this construction and destruction until he grew tired and wanted to play outside on the rocking horse. He was nearly a year old and barely able to sit up on the saddle, so I held his tiny body, my hands under his armpits to steady him, while he bounced on the plastic horse.

When my mother cooked or rested, I could play or feed Tommy, and sometimes I sat rocking him to sleep in the brown naugahyde Lazy-Boy. The blessing of having many siblings was that none of us got stuck doing everything, and the girls shared chores amongst ourselves. It mystified me that my brothers didn't do these general cleaning tasks or take out the garbage so my parents wouldn't have to do them. They didn't do their laundry either. My dad always cleaned the bathrooms and complained that we girls should pick up our long hair in the showers so they wouldn't clog the drains.

Another Vietnamese family moved to our neighborhood across Fresno Street. Châu was more or less my age, and we hung out together that summer of my sophomore year. She would be a new student in the fall at Hoover, and I was pleased about that. Her family lived in an apartment that had a pool, and we spent a lot of time there with our new friend Châu. I can't be sure, but I think it was that summer when my sister adopted an English name, Julie, instead of her name Minh Châu. I could understand her decision to do so. I, too, grew tired of being asked, "How do you say your name again?"

I occasionally thought about taking on an English name, but couldn't come up with an eloquent equivalent to my given Vietnamese birth name. For years I dreaded meeting someone with the same name as mine, and for years, I savored the fact that one of the prettiest and rarest names in the city of Đà Nẵng, or maybe even in the whole country, was Hoàng Chi. In the end, I shortened my name to only Chi, to minimize the name butchering ordeal, yet still retain my Vietnamese name.

No Girls Tennis Team

Summers were inhumanely hot in Fresno, with temperatures sometimes soaring to one hundred and twelve degrees Fahrenheit, and, usually, there were long spells of hot days in the hundred-degree range. Polluted air from miles around drained and settled into the valley basin, trapped there for days, creating an inversion layer where I couldn't see the Sierra Nevada snow-capped mountain range anymore. With some luck, the wind or rain would clear the sky so that we could breathe easily again without the smoggy air.

Our house had wall panel heaters, but no air conditioning, and so my father went to K-mart to buy a couple of oscillating floor and table fans. We minimized outdoor activities during the days and played outside in the backyard after the sun went down. We threw a blanket on a circle of a lawn, fifteen feet in diameter, which the previous owner had used for their doughboy pool. We lay on our backs, watching the sky slowly darken to unveil the bright stars. We were used to hot weather from back home, but this was stifling from the excessive street asphalt surfaces. I missed taking afternoon naps on the cool tile floor back home with my body pressed close to its earthen coolness.

My parents let us watch television freely, especially in the summers, and I watched too much of it. My siblings fought for their favorite shows, and we had to decide who got to see what. There were *The Six-Million-Dollar Man, The Bionic Woman, Charlie's Angels, The Love Boat*, and of course the NFL football games. Thông loved to watch football, and he monopolized the TV, and that's how my mother started to watch and learn the rules of the game from him. She even declared that her favorite team was the Dallas Cowboys. We never ate in front of the TV, but he did when he watched the NFL games. After one season of football, my mom began to look forward to Monday Night Football just as much as Thông did, and they would confer during the games and were equally disgusted if their team lost.

Sometimes it would get so quiet at night after Tommy went to bed that my mother would fall asleep watching TV. My brothers were out working as waiters at The Old Spaghetti Factory restaurant, and Kim Chi would lock herself in her room to sew. The only ones left were Julie and me, and we woke my mother to go to bed before turning in as well. With so many of us in a family, I didn't think we would know silence, but there were times it was so quiet I didn't know what to think. Maybe I did like the predictable chaos of our family. It made me feel safe, loved, and not lonely. Someone once said that out of chaos came order, and I did believe in the organic process that shaped my young adult life.

Our new neighborhood was quiet, a nice mixture of young and old families, and we were one of two non-white families on the block. We could walk to Gong's grocery store for emergency gallons of milk or bread, but on a weekly basis my parents shopped at Gemco on Shields and First Streets on Saturday mornings. The whole family would pile in our dad's beige Plymouth station wagon, going along for the shopping experience. We marveled over the automatic front sliding doors and the luxurious cold air shrouding us upon entry.

Compared to Gemco, the Mayfair grocery store down on Belmont Avenue on the South side of town looked tiny. Gemco was a super department store that had everything we could need or want. My mother disappeared to the food section, some of us banded together for the clothes department, and my father beelined to the electronics and appliances corners. We liked the orderliness and cleanliness of its merchandising, and the abundance of goods tempted our impulses like those musical ice-cream trucks on our neighborhood streets.

My father had strict schedules and was disciplined. He was methodical about most things he did, like shopping for food on Saturdays, having ramen with thinly sliced sautéed beef and cilantro for lunch when they got home, and after nap times he and Tommy got their haircuts at the barbershop on McKinley Avenue. He had the freedom to have a routine without risking his safety like he did back home. My dad didn't have to worry about a sudden ambush on his way to the post office once a month to buy stamps. All he had to worry about was dodging the mail trucks when he crossed the parking lot.

Ernie Pyle Elementary School was one street behind Gong's Supermarket and a mere ten-minute walk from our house. My mother walked my two little sisters to school and picked them up every day, while my father stayed with Tommy in the mornings and afternoons before he went to work. My younger sisters were at their appropriate grade levels of first and second grades and thrived beyond our expectations.

By now our church attendance had dropped to just a one-person representative. Every Sunday my father dressed in his nice long-sleeved white shirt and gray slacks and drove down to Bethel

Lutheran Church to listen to Pastor Johnson's sermon, then stayed a bit for the social hour. He read the Bible and tried to follow the teachings of Judaic-Christianity, but didn't insist that we do the same. Now and then, usually to express his displeasure with our inaction to help with household chores, he'd hold family meetings and explain the mechanics of a family's inner-workings:

- Respect the elders
- Do your part to help
- Do your best in school
- Be honest
- Have discipline
- Choose your friends wisely
- Be clean and keep your rooms tidy and orderly
- Don't harass your siblings

He'd address the major points, then get down to the nitty-gritty. He'd say that we didn't come to America for merely economic reasons, that was only a part of it. He wanted to be in America for a safe and brighter future for his children and their descendants, a place where we could pursue higher education and be positive, contributing citizens. Sure, we could make a lot more money here in America, but what he truly wanted was for us to be well-educated individuals who could think broadly, find personal fulfillment, and be a positive influence in society.

He wanted us to think independently and be leaders, not followers. He read mountains of books and newspapers, listened to various news sources, and encouraged us to do the same. He wrote to the Fresno Bee's editorial page regularly to voice his opinions, and continued to do so until they published an edited version of his letter.

We all thought he could be somewhat difficult to persuade, but then one day Tommy changed my father's life forever. He learned the harmful effects of smoking in first grade via the anti-smoking campaign at school, and one day, when he sat at the kitchen table during lunch, he pinched his nose while my father smoked his after-meal cigarette. My dad understood Tommy's meaning but asked him why he did so, and Tommy's answer didn't surprise him, "smoking kills." My father quit smoking then and there, forever, "cold turkey" as they say in America. My dad kept his promise and saved a tidy sum weekly, but sadly, he gained considerable weight in the months that followed.

My parents communicated almost as well as our siblings did. There were periods of bickering, sulking, silent treatment, battling, and of happiness and contentment. They were not accustomed to having each other around all the time. At times my father could be impatient and hot-tempered, leading my mother to assume her martyrdom stance and her passive-aggression. We steered away when they argued in their dramatic and theatrical ways. I didn't want to take sides with either of them because I didn't think a child should have to participate in adults' affairs, deciding who was right or wrong. That was their job. I just wanted them to love each other and make us feel secure, or we simply wouldn't make it.

My mother seemed to adjust as well as one could expect. She didn't speak any English and didn't drive. She stayed home with Tommy and cooked for all of us, and looked forward to her adult English classes on Tuesday and Thursday nights at Roosevelt high school, clear across town. She enjoyed the learning environment with fellow foreigners her age, trying to learn to read, write, and speak American English.

My father had his frequent melancholy episodes and still suffered terrible nightmares. He continued to grind his teeth severely, to the point that I expected he'd have nothing left between his gums in the morning. He had so much anger and resentment that if he wrote how he felt, it would be more than the contents of the Library of Congress. He lived two different lives, one of power and prestige in delicate balance with life and death in Vietnam, and the other in humbling modesty coupled with freedom and safety for his children in America. We all said that we were happy and grateful to be here, because it was the right way to be, but did that make it wrong to admit that we were impatient or unhappy with the steep learning curve of assimilation?

As for me, I must confess I got tired of the continuous butchering of my name and strangers' insistence that I was Chinese, not Vietnamese. Perhaps I should have dressed my part as a refugee, in tattered and torn clothes, with a big fat print of "I survived JFK and LBJ's Red Scare" in the front and an "F.O.B." on the back of my shirt.

Roll calls would be less painful if the teachers would ask me how to pronounce my name instead of making it up as they went and creatively altered my name to Hog Na Chai, or Wang Kai, or Hone Kee. But most of all I grew tired of not belonging, of not knowing how to integrate my ethnicity to the new society much of my waking hours. I wished there was a recipe or a playbook that I could follow with the right ingredients to yield a happy and well-adjusted teenager caught between two cultures. Instead, I toggled to the default mode of day-to-day improvisation in my new environment and made small corrections as I went. Sometimes my spastic responses fit beautifully, like that missing piece to a jigsaw puzzle. Other times it felt like a face plant on the cacti in the Sonoran desert.

Every single member of my family experienced a different kind of growing pain, a different acculturation process, and we did so privately, without even thinking to stop and consult with the others. I wanted to be a chameleon that could deftly adapt myself to my new environment without having to regroup the inner workings of my brain, heart, and soul. My mother said I couldn't join the tennis team because it would mean I'd stay after school for practice. She had issues with supervision and trust with the school. I was surprised. I thought it would be a non-issue since I was doing well in school, as well as keeping up with household chores. She said I could play tennis with my brothers and didn't have permission to sign up for the girls' tennis team, and that was the end of that.

That summer, my two brothers pooled their resources and put a down payment to buy a Ford Pinto for work, and they begrudgingly took me to play tennis, although not with them. I usually played against the wall at City College. They had met and were dating two of the Nguyễn sisters and played tennis with them while I practiced against the wall. It worked for me, for a while. They buckled at my pesky pleading and sometimes rallied with me, but I endured their exhaustive, short-tempered criticism of my backhands and serves. Their girlfriends scored copious "younger sister's points" with me by coming to my aid. They worked with me patiently, coyly applying their maternal instincts on me, which didn't go unnoticed by my brothers. It suited me fine, and I appreciated their attentiveness over my brothers' dismissive ways with me.

"Sweetie, don't you think Chi is doing so much better with her serves? Watch!" Đào cooed in her stretched-taffy voice that surely melted my brother's heart. I felt like a third wheel, standing there on the court, in their way, while waiting for a visual OK to serve. But they were in love, in courtship, and I needed to leave them alone, resuming my practice against the wall. That said, their girlfriends were generous and gave me their old tennis racquets, which started Julie and I playing at the nearby junior high school. They even loaned me their cream colored gown so I could proudly attend the Senior Prom.

My Vietnamese Friendships

Late that summer, a few weeks before school started, Dzũng and his two older brothers came to visit our family. We'd been writing each other sporadically. About every two months, one of us would write the other; then it would take another month for the other to respond. His letters became progressively emotional, uncomfortably sentimental. I stalled writing back, not knowing quite how to respond. I did like him, but it was a bit too much to hear that he loved me. We hadn't written each other for a few months, but I was thrilled to hear my brothers talk about their trek from Omaha, Nebraska to see us. I hadn't forgotten that my brothers had forbidden me to hang around boys or to have a relationship with Dzũng, but I wondered if they still remembered.

They came for three days, and then headed up to San Jose to visit other friends. I had forgotten how good it was to see Dzũng; he was a familiar face from back home, and he hadn't changed much since Camp Pendleton. I wanted so much to monopolize his time, to catch up with him, but I was under watchful eyes of not only my brothers, but also my sister, Kim Chi, and my mother. I wondered what I had ever done to make them guard me so carefully. Had I gone wrong somewhere and not known it? Were they afraid that by talking to a boy I would subsequently run off and get pregnant? Certainly, they had done everything to pique my interests with boys. The forbidden fruit was getting the best of my curiosity now.

Dzũng and I exchanged polite pleasantry and an abundance of glances. The night before he left, I was sitting in the living room reading before bedtime when he came into the room. We were unescorted, at last. He awkwardly approached me, as I was equally awkward sitting on the sofa, hands on my book, not able to read. He quietly leaned to my face and planted a gentle kiss on my cheek, but then someone walked in. Everything happened too fast for me to comprehend and absorb. Whoever came by turned the light on next to us. But Dzũng was gone by then, leaving me frozen on the sofa with my cheek still burning with excitement. They left early the next day. I guessed that it was his goodbye. The next time I heard from him was by way of a card from a gas station somewhere in Arizona. The card had a pre-printed message on the front that said, "I miss you."

The long lazy summer days drew to an end, and I felt that "butterfly-in-the-stomach back-to-school" excitement. Hours of summer television watching did empower me with some ease with English. For the first time, I understood some American jokes and could laugh at them. I didn't feel a minor cardiac arrest at the thought of having to be in gym classes. Mrs. Jacobsen's encouragement and non-judgmental companionship must have boosted my confidence.

I still only wore pants. Our driver Lai's comment from my distant past, saying that I had toothpick legs still reverberated in my ears. All my new school clothes this year came from the money I made from my cleaning job. I looked more Americanized now, and if I could carefully choose my words and pronounce them with the right inflections, with luck, no one would know that I was "fresh-off-the-boat." Americans used this word for refugees like me, even though we were not "boat people," and I hated the sound of it.

Kim Chi styled my hair from a traditional straight cut to a feathered-back, Farrah Fawcett style. I'd become overly obsessed with shoes. Never would I be caught shoeless or with only one shoe again. We went shopping for Famolare platform shoes, with the rubberized soles and designs that rippled like waves. A unicycle logo was on both the shoebox and on the thick rubber soles. I felt a twinge of guilt for spending so much money on shoes and back-to-school clothes, but justified that I had earned it and I didn't have to ask my parents to help with the purchase. My parents seemed indisposed most of the time and didn't complain about my independence when it came to clothing styles or purchases.

Julie, my neighbor friend Châu, and I experimented with plucking our eyebrows, and shaving our legs and underarms. Tears voluntarily welled up as I plucked the strayed eyebrows that dipped too far down my eyelids. My limited pain threshold stopped me from continuing further with this vanity ritual. I stood back watching the girls, squirming as they plucked.

"You guys are crazy. I would not go through that much pain for anything!" I declared adamantly, secretly wishing I could stomach the tear-jerking pain. We laughed so hard that we cried while attempting the new ritual of shaving our armpits and legs.

"Can you tell me again why we have to shave?" I implored.

"Because it's considered disgusting to have hairy legs and armpits in America." Châu continued, doubled over, then involuntarily flaring her nostrils as she gagged with raw and guttural laughter.

"True," I said. "You should have seen this guy's face in my class last year when I raised my hand in class. He turned to see who the teacher had picked and instead of looking at my face, he zeroed in at my armpit. I could have died." I agreed to the reason we had to give in to the new social etiquette.

"Hmm. This shaving armpits business is not too bad, so I don't mind doing it. But why do we have to shave our legs? I don't think I have any leg hair." I was the oldest girl and felt funny asking the younger ones for shaving wisdom, but Châu seemed eager to share her knowledge with us.

"Well, I think you should shave before your legs get too hairy and look disgusting in P.E. uniforms and dresses. Eeww, black hairy legs!" Châu elaborated.

I nicked myself with the razor while we talked. "Ouch. I'm bleeding. Agh, this is not for me. I'll just watch you guys."

Châu sweetly tore off a piece of toilet paper and folded it into an even smaller square and stuck it on my cut below my knee. I sat on the toilet with the seat down and held my face in my palms, watching the girls lathering up their legs. So, that was the secret; you lather up before you shave so you won't cut yourself and hemorrhage. I let out a sigh of relief and daydreamed about what the new school year would bring.

CHAPTER 20

Sorry I don't Understand Your Jokes

M r. Jarnegan, my junior year English teacher, arranged the seats in a large circle, consciously making the students face each other. It was the first day of school, in my first-period class, and I was too self-conscious to walk across the room. Instead, I found the closest seat to the door, about three away from the teacher's desk, and hung my homemade handbag on the chair and then sat down, too shy to look at anyone around me. I put a big binder and pencil bag on the desk and then fidgeted a little. I doodled my name on an orangey-yellow Pee-Chee folder and wrote "Composition" in all caps. I doodled some more while waiting for the teacher to start the roll call. Here we go again, I dreaded. I must put on my thick hide and steel myself from the inevitable embarrassing name butchering.

In each chair, the students' faces brimmed with renewed hope, their crisp clothes so new I could smell the starch and see the stiffness, the girls' jeans so tight that their thighs and buttocks looked like sausage casings. Some girls applied and reapplied their lip-gloss like a nervous tic, while others chewed on their number two yellow pencils. Some boys thrummed their fingers on the desks, and others jiggled their thighs. There wasn't much talking, as most kids didn't know each other, but there was the discreet glancing and browsing between the girls and boys.

A big guy sauntered in late and sat down to my right, the only empty seat left. He sprayed spittle generously as he volunteered unnecessary information to the teacher or anyone else who would listen. His name was called right before mine, in alphabetical order. Thomas, D. Thomas. He replied with a boisterous "Yo," and rocked in his desk like a trapped rat. I tried to be open-minded, but he was the kind of guy who wanted to hear himself talk, and caused quite a distraction to everyone in class.

Surprised by my eye rolling at my boorish neighbor, I recomposed and looked up, hoping no one had seen it. Everyone was in his or her pre-class daydreaming or nervousness, so my eyes relaxed and scanned my classmates for potential friends. It was then my eyes fell upon a guy directly across the room from where I sat. I did a double take, then my eyes stayed there for a long time.

He was reading Mr. Jarnegan's syllabus to the class, his eyes hidden behind the aviator-framed prescription glasses, which rested on a masculine nose. His tumbled blond curls shone as he casually brushed them back to rest one hand on his chiseled chin. He was tall, slightly thin, and broad shouldered. His long legs spilled out from under the desk and crossed casually at the ankles.

While everyone wore their new school clothes, he didn't. He had on army surplus cargo pants, blue "zories" sandals, the flip-flop kind, and a baby blue UC Davis jersey, not the first-day-of-school kind of new, with a large number in front. Apparently, he had spent his summer outdoors and had a healthy natural tan on his long, sinewy arms outstretched to cradle the back of his head as he looked up. This person exuded a quiet confidence, I thought, as if he was ready to make friends and didn't seem to care about what they might think of him.

He scanned the room just like I did, and his eyes met mine. Gulp! I looked away but not fast enough to miss his "I gotcha" broad grin. I was thoroughly embarrassed and flustered, my thieving stare discovered, but forced myself back to my previous well-behaved self for the first writing assignment.

When class ended, I consulted my schedule, and then headed for my next class quickly so as not to run into the Blue Jersey. Rounding the corner, I ran into Jackie who said she also had Mr. Haney for chemistry next period. We happily agreed to be partners and walked into class together. She'd gotten braces over the summer but otherwise looked the same. She was quick to compliment me and said that she liked my new hairstyle.

"Thanks," I said, for her boost of confidence.

We sat at our stainless-steel lab table in the classroom, which was cold as a meat freezer, and about as comfortable as a morgue. Our hands and feet were almost blue from the cold, and I was sure we looked like two apprentice morticians waiting to make over our next cadavers. We were alone in the class. Everyone else stood outside, socializing, catching up after the long summer absence.

When I saw the Blue Jersey walk in, talking to his friend with a well-coiffed "fro," I slid down in my seat. He kept talking, but gave me a slight nod with a knowing look that said, "So we meet again." I wanted to slide down in my chair a little more and hide from him. I didn't know what to say. I didn't even smile. I was socially awkward. The guys came around and sat directly behind Jackie and me.

"Hey, I'm Ron. This is my friend Chris," the guy with the "fro" said, slapping the Blue Jersey in the stomach. His friend played hurt with a slight double over while grinning that same broad grin.

"Hello, I'm Chi. This is Jackie." I said it with as much American coolness as I could muster to mask my nervousness, and then slowly turned away toward the front of the class.

Our two new friends tried again to engage us with some jokes, and Jackie laughed heartily, but since I didn't understand what was said, I felt safer not to laugh. My lack of response made Ron and Chris look like two kids who had just dropped their double scoops outside the ice cream store. I felt bad making them wilt and envied Jackie. She carried on with supreme casualness in her conversation with them, and of course, they understood each other perfectly well. There was no communication gap whatsoever between them. "I think those guys are cute and kinda funny." She leaned over to comfort me, but that didn't help much. How I envied these happy-go-lucky American kids.

When Ron introduced us, I briefly saw Chris's eyes. They were light blue and brought that spring fever feeling from within me. Oddly, I hadn't felt that sensation before. I couldn't pinpoint what that feeling was, but he stirred something wild inside me. Of course, he was "foxy," as they said then, but I thought, "No." Rather, he was ruggedly handsome, like the Brawny paper towel man kind of hand-some, or the warm and fuzzy Pendleton wool shirt kind of good looking. I could tell he was gentle just by looking at the soft corners of his smiling mouth. He seemed desperately charming in a calm yet rebellious way, sporting a hippie kind of exuberance that screamed Dr. Bronner's mantra, "For we're All-One or None! All-One!" He was different than the other guys. He wore the counterculture kind of clothes, not the mass-produced flared jeans and shiny polyester shirts. It seemed so unlikely, but for just one moment, I thought I was part of the hippie generation, being superfluously keen in vibes, auras, and telepathy. I thought I could feel the birth of our bond and felt a surge of its Herculean strength. "Snap out of it," I told myself. I'd just met the guy; he couldn't possibly have that kind of influence over me!

At lunch that day, I prodded and pried Jackie for information. "What did it mean Jackie? What were they joking about? I didn't laugh because it could have been a dirty joke, or a joke on me," I pleaded.

"It was nothing, really. It was just the way Chris said it that made it funny. I don't even remember what it was. It wasn't anything about you."

Unconvinced by her reply, I kept staring at her for further explanation. Give me some more compelling explanation please, my eyes said.

"Relax, Chi. Let your hair down. It was nothing!" She was as sincere as a friend could be.

Jackie didn't understand that I'd been uptight for too long, fortressing my vulnerability from the eager critics around me, needing to be perfect, being a colonel's daughter, keeping it honorable for the family, and that I couldn't let my hair down. It was good to hear a shy peer like Jackie telling me to relax, albeit in a very gentle way, with a slight shrug of the shoulder like it would hurt me too much if she wasn't more gentle. Even Jackie thought I was uptight. Did Chris think I was uptight? I wondered. He did say goodbye when we got out of chemistry, and I did manage to smile and said goodbye too. I wanted to let him know I liked him.

We both let out an unexpected chuckle when we saw each other in P.E. right after lunch period. I saw Chris lining up on the basketball court. His long arms and legs against the chain-link fence, arms overhead, hooked together and one knee up for an anchor. Even a wrinkled gray gym shirt looked lovely on him. His well-worn dark blue shorts revealed the hairy blond mat on his pole vaulting legs. "Be still my heart." I refrained from fluttering my eyelashes at this unassuming, Scandinavian looking guy. I adored his hauntingly handsome face, but that wasn't the sole wooing factor. It was the effortless way he carried himself, extremely confident and carefree, with a genuine smile and charm.

"You again," I said, this time unbelievably at ease, forgetting that I was in my not very flattering looking uniform and baring my recently shaven and nicked knee and toothpick legs.

"Smith right? I'm Trương, right behind you then." I scooted beside him against the fence, hoping no S or T last names would show up to come between us. He towered over me, and the top of my head came up to about his shoulders, at best. I would be perfectly happy if I could just stand there next to him for the rest of the period. I admired his locks of blond hair, seeming soft and silky, his eyelashes in pale blond contrast to his pools of blue. I wondered if he could feel that irresistible pull I felt toward him. Up from within me rose that hurricane again, and yet I relished this unexpected change in weather.

"Are you a freshman?" he squinted at me, "I haven't seen you before." His mouth moved to reveal teeth that were sweet enough to frame.

"No, Junior, you?" My answer just popped out. Whoa! Did that confidence come from me? I had no idea I was even capable of such nonchalant conversational skills. I had completely forgotten it was rude to stare, and I believed that was what I was doing, staring at him the whole time while we talked.

We had softball in P.E., and the coach assigned me to the left field, where I could go away and daydream about Chris.

He boldly came and sat next to me in English the next day, and the days after that. We brought brown bag lunches and ate together on the green field with no one around. Afterward, we conveniently lined up next to each other in P.E, sitting on the bench watching the others swing the bat. I felt bliss for the first time in a long time, ever since I left Vietnam. Having felt so alone and estranged in this foreign land with no one who understood my pain and anxiety, he was my much-needed breath of fresh air. In one fell swoop, he swept me off my feet with his casual and non-judgmental way.

209

Chris was gregarious, outgoing, and liked to make everyone laugh. He seemed to connect with Mr. Jarnegan on some mature level. The girls loved chatting with him for his polite friendliness, the same reason that I did. They also liked to catch up with him on Monday mornings, and I felt a twinge of jealousy, but these were his friends he'd had since elementary school. We were friends, and I had no claims on him. He could talk to whomever he liked. Likewise, I felt more confident now and tried a little at a time to reach out and experiment with new friendships. Before classes started, I turned and struck up a conversation with someone I didn't know, but I did it because somehow Chris had encouraged and empowered me by investing the time to listen to me and care about my feelings. He liked me and believed in me.

Lunchtime was now a much-treasured time, instead of the dreaded time it used to be. We bought cartons of milk and juice before heading out to the P.E. field. I looked forward to sitting on the grass and sharing sandwiches with Chris. He always brought the hefty wheat bread sandwiches with thick slabs of cheddar cheese, tomatoes, and lettuce. I was still not used to his bluest eyes. Where I came from, I told him, everyone had brown eyes and lashes. Everyone had black hair. Chris said something that surprised me, "But I like your brown eyes and your black hair." It was the first time he had wandered out of the friendship safety zone.

A Long Christmas Vacation

As usual, on Mondays, we always spent time catching up. "I worked on my brother's truck," he said. " I hung out with the guys, causing some trouble. Oh, and I went skiing with my girlfriend..." Chris's voice trailed as he enumerated his long weekend. My head spun. Girlfriend? Did he say he had a girlfriend? I guessed Chris had mentioned that earlier in the semester when I first met him, but it didn't register then like it did just now. He hadn't mentioned her since that first time, and I had forgotten he was attached. After all, we were just friends. He wasn't obligated to say anything else.

But Chris felt it necessary to disclose his romantic status. "We met my sophomore year, during the summer in the Youth Conservation Corps." He paused. "We've only seen each other a couple of times since summer."

I stayed silent, waiting and listening intently.

"I would have told you sooner. Just didn't know when was the right time. I want you to know that I broke up with her over the weekend." He looked down at his hands then back at me. "It feels horrible," he said. "I didn't want to hurt her feelings, but we didn't have much in common anymore, and it was the only honorable thing to do."

I felt like I had a new lease on life. He didn't say he wanted to go together, but I thought he might as well be saying it. I was selfishly happy that he was not attached anymore and pleased he could freely and honestly spend time with me without guilt. Jackie understood that I wanted to "hang out" with Chris at lunchtime. She looked at me with laughing eyes and devious smiles when she said, "It's okay. I'm fine." I coveted my alone time with Chris and we spent every possible second together, although we were just friends.

I wasn't looking forward to the end of that school year because the winter vacations had given me a preview of my severe separation anxiety, of time without Chris. I longed for his voice and laughter, and his presence. I missed his bluest eyes looking down at me in P.E. when we lined up at the fence. I needed to sit and look at the way he ate his cheese sandwich with lettuce and tomatoes. I spent time writing poems. Many that read alarmingly like lovesick poems. These I kept for myself and didn't share with anyone.

Every time we came back to school after a holiday, we'd talked non-stop. "I helped Mrs. Jacobsen set up for her Thanksgiving dinner one day, and came back another day to put decorations away," I told Chris. "You know she has decorations for every holiday on the Hallmark calendar, but this kept me busy." I paused. "I like her a lot, you know. She is such a thoughtful person." It sounded strange, but I continued. "I'd like you to meet her someday. Maybe the next time she picks me up to work on Fridays." I didn't know why I said it, but I wanted to share some parts of my life with him.

"Sure, she sounds pretty nice." Chris agreed. I knew he would. He was always outgoing and sociable, never exhibited angst meeting or making new friends. His friendliness magnetically pulled me in like quicksand, and I was dizzy with that springtime pleasure. My desperate and woeful withdrawal sans Chris during the holidays made me painfully aware of how attached I'd gotten to him. No more school vacations this year! I wasn't ready to go for another week without Chris again. How would I manage my summer this year?

One day, Chris had to go to his optometrist on Fresno Street after school. I volunteered to walk with him since it was on my way home, and I would do that instead of taking the bus. It had only been two months since we'd met, and we hadn't been anywhere off campus, not even at lunchtime. We walked next to each other, and this always made me realize how much taller he was than me. I wasn't sure how far down Fresno we had to walk, but I hoped it would be a long way. While we were walking on the street, side by side, it suddenly dawned on me that I felt overwhelmingly protected. That's what it felt like to have him around, protected. It was like having a big bodyguard who was also your dearest friend, for that's how I felt about him.

Our arms lightly brushed now and then as we walked, and I felt his arm's hair on me. Electrical storms. That's what was going on. My feet could carry me a long way, as long as he was there walking with me. Did friends feel these kinds of feelings about each other? Was this something people felt all the time? I needed someone whom I could consult with, so I'd know what this feeling meant. We were friends, weren't we?

I felt crushed when Christmas vacation came. We left at the end of the day, and Chris said, "Have a good holiday, Chi." I liked how he said my name.

"You too, Chris." I wanted to say, "I will miss you terribly," but I didn't. "What is it?" Chris asked. But I knew to say, "Oh, it's nothing."

I pined and wrote more poems during Christmas vacation. I wondered if Chris missed me as much as I missed him. I conjured his image in my mind, reconstructed his beautiful smiles, and how his lithe body moved across the baseball field. I felt that same bittersweet feeling I'd had when I'd first gotten my period, oddly enough. Like stepping across a new threshold, another rite of passage. I hated missing him but at the same time didn't mind wallowing in this almost uncanny feeling.

Contradiction filled me. Whatever happened to the stubborn and aggressive traits of a Tiger — determined and persevering to succeed? But there was nothing for me to do, and nothing to solve. I must wait and be patient for this holiday to end.

Our Best Christmas Yet

After saying, "Good-bye, see you next year" to Chris, I rode the bus to the fabric store and bought fabric to make my two youngest sisters pajamas for Christmas gifts. I loved them, I imagined, like they were my little babies. I wanted to dote on them and protect them. Both wore bangs and bobbed haircuts, faces bright like porcelain dolls. They wore matching clothes to school and were only one school grade apart. I felt comforted by the fact that they had each other for moral support and seemed to acclimate to their new culture rather well.

I chose five yards of cozy teddy bear print flannel, white buttons, and two yards of the elastic band. That morning I had told my mother I was going to the fabric store after school and asked if she needed anything. Yes, she would love a skein of navy blue yarn to finish Tommy's sweater, giving me the paper label to match to color and yarn type.

I reached into my purse to get the sample label and thought of my mother knitting the cabled pullover for Tommy while sitting in the brown Lazy Boy chair. I imagined Tommy drawing Mr. T or the Dukes of Hazard on a piece of lined paper. Julie was probably doing her daily primping in front of the mirror like most teenage girls did in high school. "Use the other bathroom," she would say to the younger siblings, "I'm busy right now."

Kim Chi was at work at American Safety with Thọ, and my father was at Vendo pulling a swing shift, while Thông was at the car wash for his after-school job. We each had a job to do, and no one complained. I worried about a lot of things in those days, such as the press my dad operated. It was a massive and dangerous machine, and if not managed properly could sever limbs and take a life. I worried about him falling asleep at wee hours and getting his hands cut off, because it was a monotonous, routine job. I worried about him getting in a car accident driving home on Fridays at two in the morning.

Kim Chi and Thọ had to postpone college to assemble car safety belts so we could live in a safer area and go to school in a better district. I was too young to work a full-time job, or I would have pitched in to help out with our family finances. I reminisced about the days when we had our clothes tailor made, and a seamstress showed me how to measure and cut fabric, how to stitch and back-stitch at the beginning and end of each run, how the seams needed to be pressed open on the inside for a crisp finished look. I also learned a lot of sewing techniques from Mrs. Rice at Tehipite Jr. High, who patiently helped me with sewing projects so I could now make pajamas for my little sisters.

One whole week without seeing or talking to Chris would be a long time if I didn't occupy my mind with something else. I worked on many of my hobbies to overcome this newfound distraction and challenge. I resisted writing poems because that would only sink me further into my melancholy. I planned to sew, draw, read, and play tennis with Julie. I would ask my mother if she would teach me how to cook, and would ask Kim Chi to teach me how to bake and decorate cakes. I'd go to the mall with Châu and Julie. I'd do anything but fall into the Chris-wallowing-pit.

I locked myself in my room for the whole day to sew my sisters' Christmas gifts. The newly installed short-hair carpet in my garage bedroom kept it warmer now, along with the floor heater, and I sewed late into the night. I cut the fabric and removed the pins from the modeled shirts and pants and I decided that I would continue the sewing another day as it was getting late. I needed to stretch this out a little since there was still plenty of time before Christmas day. I asked my mother, and she agreed to teach me how to do the cable knit if I bought another set of knitting needles and skein of yarn, but for the time being, I helped her roll the new skein into a ball to make it unwind smoothly for her knitting.

As it turned out, I ran out of time and worked frantically to sew buttonholes by hands, all ten of them, and sewed the buttons on. The interfacings, or lining of the collars, needed careful hand stitching and were time consuming, and I ended up sewing hemlines by machine instead of by hand as I had previously hoped to accomplish. When I inserted the elastic band and sewed the ends together, I sighed with relief and took the time to snip the loose threads and press the pairs of pajamas for better presentation. I finally wrapped the PJs. First in white tissues, and then in colored paper, and I tied ribbons on each gift. I'd bring them out on Christmas morning to watch the fun game of my sisters guessing the contents.

They wore my gifts on Christmas morning and sat playing with their new Barbie clothes design template. Watching them moving with ease with their new pajamas gave me enormous satisfaction. They fit! All of my experimentations, cutting up my mother's "spared" aprons since I had no patterns, had actually helped my sewing ability. I was satisfied that those cute aprons had served as a means to a good end.

Vendo gave their employees a turkey for Christmas and Thanksgiving. My mother experimented baking with the big bird, trying to get it to look crispy brown like the ones that we'd seen on TV and the supermarket ads. She bought all the trimmings and made those too, but most of us didn't care for the tart cranberry sauce, though I loved the creamy mashed potatoes and gravy. My mother didn't have recipes, or more truthfully, we couldn't translate all the steps in the recipes for dishes like creamed corn, green bean casserole, baked yams and stuffing, so she made everything to the best of her ability. She made everything from scratch, except for the canned cranberry and the gravy. Each Thanksgiving, her American cooking improved, but we still had our authentic Vietnamese fried rice, my mother's most fabulous egg rolls, and a green salad with Vietnamese herbs the way my father liked with big slices of tomatoes.

Like most American families across the country that day, we had our share of leftover turkey. We sprawled around our living room playing board games, and went to Fresno City College to play tennis in the afternoon. My backhand and serve had improved, but I was still no match for my brothers. I still practiced against the wall and played with Julie most of the times. It was December, and yet we still drank iced tea and water on the tennis court. The sun was out after days of oppressive, constant overcast. We sat there fanning ourselves, feeling content, and agreed that our family had a successful year in America.

CHAPTER 21

Learning the Ropes

We had a lot to be thankful for that year. Thảo reunited with his family and started their new life together in their apartment on Ashbury Street in San Francisco, not too far from their family's flat at Haight and Ashbury. Our anticipation and excitement reached a crescendo. Everyone sobbed, our bodies shook, and tears flowed like a river when we finally saw Thảo, after two years of separation. The last communication we'd had with him was via my father at Cam Ranh Naval Base on March 30, 1975. Early the next morning, on March 31st, the North Vietnamese People's Army Vietnam (PAVN) had rolled in and gained complete control of the Phù Cát Air Base by that afternoon. Although my brother tried to escape, he was captured as a Prisoner of War, suffering their punishment and "re-education" for the next two years.

I thought he looked like he'd aged a hundred years, though he still had that charming Elvis-crooked smile lurking beneath the depth of pain. We stayed up all night, listening to the stories of his life after the fall of 1975. It was worse than I could have ever imagined, the kinds of torture he had to endure and the many changes that took place once the Communists rolled in and raised their flags.

In preparation for receiving her husband from a refugee camp in Mandaluyong, Philippines, where he stayed after his successful escape on a fishing boat from Vietnam, Liên quit her white collar job at Bank of America and worked as a cook for the Missionary French Priests, whose office was near her apartment. In her traditional way of thinking, she didn't want her husband to feel inferior or ashamed by being unemployed while she was out working at a white collar, professional job. She didn't want to have the economically dominant role while her husband depended on her as he got his bearings in his new country.

We were overjoyed that Christmas, because, before Thảo reunited with them in America, Liên had to manage on her own and rode the Greyhound bus with her two kids to visit us in Fresno, after attending Mass with her family. She visited us regularly, about once a month, riding the bus roundtrip from San Francisco. We always looked forward to seeing her because we missed her and the kids, and she always brought precious Vietnamese food ingredients that we couldn't buy in Fresno's Chinatown.

That year, on my sixteenth birthday, Thảo thoughtfully sent a lovely birthday letter in his perfect handwriting, wishing me a sweet sixteenth birthday. My brothers' girlfriends and Kim Chi thought it would be fun to give me a birthday party. It was mostly a family party with a few friends. I wished Chris could come to my sixteenth birthday party, but no one in my family knew about him. I hadn't told anyone. I hadn't thought of how my parents would feel about my fraternizing with an American boy. I knew very well that my father worried about his children "losing their roots", losing our Vietnamese culture. Having an American friend for whom I had such intense feelings would not be welcome news to my parents, as it would mean that I took steps on becoming less Vietnamese, and more Americanized, thus losing my cultural identity and history.

Kim Chi baked and decorated a nine-inch, two-layer cake for me that had plenty of pink roses and pastel green leaves draping off the side. My mother made Pâté Chaud with meat fillings, and also made her famous egg rolls. After lunch, my parents retired to the living room leaving the kids to their fun.

My friends brought Hallmark gifts of a letter holder and opener that had cute little Beatrix Potter mice dressed in lovely ruffle dresses and stuffed animals. I felt incredibly special. I'd never had a birthday party, nor this much attention lavished solely on me before. When I blew out the candles, I secretly wished that I would be with Chris forever.

"So, you are a Pisces," Jackie declared when I told her about my birthday celebration.

"What is a Pisces?" I asked absentmindedly, as I balanced the equations in chemistry. My mind was elsewhere. I waited for Chris to show up, but the bell rang, and he was still not here. He didn't show up for English class either. This semester we signed up for poetry together, and Mr. Jarnegan read a poem of Phil Levine's that Chris would have liked. I'd eagerly waited for him that morning so we could do our typical Monday morning catching up and to tell him about my unexpected birthday party treats.

"You don't know what a Pisces is?" Jackie said it so loudly that Mr. Haney threw her an inquisitive look above his bifocals. "Are you serious?" She whispered this time, staring at me with those doe-like eyes. "It's one of the twelve astrological signs. You were born in late February, and that makes you a Pisces."

I shrugged, trying to sound American. "So? What's the big deal?"

"Well, don't you ever read the horoscope?" Jackie persisted.

"You mean to see what the future brings?" I inquired to keep Jackie on a roll.

"Yeah, I'm a Scorpio. We are compatible. You get it?"

Oh, what a revelation. I didn't need a horoscope to know that Jackie and I got along pretty well. But now I wondered about Chris's horoscope sign and mine. What would the future bring for us? I didn't need to read the horoscope to know that we were compatible and that we liked each other a lot, but I wanted desperately to know if we could stay together without my parents' blessings.

Ron mumbled something about "Where the heck is Chris?", his deadbeat lab partner, not showing up to do his share. They were "tight" as Ron said, good buddies, and he joked almost as much as Chris did. He said he really dug Chris, and that he was a cool dude. Ron said impetuously, "Hey, Chi. Are you guys going together?" That made Jackie snap her head my direction like a soldier at attention.

"Yeah, so are you and Chris …?" she repeated with a stare.

"What are you guys? The going-together police?" I blurted. I hadn't thought of our relationship that way. We did spend every available minute together, almost attached at the hip, but no, we were not "going together" as they said.

"But really, no. We're just friends."

"Aw, dang it! You'd make a cute couple." Ron said, his disappointment showing, as was Jackie's. They were ready for juicy gossip. "Well, you two should," he said. "I thought you guys were already going out by how much Chris talks about you."

"Nope," I said as though it was a non-issue, but the truth was, it had been the issue ever since I'd met him that fall. I just didn't know what to do about it, or if there was anything to be done.

I was ecstatic to see Chris in P.E. that day. He was late lining up, springing his long legs into his place at the fence after coach Hannah had already started the roll call.

"Smitty! You're late. Don't let it happen again." He yodeled in his deep operatic voice.

Chris had the look of someone who hurried not to miss class. He had beads of sweat on his forehead before P.E. even started. We had archery that semester, and coach Hannah lectured everyone on safety measures, choosing the right bows, wearing the armguards and finger guards.

"Ok, troops. Go get your gear and line up behind each target." It was the first chance we could talk, as we collected our bows and gear.

"Where were you this morning?" I asked, realizing I sounded a bit demanding.

"I had to go to the dentist, but then my mom's Suburban wouldn't start, so I had to mess with it until it did." He put on his arm guard and looked squarely at me. "I'm sorry...if you were worried." He sounded like he was explaining it to his mom.

"No, I was wondering, that's all. Just wanted to catch up." I lied, but not very well. I thought he could see right through me.

Chris was skillful with the bow. When I complimented him, he said that he and his brother came over to practice archery on weekends sometimes, using the school's hay bales. He pointed to the fence in the distance, "See that dovecote over there? That's my house on the other side of the wall. I usually hop over it and walk to school." He joked so much that I thought it was another effort of his to make me laugh. That's what I adored about him. He was always making me laugh, and I couldn't have done that if I hadn't felt comfortable enough to lighten up. You couldn't laugh if you were uptight, it wouldn't come out right.

"You're teasing me right?"

"Oh nooo, I really live there. On Saturdays, the marching band is my alarm clock, right at eight o'clock, I get to wake up to the Hoover Patriot's fight song."

I laughed, snorting involuntarily. I hadn't meant for him to hear me this way. Oh, dear God, that was so embarrassing, but he didn't let up. He fed my hysteria by marching around with his bow like the

221

Patriots with their bayonets. I punched him on his arm and said to stop it before coach Hannah sent us both running around the track for punishment.

Chris was my partner in archery and helped me with aiming and corrected my postures for improved accuracy. I enjoyed how closely he stood by me, hunching over my sighting, his bouncy hair brushing my cheek, making it burn hotter than the intense sun. I felt his breath on my neck and ear, sending shockwaves through my poor feeble soul. I found P.E. pleasurable because I had an attractive and helpful partner. I could stay there like that forever.

"Can I call you sometime?" Chris asked out of the blue one day in poetry. Mr. Jarnegan was reading the lyrics to "Stairway to Heaven" to the class, followed by "Eleanor Rigby". I would love it if he called me, but I wondered what my mother would say. I knew my mom's napping patterns, usually in the afternoons when I got home from school, and she went to bed early after putting my little brother Tommy to sleep. That was when it would be safe for Chris to call.

Intuitively, I knew my parents would be displeased that I had an almost-boyfriend. For them, it would go against everything in our culture, and they would think I was too young to have an almost-boyfriend. I felt a deep sense of deception in hiding my friendship with an American boy, but I didn't want to get in trouble with my parents. All I knew was that I liked Chris, and that he made me feel good about myself. He wanted to make me laugh and feel important and loved. I enjoyed his warmth, his thoughtfulness, his carefree and jovial ways, not to mention his drop-dead good looks and charm.

I was in bed cradling the phone, whispering to Chris about my trying times with my mother and Kim Chi. The long phone cord from the nightstand twisted like a strand of taffy and lay on the floor next to my bed, like the twisted feelings I had inside talking to Chris this late at night. I knew for sure that wanting to spend all my time chatting with him would be problematic for my parents. These secretive phone calls were not okay with my parents. What to do? I didn't want to upset my parents, yet I couldn't stand being without Chris either. I'd come to enjoy his company to the point of hopeless dependency. There was a word for this phenomenon. I thought it might be love, but that sounded so grown up and overwrought with sentiment.

The minute I admitted that my new entanglement was 'love' was the moment I felt relieved. It was a discovery, but not a shocking one. It was difficult for me to admit and submit to falling headfirst without questioning why, when or how. I just acknowledged that I was head over heels in love with him, from the moment I first saw him in his blue jersey in Composition. He had innocently and inadvertently cast a love spell on me. It was his grin that sealed the deal for me, and now I had hopelessly fallen off that cliff of no return.

I had never been in a quandary of not knowing the right course of action to take. The decision of leaving Vietnam was made for me and was black and white. It was not a moral decision of right and wrong, of faithfulness or betrayal, of truth or deceit, or of choosing whom to please. I'd always been a loyal and obedient child, and I had given up what my heart desired to please my parents, to honor them, do the right things by them, and to keep them happy.

But this was where the gray areas came into play. I didn't see the demarcation of good and evil. Was there just one right answer? Was there even a correct and incorrect answer? Was there anyone I could confer with who understood my predicament, my need to please all concerned? I needed someone who mastered both cultures to guide me in the right direction.

I needed to be with Chris. I needed my parents' acceptance and approval of my being with Chris, while still loving me for my choice, for my judgment. I loved them both and I didn't want to choose.

I couldn't speak for Chris, only for myself. I felt that we both remained friendly, trying hard not to overstep our boundaries. I could have quickly told Chris how fond I was of him. Something about talking on the phone at night in the dark made it very conducive to baring my soul and rawest feelings. But I resisted and stayed proper.

Insecurity still occupied a large corner of my heart and mind, although I felt that Chris shared the deepest sentiments between us, I still wondered if he felt the same fondness for me. I wondered if he loved me the way I loved him. Until I could hear him utter the words, I remained unsure and a little frightened at the prospect of confessing my love for him. Chris was very well-liked and especially popular with the girls. They admired him and called him "Foxy," making me wonder if maybe he was nice to everyone and not just me.

I was in heaven in the poetry class. There was no place more romantic to be in love with a new-found beau than being in a class where we discussed poetry for the entire period. Mr. Jarnegan's voice rose and fell melodically on each line of *Romeo and Juliet* that made me feel like Shakespeare had written the tragedy just for us. Love was joyful for me, but I knew stormy weather loomed in the near distance. The electrical storm of my lifetime was building and gathering voltage, ready to ground its powerful strike. All I needed to do was devise a lightning rod to bear the jolt. I hadn't the faintest idea what to do. Should I proceed with my love confession and let it run its course?

The content of our late-night phone calls was no longer light and comfortable, no longer about Jarnegan, Haney, and Hannah, or school. It was now about us. About how we missed each other when we weren't with each other. Did this mean that we were going together? We never said that we were, but it felt like it, we had not even been out on a date. It was springtime. The sky was blue and clear with a slight breeze. It was a perfect time of year in Fresno, and a perfect time to be in love. Chris and I continued to have lunch on the lawn next to the baseball diamond. We continued to admire each other in poetry, chemistry and P.E., although more openly now. After school, Chris stayed with me at the bus stop and waved goodbye when the bus spewed its black smoke and pulled away.

Chris's hair shone so brightly in the springtime sun. He sat on the grass with his long legs drawn up next to other boys in P.E. We were listening to the coach's lectures. He wanted us to run around the track once before starting archery. He wanted us to wear our goggles and our armguards, to aim at the hay bale target, not at our adversaries on the other side of the field. I looked at the other boys and back at Chris, and my eyes stayed on him.

"I guess I'm going with Chris," I confided with Châu that weekend. "It feels like we are going together. Except that neither one of us asked if the other one wanted to go together! Isn't that strange?"

"He broke up with his girlfriend back in October," I reasoned to Châu. "Maybe he's waiting to get over that before he can ask me. What do you think about me asking Chris to Sadie Hawkins? He told me he declined an invitation to last winter's formal with someone. He didn't say whom, and I didn't ask."

"Ok, that's probably your cue to ask him since he wasn't interested in going with the other girl," she answered. "Judging from what's going on, I think he likes you too. He's all yours for the taking," she laughed heartily. "If I were you, I would ask him before someone else does. It's the girl's choice you know, so don't wait for him to ask you." She winked at me. "Wait, but what about your parents?"

Gulp. What about my parents? What would I do? Maybe it was time for me to test the water. "The fair," I thought. "The fair is coming, and Chris talked about taking me to it," I told Châu. "Maybe he could do the right thing and ask my father for permission to take me to the fair. I'm going to ask Chris today if he would be willing to do that and see what happens. What do you think?"

What a Tangled Web

Chris was willing to do anything, it seemed, to be able to take me to the fair. I knew then that he was the one for me, the one to go the distance for me. I briefed him on how polite to be when talking with my father, something he was more than capable of doing. He didn't need me to coach him. He put on his would-be Sunday's best and arrived just as we had planned. That morning, I told my father a friend of mine from school would be coming by after lunch to ask for his permission to take me to the fair. He gave me no reply, no clues by which to predict his reaction. I didn't say my friend was a boy, yet somehow I thought he knew.

I was so nervous I could barely sit still. This meeting between my father and Chris was the defining moment of my future with him. I would soon know if my dad would give us a chance. We'd been in America a little over three years and here was a boy asking if he could take his daughter to the fair. Was it too soon to assimilate in this way? Was this what my father was afraid of his children becoming?

A knock sounded on the door, and it nearly stopped my heart. My dad came to the door, opened it and walked back to let Chris in. My dad was five foot four, and Chris was six foot two. Chris extended his hand to my father and introduced himself. They shook hands, then my dad walked away. He sat on the couch with his back to Chris. Chris followed my dad like a puppy.

"Mr. Trương. May I take your daughter to the fair?" Chris mustered in his most polite and charming voice.

My father was merciless. He was forthright and concise, not wasting words. "No. I don't think so."

"I'll have Chi back by..." Chris continued his futile attempt to persuade my father.

"We are such different people. It would never work!" Those were my dad's final words about the subject, and he walked away, leaving Chris standing there at a loss for words.

My mother and siblings were watching from the sideline. My mom stayed quiet in agreement with my father. She gave me the silent treatment and acted as though I wasn't there. My two younger sisters sat on the sofa with eyes wide open, feeling the tension but not knowing the magnitude of the situation. I walked past Chris and eyed him to go outside, and felt my mother's eyes on me as I opened the front door for Chris. He turned and said goodbye to my mom, and then joined me on the front porch.

My father had just asked me to choose, something I was afraid would happen. I felt so sad to see how choked up Chris was standing there in my parents' living room. How could my father have been so heartless? Hadn't he seen how hard Chris tried to be respectful and polite, and that he was trying to do the right thing? I tried to comfort Chris but didn't know what to say or do. All I could say was that I was sorry for what my father had done.

Chris was not his jovial self, but he wasn't visibly upset. He was the one to comfort me instead because I ended up crying. His hands were warm, wiping hot tears spilling down my cheeks. "Everything will be okay. You'll see. Alright?" He lifted my chin up to look at him. "I'll see you at school tomorrow. Okay?" I struggled to say something without choking and watched him get into his mother's yellow Suburban and drive away.

My father was upset with me and told me not to talk with Chris anymore, that my pursuit was wrong. He and my mother gave me the silent treatment after that, making me feel more alone than ever before in my family. I couldn't see what could be so wrong in spending time with Chris. My father didn't even give him a chance, didn't even bother to get to know Chris.

At lunchtime the next day, I didn't hold back and asked him before I lost my nerve. "Chris, would you go to the Sadie Hawkins Dance with me...in April?"

"What? We can't do that! Your dad just told me yesterday to take a hike." Chris wasn't mad, just surprised that I just proposed something against my father's wishes, and then he realized the meaning of my question. "Wait a minute. I just realized that you just asked me out. Well, sort of. You're asking me to go to the dance with you?" He grinned that charming grin.

"Sure, what the heck. I'd love to," Chris beamed. "Does this mean we have to dress in matching outfits?" Not waiting for the answer, he whooped and laughed. "You're on. Sounds like a blast."

I felt like giving Chris a warm bear hug, but punched his arm affectionately instead. Now we needed to come up with something that both Chris and I could comfortably wear.

"Oh, Chi. I forgot to tell you something. Your brother stopped by my locker this morning before poetry and asked me to leave you alone, not to talk to you anymore, or he'd do something about it. He didn't say what, but I got his message loud and clear."

I was furious, but not shocked. My parents must have told him to do this, telling a boy to leave his sister alone. First, my father told Chris to take a long hike on a short pier, and then my brother threatened Chris with bodily harm if he didn't stop seeing me. They didn't know this only made me more determined to see Chris. They had forgotten that I was a Tiger, a stubborn and strong-willed person who wouldn't let anyone get between her and her goals. I was also that Pisces, who was passionate when it came to deep emotions and I could stay more stubborn than most people realized.

At that moment, I suddenly became aware of who I was. I was a TigerFish, a Vietnamese Tiger, and an American Pisces, all rolled into one, for better or worse. That's what I was, a TigerFish, and I was determined to stay with the one I loved. Too many times now my brother had intervened, and this time I wasn't giving in. I didn't want to give them the satisfaction of running my emotional life for me, especially when Chris hadn't given me any reason to think he wasn't an upstanding person. All he'd ever given me was time, attention, laughter and friendship. What was so bad about that?

"I'm so sorry." That was all I could say to Chris, no longer interested in eating my fried egg sandwich. If he were upset at my brother, he masked it very well and shrugged, "I'm obviously still sitting here with you. I'm not stopping because he asked me to!" Chris paused and lowered his sandwich to his lap as he searched for my eyes.

"You mean too much to me… I couldn't let someone tell me just to leave you, not even your father or brother." Chris grimaced and continued, "I'm sorry to be disrespectful." His words wrenched my heart, and I felt an overwhelming flood of love for him. But I sat there, speechless. I was angry and sad that I couldn't persuade my father to give Chris a chance to prove himself worthy of his daughter. I was sure I was a sound judge of character, and that they had taught me what's morally right and wrong. It was time they allowed me to make my own decisions.

Tears were my strongest defense against pain. I felt a numbness of pain throughout my body. My heart ached with love for my parents and Chris. I had to find a way somehow to show my parents that Chris was a good person. He wasn't the one with ambivalence or trepidation at the idea of a cross-cultural love. I knew they worried about me going down the wrong path, getting pregnant or being "used." They thought of the stereotypical reckless American GIs in Vietnam. I knew they loved me and wanted to protect me. Nevertheless, it was painful to see them react swiftly and decisively out of love and protectiveness for me. Ironically, this drove me away from them, I felt vengeful and wanted to make them feel the pain I was feeling.

I felt bound up like a multicolor ball of rubber bands, full of confusion and guilt. I loved my parents, yet hated what they did to Chris. I understood why they wanted to protect me, but I blasted them for their rigid and prejudiced ways. I felt guilty for making my parents worry, but I wanted them to feel the suffering that I experienced. I was disappointed that my parents didn't approve of my choice of friends, but I was pleased that I had Chris' love. It used to be easy to understand what brought my parents pleasure and dis-pleasure, but now I had no surefire cross-cultural dating template to follow or use to figure out the appropriate course of action. The only way I could keep both my parents and Chris happily in my life was to deceive, not letting my parents know about my relationship with Chris. This way they couldn't know any disappointment or feel any pain. I felt shameful of my unethical and unscrupulous decision, but it was how I could best remedy the dilemma on a short-term basis.

"Does this mean that we are going together, Chris?" I wanted to inquire as calmly as I could but I felt somewhat unnerved. We'd never held hands or kissed, and yet I was so much in love with Chris and ready to deceive my parents just to be with him.

"Chris, you are such a good friend," I began awkwardly. "You mean so much to me, too." I felt anything but eloquent. This ex-change wasn't how I pictured a love confession would play out. Chris and I had said everything to each other except that we were going together. Maybe Chris didn't want to state the obvious. Maybe he didn't want to push too far, too fast, with our friendship developing so well.

"I'm sorry to, well, to drag you into my family situation when they are so mean to you. I shouldn't have asked you to meet my dad. Maybe we should have gone to the fair without my father's permission." I didn't believe that, did I? No, I wanted my parents to like Chris, to get to know him for who he was, not as the American Advisors and GIs who had wronged us in Vietnam. He wasn't what his government's foreign policies represented.

"Oh, your parents love you, Chi. You're their precious daughter, and I'm just some white boy who's gonna take you away. I'm not saying that I'm not pissed, but hey, what can I do?" He shrugged lightly. "I wish they'd like me or at least give me a chance to speak. But heck, if I had a daughter like you, I'd be a hard-nosed Papa too. Chris was equivocating, almost as well as I was to myself.

"Well, maybe in time they'll learn to like me." He rolled his eyes in total disbelief as he commented, "You like me. You said so yourself. I couldn't be that bad if you like me, right?" There was the sly and fun-loving guy emerging from this melodramatic scenario.

"If we're good, in time, your dad will trust you and your judgment of me. It'll all work out. You'll see," Chris promised with confidence as though he could guarantee this to me. That was the difference between us. I'd had many things taken from me so quickly, I could trust nothing to be certain. But Chris, he was the most positive person I knew, and I thought I could use this change in attitude.

"That's the problem, Chris. That's the big 'if.' And what's good in our eyes isn't what's necessarily good to my parents. Apparently, just being two people from different cultures automatically means it is not good. It's not like he didn't like the way you wore your hair. Well, maybe he didn't, but it's not like it's something you could change." I felt a tirade surging but couldn't stop finishing my thought. "You see, it's not something you could help or change. You're cursed from the beginning because of your hair and your eyes. They are not of the right colors." Here I was stating the obvious and thought I had hurt his feelings.

"I'm sorry, Chris." I squarely looked in his eyes, and he understood my gaze of sorrow.

"You have me, Chi. I'm all yours whether you choose me or not. I'm all yours. My Chi."

Chris's voice was slow and quiet, almost a whisper. It was private, just for our ears, and it was more romantic than I'd ever dreamt. It was far better than him asking me to go together with him or to be his girlfriend. I was floating on clouds and glowing in the loving words Chris had just lavished upon me. I was happy for the moment, and that was enough for me.

We met at the mall that Saturday at Fashion Fair. I had gone shopping by myself before, and it was no trouble to tell my mother that I was going shopping that afternoon. Being independent of my parents for transportation had its benefits. They weren't accustomed to taking me places, and I hadn't disclosed that I wasn't shopping alone, but shopping with Chris for the dance. I knew full well that, for one, they didn't want me to see Chris, and two, they wouldn't grant permission for me to go the dance. But I did it with full knowledge that they wouldn't approve of both of these actions. It was the first time in my life I was defiant and disobedient. I was guilt-ridden.

I justified that I wasn't hurting myself or anyone else. I still loved my parents, no less than before. I didn't want them to be mad or worry about me because I was safe and because Chris wasn't hurting me as they thought he would. It was my choice to defy, not his. Chris never asked me to be disrespectful to my parents. It was all my choice. I was protesting against my father's rigid, old-fashioned ways.

I stopped at Baskin-Robbins at Fashion Fair where Chris was working until two o'clock.

"Hey, Chris." I waved in line behind a few shoppers.

"Hey, Chi." Chris quickly went back to scooping his triple scoops and making a milkshake before it was my turn to capture his full attention.

"I'll be off in a few minutes," he said. "Do you want to have a cone and wait for me here, or meet somewhere else?" Despite the silly paper hat on his ample blond curls, he was his typical charming self.

"Tin Roof Sundae, please. One scoop on a sugar cone. And I'll wait for you here if you don't mind." I wanted to watch him in scooping action. I just couldn't get enough of him.

He alternated scooping between his right and left arm just so his biceps and hands wouldn't develop unevenly, he half-jokingly said.

His veins pumped every time he dug into the tubs of frozen solid ice cream. This Baskin-Robbins location was the busiest one in town. The dessert-craving shoppers never stopped lining up, impatiently shifting their weight, looking at their watches as they waited for their turn.

Chris changed out of his uniform shirt and brown pants to his blue and red short sleeve rugby shirt and jeans. He was the tall and handsome type, and I was so pleased to be with him. I was living the American lifestyle every minute I spent with Chris. I drifted away from being a full-fledged and loyal Vietnamese that my parents would like to see. If they only knew. I felt a pang of guilt and plagued with the feeling of family disloyalty.

Our first stop was at Miller's Outpost. We looked at off-white pants and white mandarin collared shirts with thin brown pinstripes. We were fortunate to find the right fits and sizes and bought them right there and then.

"Hungry? You want a burger?" Chris asked.

"Sure. Let's sit down and talk." I agreed and took my bag as he took his. We didn't decide ahead of time, but it worked out that we paid for our clothes.

"It's like going on a date, isn't it?" Chris said. "What a great idea. Would you like to go out with me sometime? Like to a movie or something?"

"I'd love to Chris. Let's go on a date right now," I said, winking happily at him.

CHAPTER 22

TigerFish

I didn't know then, but this was the defining moment, the turning point of my young life at a mere sixteen years old. I felt like I was on top of the world, like the joyous Carpenters' song that topped the Billboard charts in 1972, which I first heard as a ten-year-old in Vietnam. "I'm on the top of the world looking down on creation, and the only explanation I can find is the love that I've found ever since you've been around, your love's put me at the top of the world." I was on top of the world, but it was a fleeting moment of youthful jubilance, defiance, and short-sightedness.

Those were the most trying days of my teenage years, transition-ing from childhood to adulthood, trying to make sense of what it meant to be Vietnamese and American, trying to create some semblance of normalcy. This was the end of an era, the crossing of boundaries and limits of cultures, norms, and expectations, testing my familial patriarchal system, and discovering how not to fall into the abyss. Looking back, I long to hug and comfort my younger self, as I had during so many struggles in my assimilation process, but there was no playbook to follow. We were the first wave of Vietnamese refugees exploring the frontier of America to claim a place to call our own and to be with an acceptably assimilated identity. Not Vietnamese, but not Americans, teetering precariously between two cultures, hanging in the balance.

As I think back, I feel overwhelmingly melancholic and sad for my frightened young self and I love her so much, but most of all I'm baffled by how she could've ever weathered all the storms ahead of her. It certainly is a testament to how strong a person can be when faced with adversity. We march onward, one foot in front of the other. We are strong, especially when it's seemingly unbearable and unfathomable. People are strong, and we must never underestimate ourselves.

Know this, my dearest daughter, life is good, but it is good because we fight fiercely for the values and ideals that we hold most precious to our hearts and minds. The good life is not free, it's your labor of self-love and self-respect, day in and day out, hours upon hours of determination and resolve. There will be many good days, even glorious days, but if and when dark days come, always hold your head high and march on with all the strength you can muster. Please come back to my words on self-love and self-respect, as this was how I pushed myself onward during my darkest hours when I couldn't see the end in sight, when I could no longer find tears to ease my pain.

When you are feeling lost and defeated, cry, do cry, feel all that you feel, but then I implore you to get back up to fight, and fight like hell to bring happiness and joy back into your life. It is you and only you who can fill this void for yourself. This is the void, the hole I told you about when I first started telling you my story.

In telling you my history, it becomes your history, so you can gain strength from it to conquer life's challenges, knowing that because I have done it, so can you, and so will your children. You may not know yet that this hole exists, but one day that existential question will relentlessly beg you to find out why you are here, where you came from, and what your mission in life is. You will then understand this hole and emptiness about which I'm trying to forewarn you. This is the reason why I desperately needed to tell you my long journey, from birth to age sixteen, when I first broke the culture barriers and boundaries and defied my family's culture and tradition to date an American boy named Chris.

He was my first love. He showed me love and kindness when I was utterly lost in a new land, learning how to read and write like a child, how to talk, how to make friends, how to drive a stick shift, and how to navigate the treacherous waters of high school and teenage angst. My parents disapproved of us because we were young, but mostly because he was an American. It was a final discussion and non-negotiable because, in my family, parents dictated the rules, and I had always obeyed them up until that point.

"Oh! What a tangled web we weave when first we practice to deceive," as Sir Walter Scott once said. Chris, your father and I went out my senior year and continued throughout college until our wedding day, immediately after college graduation. Before we got engaged, my mother gave me the silent treatment for weeks on end, my older sister snubbed me, my brother threatened Chris with bodily harm if he continued to see me, and my father threw me out, for one month.

He came in his mother's Suburban to move my single bed, desk, and clothes to a room I rented in a house with four college girls. I mostly ate at my workplace, Moy's Chinese Restaurant, and lived on tips and wages. For the first time, I took out a student loan to make sure I could afford to finish college. I ate a lot of ramen too. It made me strong — not the ramen, but the snubbing and the ostracism by my parents and older siblings.

I cried. I plunged into depression. I looked at the school pictures of my youngest brother, my sweet little sisters and cried that I would never be able to see them again. How could I? My parents were justified to throw me out, to "disown" me because I disobeyed them, and brought shame to the family by dating an American boy. I became damaged goods that nobody would want to marry. I became defiant and stubborn towards my parents. I was determined to make it without their support and approval, but it was one of the toughest things I've ever endured, to be in exile, away from my family because of my actions and choice to be with the man I loved.

I held my head high and soldiered on, on my own. I proved my older relative's predictions correct that I would be a cantankerous Tiger girl to raise. I fought like hell for what I believed in and felt wronged by my parents' disapproval. My father's unpleasant and adversarial relationships with American advisors during the war gave him plenty of reasons to be bitter and hostile towards Americans. He was not too fond of the idea that his daughter wanted to date one. During the war, my father had to work with Americans who showed disrespect for his command, combat tactics, and our people. An American advisor once ordered him to execute a losing strategy, when my father refused for the potential massive loss of lives, he angrily waved his hand in the air and said, "Do it because I have this checkbook." This advisor had recently graduated from the military academy without real life knowledge of the guerrilla warfare fought by the Việt Cộng and spoke with conviction that his way was the way forward. My father had to balance between the welfare of his countrymen, his patriotism, and the American foreign policies to strategically protect their national security interests.

I will never fully understand or comprehend the extent of my father's heroism, sacrifices, losses, and agonies in his personal life and military career. When I was a teenager, I suffered teenage angst and acted out of selfishness. I was stubborn, and I was proud. I caused myself heartache and my parents even more. There were six years of heart-wrenching days and nights until we were married. In retrospect, as a parent, I weep that I had to take sides, and in the process, hurt the people who loved me and whom I loved the most.

When those dark days come, and sometimes in life, those days have a bad habit of popping up when you least expect them, take a pause, a significant and thoughtful pause without judgment or action. Sit on your hands, be still, stay still and listen beyond all the angry noises and anxieties. Don't react hastily or harshly. Stand by the people you love; be it your husband, children, brother, parents, friends, cousins, aunts, or uncles. When they're acting out, that's when they are crying out for help. I know because I've been there on both the receiving end, as well as the one who's acted out. It's an act of desperation, and they need your compassion.

I dug in during trying times to prevail and finish college, just like the sea cypress I told you about at the beginning of my story. I didn't know then that there were so many more storms brewing on the horizon, storms that would continue to test my strength and resolve. Each time a catastrophic storm hit, and a few did, I cycled through all the phases of grief, bouncing wildly between the range of emotions, balled up in a fetal position, cried oceans of tears, brushed myself off, then continued forward. Because I'm a Tiger girl from birth and always will be, I fiercely clawed back every inch of the way to protect the wholeness of my family, keeping it intact. I will continue to do so until my last breath. I'm fierce when I need to be, but I'm kind. And above all, I'm profoundly loyal.

My story is my gift to you, my dearest daughter. I'll leave you with these lessons to fight like hell for what you believe in, to have love and compassion, and stay loyal to your family, friends, community and country.

We are strong. Our people are strong and proud. We don't give in nor do we give up. We've endured a thousand of years of Chinese domination, a hundred years of French colonialism, and at least twenty years of the American Imperialist-Military Industrial complex. Our ancestors' heads have rolled, our books have been burned or banned, our women have been raped and oppressed, our men have been tortured and killed silently in the night, our children have been left orphaned and hungry. Our soldiers have been maimed, stricken with Agent Orange, and suffered brutal battlefield deaths. Our people, our ancestors, have sacrificed for generations so you and I can prevail with dignity and with our integrity intact.

My gift, my story, now fills that void in you that you didn't yet know existed. One day, when you exchange your vows of marriage to the love of your life, know that you embody my ancestors and the ancestors of your father, who will be guiding you through life's most difficult days. We'll celebrate with you on your most glorious days. We are with you, every step of the way. We are you, and you are us. This story is my ultimate gift to you, so carry this with you, and you will always prevail and stay successfully grounded, wherever you are.

You see, once upon a time, there was a little girl name Hoàng Chi, born in an inauspicious year as a Tiger girl, but she lived the rest of her life in her mythical Piscean world where she wove East and West, Vietnamese and American, Confucian and Christianity into a safety net. And as she danced on the high wire and swung on the trapeze beneath the blue heaven, her ancestors looked down with loving kindness and guidance for her every balancing step, every whoosh of a trapeze swing. When she turned sixteen, they cast a spell and turned her into a TigerFish. From that moment on, should she fall from the high wire or the trapeze—because the fall from heaven to earth would be a long, long way—she knew she could swim.

Legend has it that on a clear day, one could see a TigerFish acrobatically arcing on a trapeze over the sky of Nha Trang where she was born. Her goldfish-like silky fins swept gracefully against her tiger's black and orange coat, as she dipped and rose, barely beneath the heavens. Some say they even saw it with their own eyes and couldn't believe that a Tiger and a Fish could peacefully coexist in the same skin, but they swore they saw it, a twinkle flickering in their eyes.

EPILOGUE

Welcome to America Brother Tâm

Here is the letter I sent to my extended family on November 20, 1994, a few days after we welcomed our brother Tâm and his new family to America.

"Thursday morning, November 17, 1994

Dear family,

I buckled the kids in their car seats and anxiously started my three-hour journey to Fresno to greet my brother, Tâm, and his new family at the airport. I had not seen him for nearly twenty years. Now with my kids, ages one and three, nodding off for the next few hours, I felt relaxed in the driver's seat, with music from Enya floating in the background. My thoughts switched gears to thinking about seeing Tâm again.

My recollections of Tâm were limited to a handful of scenes. I always thought of him whenever I heard Procol Harum's "*A Whiter Shade of Pale*", or the Beatles song, "*Come Together*". He was in his twenties when he brought this music home, and we all listened and tried to sing along. He worked, and I went to school. We didn't interact much. For the past nineteen years we hadn't had any communication from him.

Since we last said goodbye in Đà Nẵng in 1975, I had attended high school and college, got married, pursued my career, and became a full-time mother of two children. Meanwhile, he had been a prisoner of war in Vietnam a few times, and was finally released. He had also been re-married.

I wondered how our reunion would play out. I denied grieving, and postponed examining the feelings I had about leaving my birth country in exchange for life and freedom. I felt that I had no right to grieve for leaving, but could only feel grateful for being in America. Over the years, on a few, rare occasions, the subject of my sudden departure from Vietnam would surface unexpectedly, leaving me doubled over, crying hysterically, and feeling overwhelmed with grief. I didn't understand what accounted for this hysteria. Perhaps I grieved that my parents had to suffer and endure enormous pain to raise us in such a war-ridden country. Or perhaps it had to do with how they struggled raising us in our new land.

I grieved for the physical and mental pain my parents endured when a hateful and narrow-minded youth assaulted them for their ethnicity. And right in their own neighborhood! I grieved for not knowing what it would have been like to grow up in a country without a war. Occasionally, I've seen disabled American Vietnam veterans, for whom I feel a pang of guilt. For they were also victims of US foreign policies, just as I was.

I was excited for Tâm's new and hopeful beginning for himself, his second wife, and his two daughters. I didn't know what would become of our family's relationship with his first wife and child, who had escaped while he was in the POW prison camp. I admired his first wife for raising an intelligent, secure, and upbeat daughter, and hoped that this new family would still allow us to continue a relationship with the old one, hopefully still seeing them at future family gatherings.

When the United Express, twin-engine plane landed, I recognized Tâm by his height as he descended the steps to the tarmac. Finally, oh, yes, I saw my brother's face. It did not look twenty years older, but at least thirty years, evidence of a very hard life. My eyes searched for a grown woman and the two young girls who would complete the picture of his new family, whom I had not yet met. Tâm's face showed the evidence of extreme hardship, undoubtedly he had endured hours, perhaps even days and nights, of cruel torture by the Communists, especially after his failed attempts to escape. I imagined the hard life and heartaches he had experienced as he had struggled to find ways to provide for his family, which was difficult for an ex-soldier of the previous regime.

My sisters took turns embracing him over the rail of the incoming ramp as he walked past the entrance. We had the opportunity to watch him through the tinted glass windows as he walked in from outside. I was frozen in place as my sisters and Tâm sobbed as they embraced. When they parted, I walked up and reintroduced myself, and then we hugged, both breaking down crying once more. I felt spasms in my diaphragm that made it hard to breathe. I felt grateful that I had not missed this opportunity to greet and welcome him to his new home in Fresno.

Our family celebrated over dinner for both Tommy's nineteenth birthday, and Tâm's arrival. A local Vietnamese bakery gave us a cake in Tâm's honor and a cheesecake for Tommy. We sang 'Happy Birthday' to Tommy, and embarrassed him when we asked for a speech. It was a heartwarming occasion. I felt whole again, being with my family. I felt enriched, owing this feeling to my parents. Throughout the years they had been the nucleus of our family, with all of my siblings orbiting around them. They provided a cohesiveness, a focal point, and the energy for us to create our own nucleus with orbiting offspring. Although I had rebelled and questioned many of their beliefs during the different stages of growing up, I had come to respect their discipline and can relate to them now that I, too, have been a parent.

After dinner, my father asked his POW sons how they felt about their torturers. A discussion between them had never piqued my interest more, and I could have stayed up all night listening to them exchanging their thoughts. My brother, Thảo, said he did not hold anyone responsible for his misery except the fathers of Communism, namely Karl Marx, Stalin, Lenin, and Hồ Chí Minh. On the other hand, Tâm shared that when he received his release from the prison camp, he was incredibly thankful to be free, and that he did not look back to begrudge his enemy. He also explained that, even though he continued to see his torturer in his neighborhood, they just exchanged greetings and went on their respective ways. My POW brothers' message enlightened me. It was to let go of grudges, abandon worries and guilt from matters over which we had no control.

My mother remained quiet as always while the others discussed these issues. She was compassionate and generous, and was the glue that bound the family together. She had been misunderstood at times by all of us and perhaps felt betrayed for her sacrifices. I didn't know much about her life from childhood to adulthood, and I approached her one day to fill in the gaps.

My curiosity of my parents' history made me more convinced that I had to stay vigilant about writing my memoirs for my children. I could only hope that one day my daughter and son would approach me with the same keen interest in their family heritage.

I knew I made the right decision to make the trip that week and both witness and participate in this moment of my family history. As I sat watching and listening to the family discussions at dinner, I felt comforted like a child again, happily observing and learning the many life lessons that the elders had to teach the younger generations, like mine. I became more convinced at that moment that I must provide the same source of knowledge and pass on the family legacy to my children.

I felt thankful and most proud to be a Trương family member that day, and for every day after, too.

Sincerely,
Hoàng Chi Trương

ADDENDUM

In 2005, I returned to Vietnam for my first homecoming visit with my husband and two children. It was an emotional time, going back to Vietnam for the first time since my exodus in 1975. At the time, we'd just celebrated our 21st anniversary, and our children were 15 and 12 years old. We haven't been back since, and I'm glad to have fond memories of my first trip back home. It sounds cliche to say, but the trip served as closure for me and relieved me of my survivor's guilt, seeing how the country has markedly changed and seemed prosperous, at least from the standpoint of a tourist.

I reeked of Việt Kiều or Vietnamese expat. There was no use for me trying to sound or act like a local because that would be like me trying to blend in and be an American in 1975, as a newly arrived refugee. There is so much to say about my three-week visit, but I can distill it in a single sentence. After the trauma of such a sudden life disruption and the ensuing identity crisis and recovery as a refugee in America, I've finally found peace. Inner peace. That is what I've found, at last.

30 Years Homecoming Trip in 2005
Emails to Families & Friends

These are a few emails I sent to my family and friends in 2005 while visiting Vietnam after thirty years away.
Note: Natasha and Jeremy are our kids

Chris and Chi Smith *wrote:*
Sent: *Thursday, December 22, 2005, 9:10 AM*

Good morning from Sài Gòn,

It's a hyper world here. My senses heightened. The sights, sounds, tastes, and smells are incredible everywhere and at any given time, except when we are in the refuge of our rooms. We have never experienced anything like it. It's amazingly clean and very foreign to me. We are in total awe and trying to digest all that's there, like a fast-speed moving-clouds-kind of a movie. It's a culinary heaven where my tastebuds are livened up with spices and herbs I didn't know existed. People are overwhelmingly friendly, and we have to get used to the ubiquitous bowing and smiling. Crossing the street is an extreme sport that one can master with caution and practice, which may seem suicidal to a foreigner's eyes.

We will pick up Coco tomorrow. More later.
Hope our beloved pets are doing ok.

With love,
Chi and family

PS. I only saw one propaganda billboard with the hammer and sickle that says "Long live the Vietnamese communist party." Customs officers were courteous, and police on the streets carried no guns.

Chris and Chi Smith *wrote:*
Sent: *Thu, 22 Dec 2005 18:13:49 -0800 (PST)*

This rocks my world! This is our 3rd and last day in Sài Gòn. We are heading to Mũi Né this afternoon after picking up our niece, Corinne (AKA Coco per Jeremy). Europe was fantastic, but this? Unbelievably, surrealistically, sublimely, and "incandescently" fabulous. The kind of fab that will take a whole novel to describe my feelings and experiences.

To start, I was shocked that I didn't cry upon landing or on the days that I've been here. Only once, very unexpectedly, when a French song played. I don't remember the name, but chị Kim Chi and anh Trung, it goes, "Sans toi, Je suis seule. Sans toi, mon amour!" You know the one? We were in the restaurant when this song played, and I broke down crying. Don't know why; haven't figured that one out yet. Otherwise, I've adjusted amazingly well, as all of my family has.

I wish you could see the expressions on our kids' faces when we came out of the airport. I think their jaws permanently dropped, wide-eyed and speechless. The roundabout just outside was deafeningly screaming with the traffic of motorcycles and horn honking, and everyone was casual about it except us. Initially, we couldn't see our ride with her sign with our names because she was too short to rise above the sea of humanity, all told about a hundred bobbing heads, all with black hair, ten or fifteen deep, people waiting to pick up their families and so on.

A quick sketch of where we are, a blend of old French colonial, the tropics, say Mexico and Hawaii, of beautiful old architecture next to makeshift, ramshackle storefronts. The quintessential yellow uniformed street cleaners, always women, sweeping the streets and keeping them quite immaculate. Everyone wears the traditional Nón Lá hats. These hats are a contrast to the all-American ball caps. One would have to look for an imprint of Americans here, although people tell us they learned English through our Hollywood movies. People here are extremely friendly and genuine, southern Vietnamese style. The women are beautiful and slender, will hold your gaze and are not shy at all.

The people here do love to speak English to us. The service is ALWAYS impeccable, hovering and flitting about our table to the point of discomfort at times. Jeremy always gets the compliments of waiters and waitresses and their wanting to touch him. As for Natasha, they were less direct, only admiring glances but not overtly commenting on it for propriety's sake. Jeremy is still a kid, and I suppose it's okay to fuss and touch him out of adoration. Little kids love Chris, and a bunch of them affectionately accosted him with their barrages of limited English. We haven't eaten the same food twice. An adventure every day and a very pleasurable one.

Yesterday, we went to the river delta south of Sài Gòn without a tour guide. Just got a taxi and headed out and saw how a local driver navigated the rush hour traffic, which is all the time! We got to see how people live outside of the metropolis of Sài Gòn. If you're compulsively orderly like me, it will bother you to see the absence of sidewalks, building codes, tall and skinny multi-storey buildings built on top of what were once one story buildings. Everyone is a merchant! There is no lack of food stalls or restaurants. You would think that all people ever do here is eat. That said, these are resourceful and industrious people. Nothing gets wasted, and I was happy to see the recycling at its best, though I highly doubt that this is their intention to preserve the earth, only self-preservation. Either way, it rocks. The restaurants do not serve anything chicken for prevention of bird flu, so they say.

With love from Sài Gòn.

Chris and Chi Smith *wrote:*
Sent: *Saturday, December 24, 2005 11:24 PM*

What it means to have won the birth lottery.

Every day I don't write is an eventful day I risk leaving unrecorded.

The day we went rowing in the delta's tributaries was full of discoveries. Kids were fishing by hand, swimming, and diving into the murky water. Islands that raised cobras for snake wines where they will gladly behead the beast and let you drink its blood, then prepare the rest for your lunch. We settled for only viewing the thing with its hood fully extended, mouth wide opened, in the midst of gobbling another snake–all this inside a wine bottle!

I'm only recording what my family told me since I simply don't have the stomach for any of this. You may ask why does anyone want to ingest such a thing. The answer given was that it's good for your health, a little dubious sounding to me.

We went to the fisherman's village yesterday of Mũi Né, Phan Thiết. Our kids admitted afterward that they didn't know people lived that way. They continued to say that the poor people in America didn't have much to complain about, compared to what these fishermen endure.

Right on the beachfront, where one would have found a grand villa, instead, there were clumps of makeshifts shacks of corrugated tin, woven bamboo, tarps, in other words, whatever one could find. Kids came running out to say hello to us and got called back in by their parents. We found many beautiful shells on this beach, but it is littered with other unsavory debris. It's strictly a stretch of a fishing village. People squatting over the freshly caught fish, choosing them and weighing them while someone else recorded in the ledger. The fleet of brightly colored fishing boats, all with eyes painted to guide them out of harm's ways, covered the bay for as far as the eye can see. One would wonder if this is what the Bay of Monterey, California was like before it was fished out.

We have a gregarious driver who is very cautious and an excellent tour guide though that's not his job description. He clued us in on the hand signals the drivers gave each other to warn about traffic cops. Rightly so since the fines for exceeding the speed limit is equivalent to 200 US dollars. They punch your license for each violation, and with three strikes you'd lose your license.

The water temperature of the beach we're at is very nice. The wind picks up after 1 or 2 pm, and we'll try windsurfing today. Yesterday Jeremy and I played two lively games of volleyball with the local kids. Natasha and Coco, our niece, enjoyed kicking back and body surfing. They were too shy to play with a bunch of boys and us. The hotel shields us from the hard living the locals face. The kids are keenly aware that we as Americans are using way more of the earth's resources than the average citizen locally. We all concurred that we had won the birth lottery. More on that later.

We had about seven different kinds of noodle soups so far. The hot pepper is fantastically hot, and Chris found his 50 cent beer and is loving it. Natasha, Jeremy and Coco learned quite a bit of Vietnamese and the locals loved it when they sprung some unexpected 'Thank yous.' All are happy and grateful as can be, seeing the local rural kids subsistence level living.

We went to the red dunes yesterday, and it was like the Sahara with the ever flowing sands, ever changing the landscapes. Jeremy looked like a lone explorer running up and down the dunes. There were mobs of peddlers trying to rent the sand sleds, approaching from the far side. A little girl about eight years old clung on tightly with Natasha and Coco while speaking her broken English. Another boy about ten years *old hung tight with Jeremy, and they even chatted somehow. At one point, we were on the far dune and could see a wave of tourists with their accompanying peddlers coming over a hill. It was like "Shawn of the Dead"!*

Today we'll just kick it at the beach since it's Christmas. After breakfast tomorrow we'll head to Đà Lạt and should arrive there about noon.

We are still entranced with this whole thing. It's still not real. Still feeling like it's a dream. Could it be the hot peppers that we ate?

Thank you all who have been writing to us. We'll keep it coming and try not to bore you. Thanks for the advice and emotional support from everyone. I'm doing very well so far. People are still finding an excuse to keep their hands on Jeremy and studying his face with fascination.

Thinking of you all on Christmas day.

With love,
Chi and family

CITATION TO ACCOMPANY THE AWARD OF

THE BRONZE STAR MEDAL

TO

COLONEL TRUONG TAN THUC
ARMY OF THE REPUBLIC OF VIETNAM

For meritorious service from March 1968 to March 1969 in connection with operations against enemy aggressor forces in the Republic of Vietnam while serving as Commanding Officer of the 51st Infantry Regiment, Army of the Republic of Vietnam.

Displaying superior leadership and initiative, Colonel Thuc molded his unit into an aggressive fighting force and repeatedly disregarded his own safety as he boldly moved to forward positions to coordinate supporting fires and direct the efforts of his battalion commanders. Under his dynamic leadership, his regiment participated in numerous major combat operations, including LINN RIVER, MAUI PEAK, and MEADE RIVER, and was instrumental in significantly reducing the enemy's combat capabilities and material assets.

Maintaining effective liaison with other Free World forces in his tactical area, Colonel Thuc rendered invaluable assistance in planning and coordinating joint operations, and provided sound recommendations concerning the most efficient employment of available manpower and material resources. His resolute determination and seemingly unlimited resourcefulness earned the respect and admiration of all with whom he served, and contributed significantly to the accomplishment of his unit's mission.

By his leadership, superb professionalism, and unwavering devotion to duty, Colonel Thuc upheld the highest traditions of the military service.

The Combat Distinguishing Device is authorized.

The United States Award of Bronze Star Medal to my Father. 1969.

254

GLOSSARY

Political and Military Nouns & Events

ARVN: The Army of the Republic of Vietnam, also known as the South Vietnamese Army (SVA).

Điện Biên Phủ [Din Bin Foo]: Việt Minh's decisive victory against the French in 1954, which resulted in the signing of the Geneva Conference for the split of Vietnam into North Communist Vietnam, and South Republic of Vietnam at the 17th Parallel, or the Demilitarized Zone (DMZ). This battle also resulted in the termination of the French involvement in Indochina. (http://www.encyclopedia.com/history/asia-and-africa/southeast-asia-history/vietnam-war. April 17, 2017)

G.I. is a noun used to describe the soldiers of the United States Army and airmen of the United States Army Air Forces—and for U.S. Marines and sailors—and also for general items of their equipment. (https://en.wikipedia.org/wiki/G.I._(military). April 17, 2017)

Hồ [Hoh]: Short for Hồ Chí Minh.

HU-1: An Iroquois military helicopter also widely known by its nickname, "Huey." "It was developed by Bell Helicopter to meet a United States Army's 1952 requirement for a medical evacuation and utility helicopter, and first flew in 1956." (https://en.wikipedia.org/wiki/Bell_UH-1_Iroquois April 17, 2017)

Military Police or **MP.**

Tết Offensive [Tate] One of the largest military campaigns of the Vietnam War, launched on January 30, 1968, by forces of the North Vietnamese People's Army of Vietnam against the forces of the South Vietnamese Army of the Republic of Vietnam, the United States Armed Forces, and their allies. It was a campaign of surprise attacks against military and civilian command and control centers throughout South Vietnam. The name of the offensive comes from the Tết holiday, the Vietnamese New Year, when the first major attacks took place.

Uncle Cụ Hồ [Coo Hoh]: Hồ Chí Minh. Vietnamese Communist revolutionary leader, or the Father of the Vietnamese Communist Party.

Việt Cộng, VC [Viet Kong]: North Vietnamese, Communists, NVA (People's Army-Vietnam).

Việt Minh [Viet Ming]: Communist sympathizer.

NAMES

Father: Colonel, the Commanding Officer of the 51ˢᵗ Infantry Regiment (Separate), Army of the Republic of Vietnam

    Auntie Cô Ba [Koh Bah]: Father's younger sister
    Uncle Chú Sáu [Choo Sow]: Father's younger brother
    Uncle Chú Bảy [Choo Baye]: Father's younger brother

Mother: Housewife

    Auntie Bác Xuyến [Back Xu-en]: Mother's friend
    Auntie Dì Ba [Yee Bah]: Mother's oldest sister
    Auntie Dì Năm [Yee Nalm]: Mother's second older sister
    Uncle Cậu Nhượng [Kow Yung]: Mother's younger brother

My Siblings: Oldest first

    Thảo [Thow]: Oldest brother
        Liên [Lee-en]: Thảo's wife
            Tuyết [Too-et]: Liên's younger sister
            David: Tuyết's husband
    Bá [Bah]: Older Brother – Missing and Assumed Deceased
    Tâm [Tahm]: Older Brother
    Kim Chi [Kim Chee]: Oldest Sister
    Thọ [Thaw]: Older Brother
    Thông [Thom]: Older Brother

Hoàng Chi [Huang Chee] (Author)
 Chris: Husband
  Natasha: Daughter
  Jeremy: Son
 Hạnh Thi [Han Tee]: My best friend from 2nd to 6th grade
 Xuân Mỹ [Su-an Mee]: My friend from 6th to 8th grade
 Dzũng: Neighbor and childhood friend
Minh Châu [Ming Chow]: Younger Sister
Thi [Tea]: Younger brother – Deceased at birth
Mỹ Châu [Mee Chow]: Younger Sister
Hồng Châu [Hong Chow]: Younger Sister
Tommy: Youngest Brother

Family Helpers:
 Bà Hai [Bah Hay]: In-home helper
 Lanh [Lan]: In-home helper
 Chú Chiêu [Choo Cheow]: Family Cook
 Chú Tăng [Choo Tan]: Family Cook
 Chú Rổ [Choo Roh]: Family Cook
 Chú Lai [Choo Lay]: Family Driver
 Chú Thăng [Choo Tang]: Family Driver

PLACES

Bạch Đằng River: Đà Nẵng [Bat Deng, Dah neng].

Củ Chi tunnels [Koo Chee]: Located in the Củ Chi District of **Sài Gòn**, Vietnam, and a part of a much larger network of tunnels that underlie much of the country. The Củ Chi tunnels were the location of several military campaigns during the Vietnam War, and were the Việt Cộng's base of operations for the Tết Offensive in 1968. (https://en.wikipedia.org/wiki/Củ_Chi_tunnels. April 17, 2017)

Bình Thành, Ninh Hòa [Bin Tan, Neen Wah]: ARVN region. Mother's place of birth.

Đà Lạt [Dah Lat]: ARVN region. Father's Military Academy.

Đà Nẵng [Dah Neng]: ARVN region. My School years 1966 to 1975.

Hà Nội [Hah Noy]: The Capital of Communist North Vietnam.

Huế [Whey]: ARVN region. Near Đà Nẵng.

Khe Sanh [Kay Sahn]: ARVN region.

Kôn Tum [Kohn Toom]: ARVN region. My parents' first home.

Nha Trang [Na Treng]: ARVN region. My Birthplace.

Nguyễn Trung Trực Street [Wen Troong Truk]: ARVN region. My parents' house in Nha Trang.

Quảng Trị [Wang Tree]: ARVN region Sơn Chà: [Sun Chah] South ARVN region. Near Đà Nẵng.

Sài Gòn [Sy Gone]: ARVN region. Capitol of South Vietnam.

Vũng Tàu [Voon Tow]: ARVN region. Destination of our boat trip from Cầu Đá (Chutt, Nha Trang).

COMMON NOUNS

Áo dài [ow yay]: The traditional Vietnamese dresses for both women and men (mostly women).

Bánh In [Bahn Een]: Dry and dense sweet rice cakes.

Bánh Tét [Bahn Tec]: A sweet rice cake with seasoned pork and mung bean filling.

Bé [Beh]: Little one, e.g. "Bé Chi."

Bún Bò Huế [Boon Baw Whey]: A specialty and signature noodles soup from Huế.

Dưa món, củ kiệu [Yuh Mung, Koo Kew]: Pickled daikon, scallions, and carrots in fish sauce to eat with Bánh Tét for New Year's.

Phở [fuh]: A specialty and signature noodles soup from Hà Nội region.

Tết [Tate]: New Year.

Tiền Lì Xì [Tin Lee See]: Money gift in red and gold envelopes for Lunar New Year.

Nón Lá [Non Lah]: Traditional conical hats worn mostly by women.

Xôi Vò [Soy Vah]: Sweet rice, mung beans and coconut.

COMMON PHRASES

Trời Đất ơi! [Juh Dak Oy]: Roughly means "Oh, My GOD!" The direct translation is "Oh, my Heaven and Earth!"

Thưa Ba [Tou Bah]: A respectful and proper greeting to one's father.

CPSIA information can be obtained
at www.ICGtesting.com
Printed in the USA
FFHW021249171218
49915491-54529FF